Joe Clark

Joe Clark
A Portrait
David L. Humphreys

A TOTEM BOOK
TORONTO

First published, 1978
by Deneau and Greenberg Publishers Ltd.
Ottawa, Canada
This edition published 1979
by TOTEM BOOKS
a division of
Collins Publishers
100 Lesmill Road, Don Mills, Ontario

© Deneau and Greenberg Publishers Ltd. 1978

Canadian Cataloguing in Publication Data

Humphreys, David L., 1939-
    Joe Clark

Includes index.
ISBN 0-00-216169-9 pa.

1. Clark, Joe, 1939-   2. Politicians•
Canada - Biography.

FC626.C53H85 1979   328.71'0924   C79-094174-0
F1034.3.C53H85 1979

Printed in Canada by Universal Printers Ltd.,
Winnipeg, Manitoba

To
Cecilia and Christine

CONTENTS

ILLUSTRATIONS
(In centre section)

PREFACE

I had known Joe Clark for eighteen years — the span of his political career — when he was elected to the leadership of the Progressive Conservative party in February 1976. I believe today as I did then, that the country doesn't know the Joe Clark I know. I offer this book in the hope that it will help Canadians get to know one of their political leaders better.

It is too early in Clark's career for any definitive biography. I hope this book will help others who will want to write about Clark.

I have not ignored his faults or failures. He appears, warts and all, as I know him.

While I had the advantage of being able to draw on personal experience, there were gaps in my knowledge. For helping me fill them, I am grateful to Joe Clark particularly for allowing me to publish excerpts from his letters. I am indebted, too, to Charles and Grace Clark of High River and to Peter Clark of Calgary. For assisting with research, my thanks go to Robert Hill and Jim Witte of Edmonton, for reading the manuscript to David Williamson of Winnipeg and Murray Goldblatt of Ottawa. I am grateful for the assistance of others, too numerous to mention, from coast to coast. Any errors or omissions are my own.

PROLOGUE

Did I think it was hopeless? Never."

Joe Clark, leader of the Progressive Conservative party was musing on his leadership after nearly two years of nerve-testing trials and modest triumphs.

"I knew they were underestimating me."

The elusive "they" has been used often by Clark's illustrious predecessor John Diefenbaker to describe his critics and tormentors. "They" had not disappeared but, rather, lurked quietly in the shadows to criticize, correct and condemn leaders of the Progressive Conservative party who had the misfortune to fall from public favour. "They" were the politicians, the party foot-soldiers and the press.

Clark knew they were wrong and believes he has proved it. When he gambled a lot of time in Quebec only to lose all five byelections, when everything went wrong on a mismanaged tour of British Columbia, when the Gallup poll dropped his party to only 27 percent approval in its national survey, Clark lived one day at a time and kept his own counsel. He believes that he will make up for lost points during the course of an election campaign.

Clark knew he was not alone. After all, when he was

"up" in public favour during most of 1976, Pierre Trudeau was "down." Liberal rank and file and the press began to talk about a successor. Almost every leader in a western democracy, in power or in opposition, has faced the same problem.

Kingman Brewster, former president of Yale University, and U.S. Ambassador to Great Britain, says the western democracies are infected with what he calls "now-ism." "Now," after the Mogadishu hijack rescue, West Germany's Helmut Schmidt is steely and irreplaceable. Six months before he was perceived to be tired and grey. "Now," after the split of the French left wing, Valéry Giscard d'Estaing is refreshing and far-sighted. Six months before he was discredited and doomed.

"Now" Jimmy Carter is floundering and racked with doubt. Six months previously he was hailed as the best thing to happen in American politics since Roosevelt. And so, "now" Pierre Trudeau is the man who can deal with Quebec, just as he was seen to be in 1968. Six months before he couldn't hold a cabinet together.

"Now" Joe Clark can unite his party after all and he can hold his own with Pierre Trudeau. Six months before he was young, inexperienced and not quite tough enough.

During his first two years, short-term crises buffeted Clark: the Battle of Bow River, the defection of Jack Horner, the Quebec byelection losses, the bad cycle in the opinion polls and the accompanying criticism. Against these troubles the new leader could point to long-term successes: the uniting of the caucus, the introduction of a caucus executive policy group and the restructuring of the party's national finance office, natural moves for a leader with sixteen years apprenticeship in the back rooms. And the support of the country's five Conservative provincial premiers.

There was much more negative than positive news about Clark during his first two years. His term began with the honeymoon most new political stars enjoy with the media. He "made" the covers of *Macleans* and the last Canadian edition of *Time.* The media sought out his wife, Maureen McTeer, for interviews and she obliged with frank opinions on many subjects. There were several profiles of Clark. But it appeared to many that his wife was the stronger personality and she became a controversial figure. Then the news took over, chronicling the new leader's misfortunes and, less thoroughly, his recovery. Throughout the period there was no serious attempt to answer the question posed by the *Toronto Star*, "Joe Who?"

The media gloried in caricatures based on Clark's youth (thirty-six at the convention) and superficial references to his background. The kid on the skateboard. The idealistic boy politician from High River.

The Canadian public saw Clark regularly in their newspapers and on television. He became a national figure, a young politician with a serious opinion about every political issue of the day. He is a television image, a prominent actor on the national stage. But Joe Clark the man is neither known, nor understood. Certainly he is widely recognized. Many Canadians even know he comes from High River in Alberta. Reporters have been to his home town to talk to anyone who could remember him. But the results have been a column here, a tentative profile there, and a few questions during a half hour of "personal" television. In other words there have been glimpses revealing a bit more of the caricature.

High River is the beginning of the Clark story. What kind of place is it? What kind of home does Clark come from? The little town and the home moulded his character indelibly. And an understanding of the man behind the political figure begins at his home in the foothills.

1
HIGH RIVER

> Its distinguished sons, if any, will be able to
> contribute to their home town only an occa-
> sional visit and a free performance — to a full
> house, for pride in its sons remains even
> though the town cannot keep or use the boys it
> is proud of.
>
> Wallace Stegner in *Wolf Willow*.

WALLACE Stegner's book about a small town on the prairies has been close to Joe Clark for more than a decade. Stegner wrote, not about High River, but about a forlorn place called Whitemud in Saskatchewan. *Wolf Willow* is a lament for times past, good times for a small town and its frontier rangeland. It is a key to understanding Clark, who quotes from its pages regularly. When he became leader of the Opposition, he sent copies to aides and friends. *Wolf Willow's* message is simple: small is good and worth preserving. The frontier pioneer spirit, sturdiness, self-reliance are worthy virtues.

Clark learned to know and love his own small town. He still loves it. Unlike Whitemud, High River has always been a place with a future — ever since its birth as a good spot to ford the Highwood River. Back in 1882 it was known as "the Crossing."

Clark lived there only until he was eighteen but he has

returned often for visits. In the spring of 1965 he took me with him. We turned off Highway 2 South at Alderside, half a dozen houses and a grain elevator, to drive along the old highway, straight and flat for the eight miles to High River. It was pot-holed in those days of Social Credit rule, for even then this was Tory country.

Joe insisted we stop on the shoulder of the road for a few minutes to admire the expanse of rolling rangeland and foothills with their backdrop of glistening snow-capped Rockies framed with a rich blue sky.

We sped along to the house Joe's grandfather had built on the original Macleod Trail and where his parents, Charles and Grace Clark, made their home. As we drove west to Pekisko Creek, Joe pointed out the landmarks of historical interest. The old log store, known as Robber's Roost by the hands at the nearby Bar U ranch because of its steep prices. The Bar U itself where cattle and horses have grazed as far back as the 1890s. When the ranchers tired of eating beef three times a day they would go up the river to fish for trout or grayling, or perhaps bag a duck or prairie chicken. The Bar U, founded by George Lane, also a pioneer of the Calgary Stampede, is but one of many historical ranches. Beyond the Bar U is the EP, once owned by the late Duke of Windsor, now the property of the Cartwright family, ranchers long before "Bonanza" came along. The A-7 is the home of the Cross family, perhaps better known as founding owners of the Calgary Brewery. On we went, past the Anchor P, the Bar S, all historic names and brands. Eventually we reached the Hump — the summit of one of the hills.

The view is breathtaking, facing all points of the compass, from the vast acres of grassland to the east to the mountain majesty to the west.

Joe's father described High River as a beauty spot,

with grain on one side, cattle on the other and a creek running through the town. When he spoke at the opening of the town's Pioneer Square in 1973 he mentioned the good sense of the town's founders. "Here was a place a man could tether his horse, where he could build his house and watch each morning an eastern sun unveiling a vista of splendid nature, framed by peaks — offering adventure too." Joe's grandfather, celebrating his fortieth anniversary as a weekly newspaper editor wrote: "Our rich countryside never fails to satisfy the eye; the infinite variety of our seasons in all their unpredictable whimsies; the backdrop of the eternal Rockies; the high clear skies, and the Chinook arch which is our sky symbol of hope."

Joe Clark knows this wheat and cattle country — or his little corner of it — intimately. Perhaps he is, as one Ottawa columnist wrote, "a man who would rather read than shoot," but the description is misleading in the stereotype it suggests. Joe Clark may be a reader, and he may now be a city dweller, but he is, and will always remain, a man whose roots are deep in this western small-town country.

Eastern writers love to stereotype westerners. For a long time Jack Horner was always described as a "rancher-politician" by writers who would never have dreamed of calling Pierre Trudeau a "professor-politician" or John Turner a "lawyer-politician." The writer who thus qualifies a politician invites the reader to draw certain conclusions. Presumably a man who would rather read than shoot is bookish (a derogatory reference in macho Canadian politics), intellectual (suspect, not a true representative of the breed), effete (might he be weak?). But even a small prairie town is a microcosm of society; it contains merchants, bankers, undertakers, postal clerks and newspapermen as well as the ranchers who may surround it. Most aren't out shooting up the countryside and bucking broncos. They are nonetheless authentic small-town westerners. Joe Clark is one of them.

Joe grew up on the edge of a town typically western in some ways, but endowed with more than average beauty. The CPR line south from Calgary runs through it, with a stereotype station on one side and stereotype grain elevators on the other. Its business district covers four or five blocks sandwiched between Railway Street and the Highwood River. One of the blocks has been demolished since Joe left, to rise again as the redeveloped Pioneer Square.

The square sits on the site of what were the oldest, most deteriorated buildings of High River, among them the town's first house. High River rejected Ottawa's proposals for rebuilding the square (and, consequently, the federal financing that would have accompanied acceptance), and, true to character, struck out on its own to produce single-storey buildings architecturally complementary to their venerable stone neighbours, which date back to 1907.

One of the neighouring buildings, modern by High River standards, is the Times Building, a one-storey brick structure built by Joe's grandfather in 1927. It was patterned after a CPR building that had recently been completed in Calgary. The various hues of the brick blend harmoniously with the sturdy old stone and wooden structures which house the variety of stores and offices you'd expect to find in a town of three thousand.

For a rangeland community High River is rich in trees, many of them planted by Joe's grandmother, who formed the Civic League in 1907 with beautification in mind. The Clark home, a two-storey frame structure with a spacious verandah, is set on a large lot with a flag pole on the lawn on the northern side of town. Newer post-war homes, most of them indistinguishable from those in any

Canadian suburb, line the streets a stone's throw away.

Nearby is the George Lane Memorial Park and the golf course where Charles Clark loves to play. The park is named for George Lane of the Bar U and the Calgary Stampede, and in its grounds are the remains of the famous Medicine Tree. Actually two cottonwoods, which stood side by side and were joined by a large branch ten feet above ground, the tree was considered sacred by the Indians. It stood several miles away on the banks of the Highwood until it was blown down in 1958.

Essentially this is the High River Joe Clark can't leave behind. He may never live there again but he has taken the spirit of High River with him just as he has taken his father's photographs of High River country to Ottawa and hung them in his den in the official residence of the leader of the Opposition. He hopes to hang them some day in the prime minister's residence. It's an appropriate attachment for a man with his sense of history. For seventy years his family's history and the town's have been inseparable.

Joe Clark's grandfather Charles was born in Kincardine, Ontario, in 1869, son of a Scottish immigrant. He worked for his brother Colonel Hugh Clark, editor of the weekly *Kincardine Review* and later a member of both the Ontario legislature and the federal Parliament. In 1899 Charles Clark was one of the first party of eastern newspaper editors to tour the west, then on the threshold of a wave of settlement. The tour aroused his interest.

The Boer war broke out and Charles Clark volunteered for service in South Africa. He later described his war service as "a rugged experience but it had compensating features." Those included personal meetings with the brass — Lord Kitchener, Lord Roberts, and General DeWet. On his way home he attended the coronation of

King Edward VII in London.

Back in Canada, he headed west to Calgary in 1903 with a dream of ranching. He dabbled unsuccessfully in horse trading and real estate through a hard western winter. In 1904, in Okotoks (pronounced Oh-kuh-toaks), a small town twenty-five miles south of Calgary, he discovered an abandoned newspaper plant with type strewn all over the floor. He located the owner, sorted out the mess, and published the first edition of the *Okotoks Review.* The town and paper were not flourishing though, and Clark cast envious eyes on High River, a larger, more prosperous town a few miles farther south.

In 1902, Bob Edwards, probably the wittiest, most notorious weekly editor the West has produced, had founded the *Eye-Opener.* Charles Clark got to know Edwards just as he finally ran into trouble with his readership. Edwards had set the tone of his editorship — irreverent and satirical — in his very first edition.

"The management has decided on the name, *Eye-Opener,* because few people will resist taking it. It will be run on a strictly moral basis at one dollar a year. If an immoral paper is the local preference, we can supply that too but it will cost one dollar and fifty cents."

The following year Edwards had not lost any of his enthusiasm for the town. He commented that High River was "favoured by location and nature with everything calculated to make it one of the most delightful places in the West. Beautiful for situation with a health-laden breeze floating down from the mountains, High River has little to complain of in regard to her share of nature's bounty." But it didn't take long for relations between the irreverent, hard-drinking editor and the town's righteous citizens to deteriorate.

The breaking point came over a bit of mischief at the Methodist church. The gramophone was still a novelty and a travelling salesman persuaded High River's minister of the advantages of using a gramophone to play hymns. A demonstration was agreed upon and the salesman set up the machine, with records, in the church on a Saturday night, then repaired to Jerry's Bar to celebrate an anticipated sale. At morning service the following day the first hymn suitably impressed the congregation. The second hymn, however, turned out to be not "Nearer My God to Thee" as announced, but "Just Because She Made Them Goo-Goo Eyes." An irate minister announced, "The resignation of the gramophone choir is accepted. Let us pray." As a prank, somebody had substituted the barroom song for the hymn. Town gossip blamed Edwards for the incident, although no proof was established. Edwards was deeply hurt by the subsequent whispering campaign.

Deciding to fold his tent and move to Calgary, Edwards gave Charles Clark advance notice. Other newspapermen were watching the High River market, but thanks to Edwards' tip, Charles Clark had his plant established in an old drug store before the fiery editor withdrew. Edwards continued to publish the *Eye-Opener* in Calgary, always irreverent, sometimes wayward, until his death in 1922. The *Eye-Opener* is still remembered in the West for its irrepressible editor and his satirical approach to the sacred cows of his day.

Charles Clark opened the *High River Times* as a serious, politically independent weekly on December 5, 1905, four months after the founding of the province of Alberta.

In its Golden Jubilee edition, published August 18, 1955, the *Times* commented, "The district was ready for a paper which would publish with some degree of regularity, and would print news impartially rather than indulge in brilliant though erratic attacks on all and sundry. In other words it would welcome a little orthodox newspapering."

High River was then a town of twelve hundred, a trading and social centre at the time of its incorporation, which took place just two months after Clark founded his paper. It had a general store, the High River Trading Company, a drug store, a hardware store, two hotels, a barber shop, a blacksmith, and twenty-three real estate agents.

Pickles and whisky were dispensed from barrels. In wet weather carts sank to their axles in mud on the streets. Cattle roamed at will. A small plant supplied electricity to the businesses but lamps and candles were the usual source of home light. There were few wooden sidewalks. Grandfather Clark's bride had been a nurse in Paris before she joined him in High River. When someone remarked that her Paris gowns would be inappropriate for the mud and dirt she replied, "We'll build sidewalks."

Those first years of the century were good to High River and to many other small towns. Farmers harvested bumper crops. Trainloads of settlers poured in. Railways brought new small industries and credit was easy. Grandfather Charles Clark summarized the atmosphere of the time in his fortieth anniversary edition in 1945.

"In its youth the town had dreams of greatness, of railways, industries, oil wells and so on, all of which were championed vigorously by this paper, and are worth recalling even though they came to naught. Plenty has happened in the community without much spectacular nature and most of the developments have been of an enduring quality."

The *Times* itself progressed gradually. The purchase of a Linotype machine in 1917 was "a revolutionary change" that reduced the staff of six who had set the type by hand. Electricity replaced gas power in 1925. Two years later the present Times Building was built. J.S. King, president of the British Newspaper Society, who headed a party of British editors touring Canada, laid the cornerstone.

Grandfather Charles was a Baptist who married a Roman Catholic woman and became an Anglican later in life. He persuaded the Anglican bishop to confirm him without the benefit of Anglican instruction. He had met his wife, a native of Bay City, Michigan, while she holidayed in Kincardine. The wedding was held in Bay City in 1906. The new Mrs. Clark's two sisters and a brother came to High River with her. All three of the sisters married Protestants. In those days, mixed marriages raised eyebrows in many small towns, but not in High River.

It was a time of social mobility. Towns like High River went out of their way to attract settlers under Clifford Sifton's immigration policy for developing the West. Many towns attracted Ukrainians or other European immigrants. High River attracted Englishmen. The big ranch country opportunities were widely advertised in England and during the 1890s High River attracted a lot of "remittance men," young men of well-to-do established families who preferred to keep their sons abroad in the colonies rather than put up with their embarrassing habits at home. They may not have been the cream of English society but the remittance men brought with them some of its culture. Polo, a common game in the area for years, was played by Joe Clark's grandfather and father. White linen tablecloths and full place settings and white tie parties were the order of the day in the Clark household and in many others. A piano graced the living room of the spacious wooden house that grandfather Charles built in 1909.

His only son, Charles A. Clark, was born in the family home in 1910. (The home was passed from father to son, and Joe's father and mother still live in it.) Joe's father grew up there, attended the High River one-room school and learned the weekly newspaper business from his father. As a youth he swept out the office or did "anything that came up." He began to work at the *Times* during the Depression when the paper would accept three bushels of wheat or two chickens instead of cash for an annual subscription.

He got to know Grace Welch, the daughter of a lumber merchant in another small Alberta town, Wainwright, when he went to the fledgling University of Alberta to study liberal arts. Several years later Grace Welch took a teaching job at High River and found herself living near the Clark home. Her friendship with Charles blossomed and they married in 1937. They had two sons, Joe, born June 5, 1939 and Peter, November 18, 1942.

Grace Clark remembers that one of the first meals she had to cook as a bride was for two guests of her father-in-law, one of whom was Arthur Meighen, then Conservative leader in the Senate. As a child, young Joe was frequently introduced to interesting or important guests before being packed off to bed. "Sometimes I crept back down the stairs to listen, just because they were such interesting characters," Joe recalls. There was Guy Weadick, cowboy founder of the Calgary Stampede. "He had long, shoulder-length hair and looked like the Oklahoma cowboy that he was. I remember he was always loquacious." Another frequent visitor to the Clark home was John Fisher, who became nationally known as Mr. Canada for his stories about life in the country's regions. He was usually in High River to work on stories about ranch life. Both Weadick and Fisher usually brought matchbooks from far and wide for Joe, who made a hobby of collecting them. "There were so many they darn near crowded him out of his room," his father says.

What he remembers most clearly about his grand-father's funeral in 1949, Joe says, is the number of out-of-town notables who came to pay their respects.

After church on Sunday the Count and Countess deForas customarily came to the Clarks for breakfast. They were immigrants from France who farmed a few miles out of town. Their daughter Odette rose to become an international opera singer. A more typical immigrant who dropped by the Clarks was W.K. Runciman, who had come from England, and who was able to bring the latest news from his brother, a British cabinet minister.

His father believes Clark's political interests are the natural result of the feeling he has had since childhood for people.

"Joe was old enough and interested enough to appreciate the sturdiness and the ideals and dreams of these men and women," his father says. "He was in the right place, for here they were still active, dreaming still, still planning for the future of the country they adopted. And they were from all walks of life."

His father introduced Joe to the outdoors early in life. Not all of these experiences were pleasant. He almost drowned when he was three when he was out fishing with his father. The bank gave way, plunging him into the stream, but he managed to grab his father's fishing line and was pulled to safety. The experience left him with a fear of water that lasted for years.

As a boy he liked camping but not fishing or hunting. He was enthusiastic about outings with his family. He liked to track down places or things of historical interest.

Joe was not the outdoors type but he enjoyed the outdoors very much. There is no contradiction here. The first alludes to athletic qualities, the second to the ability to observe and appreciate one's surroundings. (During one attempt at image-building early in his leadership, Clark's advisers arranged for him to be photographed in the Yukon, supposedly catching a fish. It was a phoney, false image, although the setting — Clark at home on a forest-encircled lake — was appropriate.

His interests at school extended to sports, particularly baseball. But his concern was more in knowing about sports than in playing them. His brother Peter was the enthusiastic kid on the ball diamond or the rink. Joe preferred to read about games. His parents gave him Frank G. Menke's *Encyclopedia of Sports* as a Christmas present in 1954. Soon he knew all about the big leagues, all the records, and all the players. At school he showed his first journalistic talent reporting local sports for the *Times*.

Joe and his brother Peter shared an interest in singing. Their father was musical. He played the ukelele when the spirit moved him and for a time he had an organ in the house, which he played by ear. For many years he sang in the choir at St. Francis de Sales Roman Catholic Church. Joe and Peter sang solos at the annual Christmas midnight mass. They also entered the town's amateur nights and usually won with their rendering of "Mocking Bird Hill."

High River was small enough for everyone to know everyone else. Joe was the paper boy and some of the older residents remember that he delivered the *Calgary Herald*. One, Margaret Henderson, says he was a polite youngster who made a lot of friends along the route.

With his friends he went through cubs and scouts and air cadets. "I was never a sixer in cubs. And contrary to some newspaper reports, I did learn to tie a reef knot, but that was about it." He recalls that he was in the air cadets because it was the thing to do. He never really liked the regimentation. He enjoyed flying off with his friends to

summer camp at Abbotsford in British Columbia, but on
weekly parades he disliked the discipline and marching
and found himself getting more and more floor-sweeping
assignments. "Finally there was some disagreement and I
was told to leave."

High River High School in the mid-fifties nurtured
leadership and discipline in its students. The principal,
George Harper, ran the school on strict English
disciplinary lines. Shirts with ties were compulsory for
the boys. Harper preferred jackets but did not insist on
them. He even disliked the western-style string ties
favoured by some students. He lectured the new Grade 9
students every year, leaving them with no doubt that they
were the lowest on the school totem pole. And just in case
they did doubt it, Harper subjected them to a fagging
system under which seniors could assign menial jobs to
juniors. A junior at the time (Alan Hughes, now an actor)
says he can't recall Joe ever taking advantage of the
system. He doesn't remember anyone ever carrying his
books or shining his shoes.

Joe Clark succeeded in Harper's school, despite his
lack of athletic prowess and his failure at air cadets.
Harper ran the cadet corps and it was generally believed
that boys who wanted to be in his good books joined and
succeeded in cadets. Joe was the exception, probably
because he was no trouble in school and Harper knew
and liked the Clarks. Joe was one of the few who usually
wore a jacket; he was clean, crisp and fastidious.

In his last year of school, Joe became president of the
student council. As student president, he had to answer
a wave of grumbling over an increase in student
association fees. He appeared in the Grade 9 classroom to
speak on council matters and to check on non-payment
of fees. One Larry Fisk quarrelled with Joe and urged his
fellow students not to pay the fees. Joe called in the

treasurer and asked, "Has Larry Fisk paid his dues?" Told that he had indeed paid, Joe dismissed the issue with the comment, "I thought so — they're usually the ones who make the most noise." Whereupon the meeting moved on to other subjects.

Joe's respect for the English language was evident in high school. In Grade 10, he became editor of the *Reflector,* the student paper. And he was an outstanding English student. His mother gives credit to teacher Mrs. Florence (Faunnie) Miles. "She had a sincere love for the English language and an ability to transfer that feeling to her students." Mrs. Miles kept a file of Joe's essays and used them at times as an example for other students. Joe agrees that Mrs. Miles was the teacher who exerted most influence over him during high school. She had come west from Cape Breton with the intention of teaching for a year only but she settled in High River. Another of Joe's teachers, retired now, was Martha Houston, who taught him both English and French. He was good in English, just average in French, she recalls. "He was always able to express himself well, both in writing and speaking. He was a very good writer."

In public speaking exercises most students had difficulty stretching their speeches to fit the allotted five minutes. Joe ran over. In Grade 11 he won a public speaking scholarship which sent him to Ottawa with the Rotary Club's "Adventure in Citizenship," an annual project which still brings bright young Canadians to the national capital for a first-hand look at the federal establishment.

During his stay, Joe passed up the visits to the art gallery and the museum. Instead, he preferred to wait for hours for a chance to meet George Drew, then Opposition leader, MP John Diefenbaker and Alberta Senator Donald Cameron. Already his interest in politics was evident.

It was the year of the infamous Pipeline Debate and Joe Clark watched from the House of Commons gallery as the St. Laurent government imposed closure to cut off debate. Today, his mother remembers vividly his return. "That visit impressed Joe," she said. "When he returned he said we didn't have democracy in Canada. The Liberals had their tremendous majority. He felt that the Opposition were doing a good job but they had to be stronger. I don't think he saw himself then as the person to bring that about." But his father adds, "It may have persuaded him to do what he could to serve the kind of Canada he had learned to appreciate."

The growing depth of their son's commitment began to be apparent a year later. Events moved quickly in Ottawa, with the resignation of Drew and the election of Diefenbaker as his successor. Diefenbaker held a meeting in High River during the heady days of the 1957 election campaign. It was an afternoon meeting at the Town Centre and Joe was determined to be there. He rushed home to drop his books off after school before going on to the meeting to shake hands with the new leader whose acquaintance he had made a year earlier.

As his fascination with politics grew his interest in sports continued unabated. When his mother asked him if he was studying hard enough he would say it didn't really matter because he could always get a job as a sports reporter at the *Calgary Herald*. He did work in the *Herald* sports department for the summer after he finished Grade 12, but by September he was eager to move on to university.

Joe's departure for university was more than just the routine break from home of a youth reaching maturity. The Clark family was proud of its contribution to the life of High River, particularly the weekly newspaper, over two generations. Joe had raised expectations with his work for the *Times* that the paper would pass to another generation, that both the paper and the family would continue to thrive in High River. Celebrating its fortieth year under Joe's grandfather in 1945, the paper noted there were few, if any, other Alberta weeklies which could claim similar continuity of publication. "And there is every prospect that the *Times* will continue for many a year in the same family. Charles Clark Jr. is business manager of the *Times* and grandsons Joe and Peter are already showing interest in the revolving wheels of a printing office." A decade later, the *Times*' Golden Jubilee edition reported, "It is an encouraging evidence of family continuity that young Joe Clark has been contributing to the paper in special assignments during the past year."

Joe's father and mother, children of the Depression, aspired to open doors to their children that had necessarily been closed to them. Charles Clark reflects, "You were glad to get what came along — you had no choice but to preserve what you had." Grace Clark felt it was wrong for parents to plan for the careers of their children and even though they had a prospering family business they did not press either of their children to join it. "We were somewhat unusual in that regard," Grace Clark says now, "we even sent our sons to Europe. We were always afraid of provincialism. We wanted to open their eyes and we wanted them to travel as far and wide as possible."

By the time their father retired both Joe and Peter had decided not to take over the *Times* and Charles Clark sold it to one of his long-time employees. Peter had never been interested in journalism. He went into law and practised successfully in Calgary.

Joe's decision wasn't as easy. He had grown to appreciate the people of the small town, High River, and their heritage. He had been interested in writing for the paper and completed many assignments for it. But by the time he went to university his political interests were awakening. Eventually they triumphed and Joe and his parents recognized that small-town newspapering and national political ambitions did not complement each other.

Joe's room at home remains very much as he left it, seven-foot-high bookshelves crowded with old novels — Steinbeck, Greene, LeCarré — texts and back copies of the university paper he edited. One book is *The Fine Art of Political Wit* by Leon Harris, and it's inscribed by a friend who hoped that during Joe's political career he would never lack for humour. He came by a sense of humour honestly, from his parents.

One cannot do better by way of illustrating the quiet humour of the Clarks than to quote from a profile of them by Iris Fleming in the *Globe and Mail* of Toronto. People who know them well, wrote Mrs. Fleming, wish their humour would show up on television (a comment which is also being applied to Joe). "But they are asked sober questions about their son and they reply in kind."

Charles Clark speaks in a quiet, almost tired-sounding voice; his droll humour comes out the same way and can easily slip by unnoticed. Grace Clark's humorous responses are straight-faced.

"I mentioned the possibility of their home being designated a historic site in years to come.

"'Then I'd better get busy and tidy up,' Grace said.

"'I'll cut the grass,' Charles added.

"We discussed their small vegetable patch. The radishes have always given them trouble. They grow hard and woody. Too bad they were wasted. 'Not at all,' Charles Clark deadpanned. 'we burn them in the fireplace; it saves on wood.'

"We talked about the art course he'd taken — he's always taking some course or other — and I asked where his paintings were. 'We hide them,' Grace Clark said."

Iris Fleming also quoted a famous Charles Clark story about his visit to Spain in 1970. He had taken Spanish courses. Just arrived in Spain, the Clarks stepped out on their hotel balcony to look about. A man on the next balcony smiled and said, "Buenos dias." Anxious to return the greeting, Charles Clark replied, "Adios." They never saw the man again.

The High River Joe Clark left behind now has the problems peculiar to towns near booming cities. An endless procession of city-dwellers, ready to pay through the nose to escape from Calgary during 1976, pushed house prices in High River up to an average of about seventy thousand dollars. The town has become increasingly a bedroom community, with an estimated 40 percent of the population commuting the thirty miles to Calgary, rather than the proud ranching centre it once was. But much of the character Joe knew remains.

When Clark began to feel the strong pull of politics, he realized that he would likely never live again in a small town like High River, but he has never forgotten his roots. Time and time again after leaving High River, he has taken up the problems of the small towns and cities of Canada and their plight in the face of the growing scramble to urban centres.

In 1971, just before he sought the federal nomination in Rocky Mountain riding, Clark wrote several freelance pieces on the plight of small towns faced with rail line abandonment. In one, published in the *Globe and Mail* on July 21, 1971, he asked: "Who can prove the CPR deliberately discouraged passenger service? Or that it didn't?

"Who can assess the effect on the towns of southern

Alberta of the disappearance over a decade of passenger train service?

"Who can predict the future result of forcing a reliance on bus and air travel service and the private automobile?

"The small town can't make these calculations. The CPR wouldn't want to. The CTC [Canadian Transport Commission] doesn't.

"So, in practice, these questions are ignored and the transportation future of a region is decided at hearings which the affected communities think it would be futile to attend."

In November, he wrote a second article in the *Globe and Mail.* It served both to earn a few dollars when he was running for the federal nomination in Rocky Mountain and, once again, to explain the problems of the small town, this time High River itself. The town had attempted to use federal government assistance to rebuild a block. When Ottawa's plans for the rebuilding didn't suit the town it rejected Ottawa's help and rebuilt on its own.

He asked his readers to imagine the demolition and rebuilding of one quarter of downtown Toronto or Montreal without federal or provincial help.

"Demolition has been going on all summer, and in September new trees were planted in a new town square. Of course one quarter of downtown High River amounts to only one block.

"But the High River experience offers two larger lessons.

"First a community can act on its own — one block and $150,000 might seem like peanuts to Toronto, but it's a major proposition for a small town.

"Second, High River's experience suggests a serious inflexibility in Ottawa's approach to community renewal — a tendency to treat different communities as though they were the same."

He wrote these words during a period of preliminary campaigning for the Rocky Mountain nomination. He passed up opportunities to seek urban nominations — he had lived in Calgary Centre, being vacated by veteran Tory Douglas Harkness — in favour of the rural and the rugged. The sentiments so vividly expressed by Wallace Stegner in *Wolf Willow* stayed with him. His distinctive political style by this time had become rooted in the politics of country against city and of small against big.

As a candidate in his first election, he steered through the federal party's policy committee a brief concerned with the protection and development of small towns. The *Edmonton Journal* reported: "Engineered and put forward by Joe Clark, PC candidate in Rocky Mountain, the brief is designed to recognize and develop the importance of Canadian towns and communities under ten thousand population.

"The brief calls for:

"Systematic change of national policies which in fact now hurt, or with change could help Canadian small communities.

"Meetings between federal and provincial governments to develop a national policy for small towns and rural communities.

"Consideration of instituting a 'towns test' to assess the effect of every new piece of legislation on small towns.

"Public servants whose decisions seriously affect small towns, should, wherever possible, have personal experience in small communities, and should be required to spend an annual two-week sabbatical in a different rural community.

"There should be a small agency of lawyers, economists and other professionals independent from the federal government established, available to aid small local governments 'in major confrontations with groups whose expertise or power is disproportionately wrong.'"

Again and again Clark was to speak on the themes outlined in that brief. For example, as leader of the party, he proposed in November 1977 before an enthusiastic Edmonton audience that senior public servants be forced out into the field for two weeks each year.

In his travels seeking the leadership the strongest impression he left upon scores of delegates was that of a man who sincerely cared for the small town, the small business and the ordinary person against the powerful.

2
POLITICAL BEGINNINGS

JOE Clark's interest in politics was well aroused when he went to the University of Alberta in 1957. He had already met John Diefenbaker and Alan Lazerte. Clark has publicly given credit to Diefenbaker for awakening his youthful interest. But Lazerte?

Clark had displayed an interest unusual for a seventeen-year-old when Diefenbaker campaigned in High River in 1957. He had met Alan Lazerte, a paid organizer for the Alberta Progressive Conservative party, the year before when he visited High River on a tour of southern Alberta. Lazerte talked of the provincial party's shortcomings and its need to emulate Diefenbaker in reaching out to people, but neither attached much significance to the conversation.

During his first year at university Clark followed Diefenbaker's revival of the federal party closely. Like many Alberta Conservatives, he hoped the party's federal success could be extended to the province. I first met him in May 1958 when I was a reporter for the *Edmonton Journal* and Clark turned up as a summer student. When assignments were complete he was not one to sit around the newsroom. His interest in politics led him to attend all the political meetings he could.

On one occasion he went to hear Lazerte speak as a candidate for the leadership of the Alberta Progressive

Conservative party. Although encouraged by Diefenbaker's 1957 election victory, the provincial Tories were
deep in the wilderness. They had not had a full-time
leader for twenty-two years. The party's affairs had been
managed by a handful of older members accustomed to
working privately.

Lazerte campaigned for both an open party and open
government. For example, he said decisions about
spending party funds should be made by the entire
executive, rather than by the treasurer alone. As an
organizer Lazerte had found many Alberta Conservatives only nominally supporting the party because they
were content with the small-*c* conservatism of Social
Credit. In that atmosphere the party organization had
become too inward-looking, serving its officers rather
than they it. Or so Lazerte thought.

His campaign was revolutionary for the Conservatives
at that time. His theme was open politics and concern for
ordinary people. He drew most attention for a proposal
to refund to farmers the capital costs they were being
charged for rural electrification programs. Social Credit
said the programs were co-operative, each farmer a
shareholder. But Lazerte pointed out that the power lines
eventually became the property of the power company.

Clark worked in the Lazerte campaign. It was his first
taste of active politics. Lazerte, now a lawyer in Powell
River, British Columbia, says Clark was one of his
hardest-working supporters. In a close result, Lazerte
came second on the fourth, decisive ballot, losing to
W.J.C. Kirby, then a member of the legislature.

(Lazerte stayed active in the party. He became the
federal candidate for the B.C. constituency of Powell
River in the election which was expected to be called
during 1978. At a candidates' school in Ottawa in
February 1978, Clark joked, "Alan, twenty years ago I

bet you never dreamed that I would be your leader today, that you would be a candidate and that one of your fellow candidates would be Gordon Taylor." Taylor was highways minister in the Social Credit Alberta government Clark and Lazerte were fighting in 1958. Ironically, Taylor became the Tory candidate in the southern part of Clark's Rocky Mountain constituency which became Bow River in the redistribution of seats.)

As the 1959 provincial election cast its shadow, the party imported Ontario MP George Hees to conduct electioneering workshops. The main one was a two-day affair at the Banff Springs Hotel. Hees said the candidate should not go door-to-door himself; rather someone else should go ahead to see whether residents were home or were even interested in talking to him. Thus the candidate's time was not wasted. Neither should the candidate ever be the person to initiate a departure; he should arrange for a colleague to drag him away from his conversation. Finally, an opposition candidate should conduct himself as if he were "the alternative candidate," responding to the concerns of his constituents just as though he himself were the sitting member. As observers of Clark's subsequent campaigns could see, he took Hees' advice to heart. At the 1976 leadership convention Attorney-General James Foster of Alberta was assigned to drag Clark away from talkative groups and keep him on schedule.

Premier Peter Lougheed of Alberta later acknowledged that both he and Clark learned important lessons in door-to-door campaign techniques from the New Democratic Party. (But at this time, when Clark was listening to Hees, Lougheed was not even thinking about politics as he worked his way up the corporate ladder at Mannix Construction in Calgary.) Lougheed found that the NDP candidates never went alone, door to door.

They often used the terms "alternative candidate" and "alternative government" to describe themselves and their party; both of these terms were adopted by Lougheed and Clark.

After the 1959 Alberta election had been called, the nineteen-year-old Clark got a telephone call from a man named Ralph Hedlin. Hedlin had arrived in southern Alberta from Manitoba where he had been an organizer for Duff Roblin's successful rise to power. The new leader, Kirby, needed a driver who could double as assistant. Would Clark like the job? Without hesitation he agreed and for the first time showed interest in driving a car. He asked his father for lessons on an automatic transmission. Hedlin went on to found a nationally known consulting firm. Roles reversed, Clark called on him for help one day seventeen years later.

The 1958 campaign for the party leadership had left bitter division in the Alberta Conservative party, because Lazerte's new guard had attacked the style of the old. The winners now moved to heal wounds and close ranks to face the Social Credit giant. Clark recalls, "I got involved with Kirby because I was a bridge to the Lazerte people and I was young and could drive a car and write." For two months Clark drove Kirby the length and breadth of Alberta while making arrangements for his meetings and writing some speeches. Most important for the future, he compiled a thorough list of names of good and willing workers everywhere he went.

Although the party won 24 percent of the popular vote, it was reduced from three seats to one in the legislature. Clark went back to his studies, to his vice-presidency of the campus Conservative club and to his job as managing editor of the *Gateway*.

He was soon to be heard from again in a way that some critics have interpreted as stabbing his leader in the back.

He moved a resolution, approved by the campus Conservatives, demanding the resignations of Leader Kirby, President Roy Deyell of Calgary, and Treasurer Ross Henderson. Clark now acknowledges that his resolution was irresponsible.

Since the election the party had made no attempt to regroup, according to the Clark resolution. It charged, reminiscent of the Lazerte campaign, that funds were under the control of one man. Nothing had been done since the election, which indeed was true.

Kirby resigned. Most Albertans took little notice. It was all evidence of a tattered and politically unimportant party in utter disarray after defeat.

It was not unusual for Clark to question authority. A year later, when he went to Ottawa as a student delegate to the national convention of the Conservative party, he was singularly unimpressed by one of the innovations of the senior members. The lobby of the Chateau Laurier had been taken over by a series of information booths, corresponding to government departments. If a delegate wanted to ask the minister something or to contribute his ideas, all he had to do, the sign said, was pick up the phone and dictate his message to the minister. Clark very much doubted whether Davie Fulton, as justice minister, ever heard the tape (he didn't) and had the effrontery to say so publicly at that convention. He could be abrasive but he could also be impressive, characteristics that were to be seen later in the House of Commons. While he disturbed some people he also picked up supporters.

Graham Scott, an Ontario student Conservative, from Toronto was at that convention. After hearing Clark address the convention he said, "Jesus — that guy has really said it and said it well." He went up to meet him afterwards. Later when Clark ran for the presidency of the Progressive Conservative Student Federation, Graham

Scott became his man in Ontario.

Clark discounts suggestions by contemporaries that, even then, he had his heart set on being prime minister. In a letter to a friend in the early sixties he observed that the office of prime minister must be tough and fascinating. But he expressed no outright personal ambition. His parents never heard him speak ambitiously about high political office. Some students say he joked . with James Coutts, who was student Liberal leader at the University of Alberta when Clark was there, about becoming prime minister. Clark says that Coutts, now principal secretary to Prime Minister Trudeau, was much more serious and single-minded politically than he but "others may have had the same view of me."

Since university both Clark and Coutts have practised politics assiduously. Coutts comes from Nanton, eighteen miles south of Clark's High River and he ran unsuccess- fully as the Liberal candidate in MacLeod in 1962. Now at Trudeau's right hand, he is well placed to influence Liberal strategy against Clark's Conservatives.

Campus politicians Clark and Coutts took the annual mock parliament elections seriously. So seriously, in fact, that they campaigned successfully to change the name to model parliament when some pseudo-Nazis began to make a mockery of the proceedings. Clark argued that the debating forum ought to be a serious exercise in parliamentary procedure and policy making. Coutts was Liberal leader and prime minister for the 1960 session; Clark became Opposition leader the following year.

A friend of Clark's, John Vandermeulen, recalls that at one of their gatherings Coutts commented, "In this game you have to be a bit of a sonofabitch. Joe doesn't quite have it."

3
THE GATEWAY

IT was business as usual in the quiet, efficient offices of the stately sandstone legislative building on that overcast afternoon of March 10, 1960. Across the North Saskatchewan River about three hundred students milled about on the campus of the University of Alberta in Edmonton.

In the twenty-sixth year of uninterrupted Social Credit rule in Alberta a student demonstration against the government was unheard of. Even intelligent political debate was rare, with an opposition force of only four pitted against sixty government members. Ministers handed down their pronouncements like benevolent uncles, wise and worldly in the ways of running the prosperous family business.

A gangling young man with a brush cut and an air of authority moved among the campus assemblage. He handed to each student an instruction sheet: "Keep in mind, this march is unorganized, unplanned and spontaneous." The young man was Joe Clark, now at the end of his year as editor of the student newspaper, the *Gateway*.

One of his last editorials had roasted the Social Credit government for failing to allocate funds for badly needed new student residences.

"Social Credit's surplus budget which makes no

provision for an expanding university population is a black example of government by opportunism. If nothing else it should indicate to the student body and, more important, to the University administration, that this government holds no sincere interest in education." It was no longer useful to appeal to the government's sense of duty or reason, Clark continued. "We must meet them where they are — on a political level."

His solution was to take to the streets over residences. In 1960 — his third year at university — he was a political activist in a place and time when activism was decidedly unfashionable.

Following Joe's instructions the student marchers were orderly and, for demonstrators, tame.

"We want residences," some chanted as they emerged from the north side of Edmonton's landmark High Level Bridge.

Somebody blew a trumpet.

They hoisted a banner proclaiming, "Our beds have cockroaches."

In the forefront as they reached the steps of the Legislative Building were Joe, James Foster, a fellow member of the student Progressive Conservative club, and Dan de Vlieger, representing the CCF (Co-operative Commonwealth Federation, now the New Democratic Party) group.

"Who's your spokesman?" asked the legislature reporter for the *Edmonton Journal.*

Joe Clark and de Vlieger looked at each other mischievously, neither wanting the dubious honour. Silently they decided to put someone else on the spot. "Coutts," they blurted out.

Coutts was the student chairman of the existing men's residence. He was also the Liberal leader on campus. Arriving at about the same time as the marchers, he had driven his car across the Low Level Bridge.

The students made their way into the building, demanding an audience with Provincial Treasurer E.W. Hinman. He welcomed them and began to explain why student residences were not being built that year. Boos and hisses greeted his remarks.

"How much money has the government handed out in oil and gas royalty dividends?" Joe Clark asked.

Hinman retorted by asking whether any of the students who received dividends had suggested putting them into a fund to build residences. The dividend scheme of cash payments to Albertans over twenty-one was the closest Social Credit came to putting its untried monetary theories into practice. Widely abused and criticized, it was abandoned after a year.

The meeting resolved nothing. The crowd withdrew quickly and quietly.

Hinman said later that he appreciated the students showing an interest but, "I regret that they have chosen a method which is usually associated with countries other than ours. I find it disturbing that they regard this demonstration as the proper way to express opinions that might be in the minority."

Dr. Walter Johns, president of the university at the time, regards Clark's editorial as the only blemish on a fine editorial record. "He said I was trying to destroy freedom of the press, and I said he was trying to destroy the university."

Dr. Johns called Clark into his office for a three-hour discussion of "the editorial." Such presidential carpeting of student editors was not unusual in those days.

Clark's interest in the residence cause may have owed something to his own experience during his first year at the University of Alberta when he had to live for a term in a converted broom closet at St. Joseph's College. He spent the rest of his student days in off-campus apartments.

Politics attracted him at university, but no more than journalism. He had gone naturally to the student newspaper the *Gateway* as a freshman to ask editor Wendy McDonald whether he might cover student council. She politely informed the confident kid from the country that the job was taken. Clark didn't mention his experience in High River and Calgary. When the senior student eventually gave up the job, McDonald told Clark, "Okay Joe, here's your chance."

Not only did he cover council well, he was willing to stay around until the small hours, one of the dedicated souls a student editor was bound to notice. The following year Clark went from junior reporter to managing editor.

At the end of that year editor Robert Scammell announced Clark's appointment as his successor with these words: "He came from the depths of his position as council reporter in 1957-58 to his present position of managing editor leaving surprisingly few knives in assorted backs."

During his second year Clark shared an apartment with Scammell, who was already a successful outdoors writer and was later to become a lawyer and prominent Liberal in Red Deer, Alberta. Scammell had observed Clark closely on the job and at home for the year. He personally selected him as his successor and successfully defended his nomination while some senior students doubted that the nineteen-year-old was ready to handle the editor's responsibility. There was a popular myth about Joe's birth, Scammell wrote in his announcement. It was that Joe's father found him one day floating on one of Bob Edward's *Eye Opener's* and nearly threw him away, thinking he was an olive.

For his own editorship Clark borrowed from Bob

Edward's prayer that he "neither truckle to the high, nor bulldoze the low . . ." and that he be made "sane but not too sane." There was also an Edwardsian ring to his first statement of policy. "If my year as editor is a quiet year I will not count it successful. At the command of a college editor are several instruments by which hell can be raised and convention attacked. I hope to use some of them, and to stir both the student body and the student mind."

Usually Clark's editorials pulled no punches in attacking what he saw as wrongs. He often projected a sense of national perspective in his comments.

Municipal political scandals in Edmonton and Calgary were fresh in the public mind as Clark took over the editor's chair.

"For the land deals of William Hawrelak, for the indiscretions of Don Mackay (former mayors), neither these men nor all their brothers-in-law nor tempters can be held solely to blame. Most of the fault lies with the common citizens who are too ready to turn the other cheek, and too unready to demand from occupants of public office an unconditional devotion to honesty and duty." (October 16, 1959.)

Criticizing the report of the Alberta Royal Commission into Education, headed by Senator Donald Cameron, Clark wrote, "The program of Alberta public schools was and will remain attuned to mediocrity. It gives all the students that subject matter which the average among them can handle easily.

"In our public schools there is no challenge for the student — be he gifted or be he average. There is instead a spooning out of information, in doses which are sometimes the minimum that can still wear the guise of education; and in the sciences and foreign languages, less than the minimum." (November 27, 1959.)

Clark first wrote of the virtues of diversity in an

editorial commenting upon the disbandment of the Arts and Sciences Undergraduate Society. The organization failed, he wrote, because it attempted to unify a diverse faculty. "It attempted to take the French student and physicist, psychologist and English major and lump them into one round ball rolling towards a common pin. The pin was not there . . . and it should never be there. Diversity is the strength of the faculty. . . . The ASUS is dead. Long live the diversity which killed it." (December 1, 1959.)

With a few words changed this comment might have come from one of his speeches nineteen years later when he was leader of the Opposition and still pleading the cause of diversity.

Another topic he discussed was one that applied to himself — the question of youth's role in politics:

"There has been little attempt made to solicit the opinions of youth, little consideration given to employing young thinkers as well as young workers. It is true, and it must be recognized, that youthful ideas seldom rest on experience, and that they are especially critical of the established. They are the products of young minds and often bear the trademark of immaturity.

"It is likewise true, and it likewise deserves recognition, that youth is not always wrong. Especially when it calls for change should youth be heeded, because young minds can analyze institutions and practices objectively; the view is not clouded by the ties of experience, nor restricted by habit." (December 4, 1959.)

During the 1959 Christmas break Joe went to the national conference of the Canadian University Press in Quebec City. I was also there as editor of the *Manitoban*. It was a significant year for the CUP, a loose organization intended to provide an exchange of news among student papers. In practice little had been done, other than by clipping exchanged papers during its twenty-two years.

During our conference we decided to set up a permanent news service, run by a full-time CUP president. We also unanimously approved a Charter of the Student Press which we imagined would help us maintain our editorial integrity against the threats, pressures in various forms and censorship by university administration or faculty. On the train from Quebec City to Montreal after the meeting we got word of the death of Quebec Premier Maurice Duplessis. The Quiet Revolution was already germinating on Quebec campuses and we were impressed by the vigour with which our Quebec colleagues argued for the charter. Clark was a central figure in the debates at Quebec's Palais de Justice that dealt with both the news service and the charter. He saw the news service as a step towards national unity and he argued that universities must break out of their stifling provincialism.

"Canada," he wrote later in the *Gateway,* "is a scattered country joined only by broad geography and a federal government. Our agricultural west squabbles with our business east, and our maritime provinces are suspicious of both. We are a bilingual nation with speakers of both tongues straining their ignorance to remain monolingual. We are a mixing pot of various religions and origins which, on some stubborn point or another, are loath to mix.

"Any nation, great or small is a unity of differences. We in Canada seem persistent, and among large western nations almost unique, in developing the differences and not the unity." (January 5, 1960.)

Clark's interests in journalism and national politics were already strong. His dream at the time, which he discussed with student friends, was to be editor of a truly Canadian national newspaper. His motivation was political in the sense that he saw the newspaper as a vehicle for national unity.

The closest his dream ever came to reality was in relation to his father's weekly newspaper in High River. As Charles Clark approached retirement age Joe looked at the *High River Times* in national terms. He knew he could not return to High River and close himself off from national affairs as a weekly editor. Could he be a national politician and a High River editor? Could the *Times* become the base for a national news magazine or something of the sort? He answered in the negative.

The January 12, 1960 edition of the *Gateway* reported the election to the model parliament of a minority Liberal government headed by second year law student James Coutts.

Clark took students to task in the *Gateway* for too often sneering at colleagues who accepted or sought positions of responsibility.

"Public service, on any level, is a bed of thorns, not of roses. The glory in it, if there be any at all, is small return for the constant responsibility, the exhausting work, the lost sleep, and ever-present complaints, for the public seldom shows gratitude to its leaders." (January 19, 1960.)

Hardly the comment of the student radical, this editorial painted the familiar picture that politicians have fancied of themselves through the ages: the self-sacrifice, the toil and the ungrateful public. And it was a life that Clark himself must have been contemplating even then. But a week later editor Clark found no inconsistency in applauding students who had made life uncomfortable for just such a public servant, Joey Smallwood. Students had welcomed the Newfoundland premier to Edmonton with hostile pickets. Clark cheered. Unlike most students, he wrote, they cared enough to protest — they were a credit to studentdom. He went on to denigrate the majority.

"So long as today's student can wangle a second-class average and a date Saturday night, his little world is complete.

"This disinterest in large and important matters is not the sign of a healthy student society. It is the student expression of a narrowness and a selfishness which are eating the innards out of the democratic life. It is the prelude to, or perhaps the product of, an adult society which glorifies narrow success, and ignores God and the freedoms." (January 26, 1960.)

In one of his last editorials Clark compared religion and politics. He found a disinclination on campus, he said, to debate either and he was disturbed. "It indicates something far more fearsome than a mere disinterest in debate. It indicates that an overwhelming number of minds are closed regarding religion and politics, and refuse to open.

"Religion, by its nature, relies on faith. In some denominations more than others, adherents are asked to accept as true what the church says — to be faithful. But being faithful should not amount to being completely unreasonable. In too many cases that is the tendency. In too many cases denominationalists will take some statement of their faith, distend it and use it to beat down reason. In the name of religion, they build walls around thought." But because it deals in unknowns, religious faith which binds was less objectionable than unyielding political faith. Most card-carrying party members' minds were closed, viewing their critics as crackpots. Non-party members simply believed the concerns of government none of their business.

"Especially in a democracy, where an informed public theoretically controls government, a society which won't think about political questions is suicidal. And any democrat who refuses to consider both sides of a political question, is contributing to the suicide." (February 26, 1960.)

Clark, a life-long Roman Catholic, was, at that time, known for a certain irreverence towards another man's religion, that of former Alberta Premier E.C. Manning. Manning, a former colleague of William Aberhart's at Calgary's Prophetic Bible Institute, conducted "Canada's National Back to the Bible Hour" from the stage of the Paramount Theatre in Edmonton. Clark did an entertaining impersonation of Manning, the preacher.

In his valedictory self-appraisal Clark admitted, "Our flamboyance has been restricted by a sense of responsibility both to our readers and to journalism. Our inclination to say 'to hell with' issues has been replaced by a dedication to important causes."

In many editorials he was addressing the same issues as many other student editors — apathy, current campus and local political stories. He was more active, politically, than most and he used the paper to express his political philosophy, for example, the defence of diversity.

The last word on his editorship belongs to a contemporary at the paper and close friend, David Jenkins, who was to work for Clark on every campaign up to and including the leadership of the Progressive Conservative party. "He was writing with the maturity of one ten years older than his age," says Jenkins. "He stood out from all the rest."

4
COKE BOTTLES AND KETCHUP

There was another side to Clark at university. He was an exceptional student editor and a serious young politician, but he was also a prankster and individualist.

Let us return briefly to his first days at university. Asian flu is sweeping the country. Clark is flat on his back in that converted broom-closet room. Campus fraternities are pursuing an annual ritual known as "rushing."

"Some of my friends from High River were called on their sick beds and invited to join this or that fraternity. I wasn't. It didn't bother me at the time. In fact I didn't really know much about them, except that they were powerful groups on campus." If it didn't bother him it was odd that during those first few weeks he deliberately chose to avoid the streets with fraternity houses on them when he went out. Friend John Vandermeulen recollects that Clark was categorically against the concept of fraternities because they tended to mould students into common attitudes and he admired diversity.

But fraternities were past their heyday and they were probably not as powerful then at Alberta as Clark imagined.

Clark did join the Blue Cow Society, whose members went around saying iconoclastic things like, "stamp out Social Credit," and the Huckleberry Hound Society, which met for the television program and a beer (or a Coke). He took no part in the usual male competition for dates on campus, but he made friends, of both sexes, easily. He neither danced nor dated unless an occasion beckoned; when it did he "just bloody well took one of his friends out," in the words of a colleague.

His social life was an extension of his everyday political, journalistic and academic endeavours and, of course, they were often related. Sometimes he would go with *Gateway* colleagues to their staff parties. Not for him the alcoholic confections of the chemistry students. He was to be found in a corner, drinking Coke and discussing issues. He also liked to sing some irreverent lines about Social Credit, like this verse from an old favorite.

> Throw a nickel on the drum,
> Save another drunken bum,
> Vote Social Credit . . .

Reading and movies were regular diversions. Mysteries and movies have always been his one total escape from politics. Joe would always go to almost any movie for diversion — it didn't matter how bad it was, he wasn't fussy.

Another diversion was his penchant for raising hell. Although he could be quiet and at times almost shy, he disliked the quiet that he thought showed apathy in the student community. Perhaps his hell-raising could be attributed to a mind described by Professor Lewis Thomas as "one that got out of its accustomed channels easily." Whatever the reason, Clark loved a good prank.

Perhaps the most successful of many pranks was the "murder" at 101st St. and Jasper Avenue, Edmonton's main intersection. This was a gangland-style killing straight out of the movies and every bit as authentic. It even had a real actress, drama student Jean Craig, who was known as a good screamer. It was timed for the mandatory dinner-hour closing of the beer parlours to catch the imbibers coming out of the old Selkirk Hotel. A line was forming for a movie around the corner. In the first scene, a car dropped off stage spectators who planted themselves among the innocent real ones. This group included Jean Craig. As a big black Ford rounded the corner from Jasper Avenue, two other students jumped out carrying pistols. Eyes fixed on a staged spectator, one of them shouted, "There he is — I'm going to kill you." Both fired blanks in the direction of the targeted student who fell instantly, tearing open his shirt to reveal a chest smeared with ketchup "blood."

Jean Craig yelled, "Oh, they're killing somebody," and screamed. Innocent spectators took the cue. A drunk lurching out of the Selkirk froze in incredulity. Other student actors picked up the crumpled "body," tossed it into the back of the car and sped off. The police descended on the corner a moment later and began to take information from innocent spectators. They set up road blocks at strategic points in the city. Throughout the evening the story led the newscasts on all the local radio stations — until the students notified the police twelve hours later that it was a hoax. Clark was the leading planner of the escapade; he played no part himself because he preferred to attend a nomination meeting.

He was messy. His apartment was littered with bottles, dirty dishes, old newspapers and assorted recent paperbacks, and junk mail. Sometimes it wasn't junk but Clark didn't bother opening it. He opened only mail with handwritten addresses and "important looking" typed addresses. There was the time he worried about getting his insurance renewed. When a friend told him it was usually done automatically through the mail, he checked some envelopes with windows — the kind he usually didn't bother opening — and there was his renewal.

Some of the unopened envelopes contained bills and his family worried that Joe would have to be bailed out. His father had a direct interest because he supported him fully in his first year and to a lesser extent in other years. His occasional visits home did nothing to reassure his parents. They recall that he turned up oblivious to the soles worn through on his shoes; they insisted that they be repaired. A second-hand Austin which Alan Lazerte gave him in 1958 was usually in need of repairs when he went home for a visit. His father and brother Peter fixed it. Joe didn't seem to care. He was busy telephoning contacts around the province or dropping in to visit them at home.

Robert Scammell says Clark set aside Sunday mornings to worry. He says he asked Clark what he was doing one Sunday morning; he replied that he was worrying. There he was, propped up in bed and drinking Coke. Clark disputes that recollection. "As a nineteen-year-old undergraduate, I just wasn't very active in the morning," he says.

Undisputed is his love of Coke. He was always, and still is, drinking it. He was even then known among friends as a "Coke-oholic." When Scammell cleaned out the bottles at the end of term he got more refund money from Clark's Cokes than from all the empty beer bottles he could find. And he ate enormous amounts of chips, peanuts, cheese crisps and candies. For a treat he would devour a canned, candied popcorn called Poppycock. His friends called it "the rich man's Cracker Jack." When he went to a friend's house for a meal he often brought a can of Poppycock.

In his third year at the University of Alberta, Joe shared a two-bedroom apartment in Coronation Court in Edmonton's Westmount district with his friend John Vandermeulen. Vandermeulen, who worked on the *Gateway* with Clark and was president of the campus radio society, was a socialite. He was always inviting friends over for parties. Clark simply moved out on those occasions. "He never bitched," Vandermeulen said, "he went to a motel for some peace and quiet." In the living room of the apartment Clark used to work at a typewriter on his desk, which was cut off from the rest of the room by a bookshelf built of bricks. He frequently jumped up to make a phone call or to look something up in a book. By the end of the year, his chair had worn deep grooves in the hardwood floor. After Clark had left for the summer, Vandermeulen had to pay the landlord to have the floor resanded.

There is little doubt that outside interests interfered with Clark's scholarship, but even though his extra-curricular activities were time-consuming, he didn't choose snap courses. His academic load was heavy. In his first year he took political science, history, geography, economics, French, mathematics and physical education. He failed French, a missing credit that was to haunt him a few years later. In succeeding years he specialized in Canadian and American history and English literature, preferring modern courses to his Shakespearean studies.

In his third year, he was accepted for a hand-picked creative writing group. It was taught by a stern taskmaster, Dr. F.M. Salter, who demanded three thousand words minimum every week; his students sat up half the night writing.

"I liked to write, although I didn't think I was very good at it," Clark says.

"I didn't think I'd ever be a great Canadian novelist or poet. I have trouble with argument by analogy and some trouble with simile which I think is essential to a poet."

He didn't want to be a writer, he said, unless he thought he could be a good one. "I think I am a better writer than most people but I didn't think I was good enough to follow a useful career as a writer so I didn't pursue that. Salter thought that my writing showed promise — more originality in style than profundity."

Clark frequently argued issues with professors, not always endearing himself to them. Sometimes a lecture would turn into a debate between Clark and the professor. Professor Grant R. Davey of the department of political science says that, although he liked Clark, "I never considered Clark a serious or committed student — attending university appeared merely as one of several devices to advance his political ambitions."

A colleague at the *Gateway,* John Taylor, says Clark had extraordinary presence of mind. He recalls a dinner at the home of the *Gateway* associate editor, Sylvia Raycheba Shortliffe. Without warning, Mrs. Shortliffe called upon him to say grace. Whereupon he treated the group to one that was long, eloquent and extemporaneous. "It was one of the most inspired I can recall hearing," Taylor recalls.

Joe has always liked to travel. As a child, on summer trips with his parents, he couldn't wait to reach the next museum. At university, distance was never any obstacle if an event interested him. He took his dog Rowdy, a black Labrador, on a two-hundred mile drive to a wedding. On the way from High River to the wedding in Edmonton, Rowdy, unfortunately, got loose near an abbatoir and rolled around in the waste. It was a smelly ride home.

Joe made a special trip from Alaska to Edmonton to attend my sister's wedding. Occasionally during university years — when he was bored, he says now — he would gather together three or four friends and drive to small towns near Edmonton. French-speaking Morinville and St. Albert were favourite stops. Joe and his friends would drop into a local café for dinner. He liked to joke with the staff. I was never present on these trips, but later I had similar experiences with him in restaurants.

On one occasion he drew my wife's attention to a man
seated alone in Kettner's restaurant, in London. His large
eyes gazed straight ahead, as if studiously avoiding his
dessert. Head in his hand, he appeared to be resigned to
something. On his plate were two flesh-pink pears,
looking like nothing so much as a pair of breasts. "Look,
Cecilia," said Clark, "that man is too embarrassed even to
look at his pears."

In a Soho restaurant, Cecilia happened to notice the
arrival of the actor Richard Chamberlain and mentioned
it to us. In a loud voice Clark said, "Who did you say that
was, Cecilia? Richard Burton?" And he went through a
list of all the prominent Richards he could recall.

A couple of years later in The Mill restaurant in
Ottawa we noticed we had no sugar on the table. Joe
complained good naturedly to the waiter that he was
discriminating against Conservative MPs. Later he
ordered a sundae that came with a choice of sauces,
including marshmallow. "Is this sauce made from
genuine marshmallows, grown in Virginia?" Clark
demanded of the bewildered waiter.

After these experiences we felt we understood what his
brother Peter meant when he said, talking of Joe's
university days, "He was never in the least averse to
drawing attention to himself.

5

DRIFT AND DIEFENBAKER

JOE Clark drifted through the first half of the sixties. He was unsettled in life. He harboured doubts about his future career. He was cynical about politics. When the period began he was completing his final year at the University of Alberta. Only five years later did he find an anchor in the embryo political organization of Peter Lougheed. During the period in between he travelled and made half-hearted attempts to study law. He successfully held national office for two terms as president of the Progressive Conservative Student Federation.

He experienced an understandable let-down in the autumn of 1960 when he returned to campus as a has-been. Most of Clark's friends were a year ahead of him. They had left and he felt alone for most of his last year.

With his heavy load of undergraduate activities, Clark had graduated with average marks, most in the sixties, some higher, others lower. He had failed his French in first year and dropped it. He returned for a further year with the hope of raising his average so he could enter Washington's Georgetown University. He was attracted by Washington as a political centre and liked the idea of studying at a Catholic university, one with a good reputation for post-graduate studies in political science. As it happened Georgetown turned down his application because he was deficient in French.

Among friends who had left was Colin Campbell, a *Gateway* colleague Joe wrote to at various times during the early sixties. Campbell was an American who went home to face the army draft. Two comments in a letter dated October 1, 1960, are indicative of Clark's frame of mind. He had been to a party, which prompted the observation, "I can't remember enjoying myself less, which suggests my party days are past." (This at the age of twenty-one.)

In the same letter, Clark also mused about the qualities that made a girl he knew unusual. "She is not a carefree girl, and they are probably easier to escort. She worries and thinks and holds her own opinions, which should, by criteria I've before expressed, make her perfect. But it doesn't seem to. I often wonder what kind of a girl I'll finally marry. If. Which might be too absolute a way of looking at it."

Joe had no clear purpose on graduation, but he knew he wanted to travel. In the autumn of 1961, with his parents' encouragement, he set out for an extended visit to Europe. His intention was to find a job in London, but he tried for weeks without success. He said the unsettling effect interfered with his sense of adventure. Finally, he got a job as a stock room assistant in the basement of Harrods, the posh department store now patronized by rich Arabs and Americans. He took an apartment in seedy Bayswater Road, then discovered it was above a gambling club and below a bordello. The coming and going disturbed him. "It was not prudishness that moved me on," he recalled, "it was just damn noisy."

In London, Clark recorded some observations on the city and its society. Coming from the Prairies, he was everywhere impressed by the antiquity. "There are buildings here constructed when the world was flat, when New York and Alberta were unknown. I walk where kings walked," he wrote his friend Campbell, "in the city of Churchill, Cromwell and the Romans." There was another, more powerful, impression. "It is of decay. The British were for so long a vigorous, colonizing people, they drew strength and purpose from their task of building Britain abroad. Today, they have no world to conquer. The nation's business and the people's thoughts have shrivelled to matters petty in comparison — labour unions demand 'tea breaks' in contracts. How much help should government give the auto manufacturers? Are old-age pensions high enough? Selfish, petty considerations glorified and expounded in a manner . . . to cause the English of Empire days shame and regret. I, too, regret this condition. Britain is a place chiefly notable for its past. Its present is uninspiring and its future promises decline. A good place to visit and leave."

Clark took the Channel ferry to Calais in mid-December. He stopped over in France en route to Spain, to return later. He noted at the time, "Spent thirty hours in Paris with a 'fille francais' met on Channel boat. Nothing came of that."

He reached Barcelona in time for Christmas. He wrote that it was a doleful Christmas, far from home and unable to speak Spanish. He regretted making the trip alone and vowed later never to do so again. Soon afterward he met a footloose American and the pair travelled the rim of Spain together. Of the poverty of Spain, he wrote: "People sleep in caves and spend the whole of the lighted day coaxing plants to grow in sterile soil. Little children, diseased and without futures, clog the streets in money-hunting gangs. Some people see such sights and have awakened in them a disgust for any social or economic system which allows such suffering to exist. My reaction was the opposite of that. I saw this suffering, and lost what vestiges of faith I had in panacea formulas which would set the world right. Only by transporting these people to less barren countryside could one relieve their suffering. And yet to transport them is to jerk loose, not only the ugly, but also to tear them away from whatever has made life bearable for generations of their ancestors. Even with bread these cave people would be unhappy in a Madrid tenement. Perhaps some Oral Roberts should fasten upon such plights as proof that perfection does not reside in this world. End of sermon. I am what I guess is best called a negative Christian, who sees not much chance for salvation in this world, but has not seen that chance denied regarding the next."

With such melancholy thoughts on his mind he made his way back to the Bordeaux region of France. He had arranged to spend several weeks with a family in a town called La Brede to learn French. He found the family taciturn in any language. Instead of learning French, Clark reported, he wasted a month, learned new ways of wasting time, and developed a taste for full French meals and long hours of sleep. About his only exciting diversion was a visit to the casino in Monte Carlo where he was promptly thrown out for not wearing a tie.

In Rome, he met a Canadian doctor attached to the immigration service who fed him and gave him a conducted tour of the historic hills surrounding the city. From Rome Clark went to Milan where a cable from PC headquarters awaited him. It offered him a job pamphleteering for the Diefenbaker government in party headquarters. He regretted missing Africa, the Middle East and England in the spring. But there were other years, he thought. When he saw the job offer he made arrangements to return at once.

He took the train through the Swiss Alps, visited London for a day or two then flew home. He described his reaction to seeing Canadian soil again. "The view from the air of Labrador, north Quebec and finally the St. Lawrence shorelines was one of the most inspiring of my whole experience. We could see only sparse settlement, most of the land below is virgin, unexploited. Even the St. Lawrence, covered by snow, seemed unpeopled, as it must have looked to the early trappers and settlers from France. I think I prefer land without people."

He offered an explanation for snapping up the new job in one of his letters to his American friend, Colin Campbell. "Though Kennedy might have scotched the myth in America, a great many back-country Canadians still believe prime ministers are born in log huts. While my hopes were never that high, I've held during the last six years a patriotic reverence for Ottawa, and have explored serious work and other opportunities here."

In the new job he was preparing pamphlets ("No government has done more for the average Canadian"), writing speeches for MPs, setting up radio and television appearances and organizing conventions.

The hours were irregular but the work interesting. "A restlessness struck me in Europe, a feeling that I was filling days without accomplishment. I bore that feeling as something of a cross during the last months a-wandering. Now I feel useful again," he told Campbell.

Clark liked working at party headquarters so much that he toyed with the idea of staying for another year before returning to university for further study. Would his job last six months or eighteen months? His lack of career still rankled. He applied without enthusiasm to the Dalhousie Law School and was accepted in the autumn of 1962. Clark ran successfully for president of the national Progressive Conservative Student Federation shortly after he got there.

He was bored by law. "Not much happens in law school," he wrote to Colin Campbell. "There's a clique of us here now that forms around one meal table to parade wit and long tales. The range isn't as great as when the *Gateway* gathered; those days, I suppose, are gone from us forever." His opinion of the student paper, the *Gazette*, was low. He found the staff arrogant, cliquish, less interesting and less competent journalistically than his group at the *Gateway*.

As president of the PCSF he had to travel to national and regional party meetings and spent a lot of time working on policy and programs. By now he was accustomed to heavy extra-curricular activities and he scraped through first year with only one supplementary examination. He made lasting friendships with other students whose interest lay in politics. George Cooper, Peter Hayden and Edward Poole, were all friends from "Dal" who were to help him substantially in years to come. But Clark did not care much for life at Dalhousie, and the next year transferred to the University of British Columbia Law School. He was attracted not so much by the law school as by E. Davie Fulton, who was then provincial leader of the party. Justice Minister in the first Diefenbaker cabinet, Fulton had been shuffled to public works in the minority government after the 1962 general election and had soon afterwards resigned to head what he hoped would be a successful attack on the regime of W.A.C. Bennett.

The British Columbia job offered Fulton a new challenge. And Fulton's decision offered Clark a new opportunity — to work for Fulton. "I thought it would be less dull," is the way Clark put it, in recalling his decision later.

My wife Cecilia and I were living in St. Boniface, Manitoba at the time. One day in June we were surprised to see a standard yellow school bus pull up outside our home, and even more surprised when out jumped Joe. He was short of funds at the end of the year, he explained, and he had found the opportunity to drive a bus from the factory in Ontario to the customer in Alberta. In fact he was flat broke. We enjoyed a good visit, did his laundry, lent him fifty dollars and sent him on his way the next day.

In the fall Clark plunged into the Fulton provincial campaign, writing a terse, daily campaign advertisement for the Vancouver newspapers about Fulton's views on the issues. They were considered by many to be the most effective publicity in the entire Fulton campaign. Fulton was arguing against the grandiose proposals of Social Credit Premier W.A.C. Bennett for the simultaneous development of power projects on both the Columbia and Peace rivers. The province simply couldn't afford both, he argued. Either the issue or the timing was wrong; Fulton failed to make any inroads in the campaign and both he and the party went down to humiliating defeat.

The Fulton campaign, rather than law school, consumed Clark's energies during the autumn of 1963. He also turned his attention, as national president of the student federation, to the incipient party unrest with the leadership of John Diefenbaker.

Dissatisfaction was being expressed in student clubs across the country and some influential Tories were seeking a secret ballot for a vote of confidence in Diefenbaker's leadership at the annual meeting of the national PC association, scheduled for Ottawa, February 1 to 5, 1964.

Meeting just before the senior convention, the Progressive Conservative Student Federation voted confidence in Diefenbaker by the narrowest of margins, thirty-one votes to thirty, with many abstentions. The students shocked the party by favouring a secret ballot.

Clark, who was seeking to stay out of the quarrel as much as possible, approached Diefenbaker with the hope of establishing a dialogue that might result in a conciliation, but to no avail.

After the PCSF convention, Richard Thrasher, national director of the party, asked Clark to undertake the delicate task of introducing Diefenbaker before his address to the convention. Clark today recalls being very reluctant.

"I said, 'Dick, we've just had a very difficult annual meeting and there is clearly a division of opinion in the student federation. I don't think I should do it.' Dick in effect said they had decided, they wanted me to do it, and I had no choice. I was under considerable duress."

It was in that reluctant introduction that Clark first came to the attention of many in the party. It was a tour de force which both saluted the achievements of the leader and faced squarely the crises of his leadership.

"I am a 1956 Conservative," Clark said.

"My inactivity before is in part explained by youth. But much more influential is the fact that in those years before, the Progressive Conservative party did not reach out to me, nor to many of you, nor to the mass of Canadians."

Clark told the story of his dropping his school books at home and rushing to the town hall in High River to hear Diefenbaker speak of his vision.

"In those years, sir, you wrought a revolution in the attitudes and aspirations of Canadians."

There had, however, been a basic disagreement at the recent student meeting over Diefenbaker's continued leadership, Clark told him. Yet it had been the leader's decision to face it in the convention.

"That is the choice of a strong, great man."

An enthusiastic, standing ovation greeted Diefenbaker. When it subsided, the leader had high praise for Clark.

"I have received many introductions in the course of the years," Diefenbaker said, "and if there were no other rewards in public life than to have done what was stated by the brilliant Joe Clark I would have been rewarded more than I could have hoped for."

He launched into a predictable, scathing attack on Lester Pearson and the Liberals. His fifty-three-minute speech ended by welcoming the vote of confidence. "If it's a secret vote, that's fine with me. I want to know where I stand. I want to know where you stand, too!"

Diefenbaker left the hall. The secret ballot resolution was easily defeated. In an open vote of confidence only a handful of delegates, notably including MP Douglas Harkness, stood up in opposition.

The issue was under control for the time being. Clark followed up with a letter which put Diefenbaker on notice that the unrest may have been silenced but it had not been resolved. Forty-six clubs of the student federation, Clark wrote, had been advised that they were free — even obligated — to speak out on the leadership issue.

Understandably, Fulton worried about Clark's year at law school. First his own campaign, then the leadership issue, had jeopardized Clark's studies. He seldom attended classes, relying on borrowed notes from friends instead. He decided to try to bluff his way through final exams with his writing skill.

He realized property law was too tough for bluff. His only hope, he decided, was to write the paper so illegibly that he would buy time while he prepared better for an oral interrogation. He scrawled twenty-five pages, and waited. Sure enough, in a few days the professor called him to say the paper was unreadable. In the oral exam Clark failed to show enough grasp of the subject to salvage a pass mark. Joe took some comfort from knowing that in constitutional law, a subject that truly interested him, he scored the highest mark in his year.

Clark had shown little interest in law. Most of his energies had gone into politics, but there was a third factor in the failure. He had spent a lot of his spare time with Penny Riordan, a petite young woman with striking reddish blonde hair who was known on campus as a zealous Liberal. The friendship became serious enough to suggest an assumption on both sides that they might marry. But they finally broke up and friends speculated that Clark couldn't accept the prospect of being married to a Liberal.

On hearing that Clark had failed his year in law, Fulton wrote to express his deep sympathy and concern at the prospect of his brilliant assistant having no career to fall back on. He also thanked him for the "tremendous help" of the election campaign.

"There is no one I know," wrote Fulton, "whose career would hold greater promise for success for himself and to his country."

Highly praised, intensely active, Clark nevertheless grew decidedly downcast.

During the year he became more cynical and restless. He wrote two letters to Colin Campbell in March when his apparent academic failure must have weighed heavily on him.

The first, written on March 21, 1964, was written from Penny Riordan's home. "I am wearying of the university-leech existence," he wrote. "I begin to feel guilty at not harnessing myself to some productive outlet, i.e. guilty about not working, more precisely I suppose about not earning."

The letter contains a cynical sentence about a woman they both knew who "has capitulated her individuality, and is a mother and cocktail-party wife."

He concluded on this jarring note:

"I'm a sort of unhappy swimmer in the stream of affairs — however consuming my activity, I'm bothered by questions about its ultimate utility, its ultimate sense. I'm less parochial than before, if only in the sense that I no longer am convinced about North America's Manifest Destiny. Activity pleases me, but much as knitting pleases the owners of need-to-be-busy hands. As knitters never seem to do, I sometimes sit back and wonder about all the things I'm busy in. Rambling? When you're abroad, walk alone some night along the Mediterranean shore, listen to the buzz of peasant chatter in a Spanish street, then ask if you want the U.S.A."

The malaise continued. He wrote again introspectively on March 31. This time almost the entire letter was devoted to his personal angst.

"Really can't understand why the hell I locked myself in law school. With a little confidence and perseverance two years ago, I could've embarked on graduate work and now be almost Dr. Clark. The roads not taken. Why should such a cynic have been raised in my circumstances? That question bothers me more than I show. Much of my lack of (bow to the sociologists) direction is rooted in the fact that there is nothing I really want. Some people at my place in politics should be animated by the desire for the power of the top. I should want to write, or be a successful lawyer, or raise kids with whom I can reciprocate pride, or put out a good country newspaper. But these move me as little as the other 'shoulds'. I suppose I'm part of a North American phenomenon, but there's little comfort in that.

"You'll perhaps not remember, but your last letter remarked on the rearing up of altruism, your desire to be of service. Even that I no longer have. And I was one not

long ago fired by the thought of the Peace Corps, and of
Parliament in its highest sense. Perhaps this too is just a
period, a dry period which some rain of purpose will
dispel.

"A remarkable film was put out by the National Film
Board. *The Drylanders,* a chronicle of one farmer's
experience in the lush days of settlement and the harsh
ones of Depression disappointment in Saskatchewan.
Here were people to whom the hopeful better future was a
tangible goal, and hard physical labour its just price.
They suffered much from nature, but their suffering was
not as notable as their strength. I wonder sometimes if
our soft and cynical generation requires a Depression or a
war."

Clark looks back on those years as a period of drift in
his life. "I wasn't very enthused," he says with understatement. "I literally couldn't find anything else to do
but I felt I had to have a career so I was going to be a
lawyer. I was interested in politics. But it's not true that I
had politics so much on my mind that I set my course
single-mindedly on it. What was really happening more
particularly was a kind of drift of the kind which was
prevalent during that period."

His spirits were at a low ebb when he left Vancouver in
the summer of 1964. They began to lift when he resolved
finally to abandon his law studies. He returned to the
University of Alberta as a graduate student in political
science.

6
LOUGHEED

IN the fall of 1964 Peter Lougheed was thinking of entering politics. He had impeccable credentials for leadership. He and his wife Jeanne were personally attractive. He had money. He retained an athletic demeanour from his Edmonton Eskimo football days. His grandfather had been leader of the Senate under Borden. He was Harvard-educated. In the post-Kennedy period there seemed to be no better credentials for an aspiring politician. Except that Peter Lougheed had served no political apprenticeship. He was starting right at the bottom; fortunately he knew it.

In 1963, in the first election since Clark drove Kirby around the province in 1959, the Alberta Conservatives again failed to make any gains under the flamboyant leadership of Milton Harradence, a Calgary criminal lawyer who flew his own Mustang fighter in the campaign.

Lougheed discussed his ambitions with friends, attended the party's annual convention at Red Deer (it was the first political meeting he had ever attended) and in late 1964 formally launched his campaign for the leadership.

Clark turned up at one of Lougheed's campaign meetings in Edmonton and afterwards Lougheed invited Clark and Lou Hyndman, a prominent Tory he had met at Red Deer, to his room for a discussion. Clark regarded Lougheed with some suspicion as a wealthy Calgarian. Clark's sympathies inclined more towards a populist view, but he had not found any other candidate he regarded as more suitable.

Clark next met Lougheed after he had won the leadership on March 20, 1965. Joe's father, Charles, a lifelong Conservative, introduced Lougheed to the convention with, as Lougheed wrote later, "the right combination of sincerity, imagination and eloquence."

Clark had just successfully completed the first of three years in a political science master's degree program at the University of Alberta in Edmonton. He was to return for two more years, paying his way by working part-time as a teaching assistant. But in the spring of 1965 Lougheed began to build his organization and Clark wanted to be where the action was, in Calgary.

Although Edmonton was the capital, Lougheed and most of his advisers were Calgarians and continued to make Calgary their headquarters. Joe wanted to move to Calgary for the summer, but he needed a job. I was then managing editor of the *Albertan* . It was a morning paper with pay scales well below those of the afternoon *Herald* and there was often an opening for a new reporter. Clark was well qualified for desk and writing work and I hired him at ninety dollars a week and put him up at my house until he found his own room. We both knew that this would be just another short-term job in a varied career, but it was nothing new for the paper to have staff coming and going.

Joe was a meticulous editor, although impatient with the demands of fitting short words into fixed spaces. He was appalled by the austerity of the place and the consequent load placed on the staff. Anyone absent, as Clark often was, was sorely missed. He was forever going off on mysterious little errands, not always restricted to Calgary. During that time, Joe caught airplanes much as others catch buses — frequently and on the run.

My wife Cecilia got used to speeding along the Blackfoot Trail to get Joe to the airport with only minutes to spare. As if that were not bad enough, he would disappear into a newsstand or the washroom, as the final minutes to flight time ticked away. Sometimes he missed the plane. We decided he took delight in playing "planesmanship," in which winning was being the last person on board.

I assigned Clark to write a feature to mark the thirtieth anniversary of the election of Social Credit on August 22, 1935. He produced an incisive article.

"Of those who lived through it," he wrote, "no one is impartial about that election of thirty years ago, August 22, 1935, when Alberta elected the first Social Credit government in the world.

"If they themselves were followers of Aberhart, it will always be a watershed in the story of the people's struggle with adversity. And if they were among the minority which opposed, they will remember hooligans, emotion run amok and a stab of fear."

He said there were two basic reasons for the Aberhart success. One was the background of utter desperation. The other was Social Credit's organization.

"If Aberhart was a prophet on the public stage, he was also almost a genius in the private planning room. The tours that he and Manning began alone mushroomed, and working people drove and spoke all night and were back at work in the morning, and the unemployed went on the road full-time, eating and sleeping where they could, spreading the gospel."

He also recalled the success of Aberhart's radio broadcasts, specifically his twice-weekly "Man from

Mars" scripts. The "visitor from Mars" wondered out loud why Albertans endured their misery in the midst of plenty.

Clark remembered the Man from Mars several years later, during his own campaign for the Conservative leadership in 1976, although he changed the planet and the sex of the creature from outer space. In several speeches he asked his audience to imagine what conclusions a "Person from Pluto" would draw if she landed and looked around.

"She would see a family allowance program, costing millions, and applying regardless of family wealth, and would conclude that we needed population so desperately that we subsidize birth, while the rest of the world tries to control it. She would see an unemployment insurance program which offers an incentive to some to work for only eight weeks every six months. She would see a freight rate structure and transportation system, and grants program, which concentrated population and production in a strip along the St. Lawrence, and would conclude either that the rest of the country was uninhabitable, or that we like living in each other's back pocket. Then she would see a regional economic expansion program, which encouraged industry to settle in the very regions the rest of the structure encouraged industry to avoid, and she would conclude we didn't know what we were doing, which, unhappily, would be the correct conclusion."

The *Albertan*'s hours left most of the day free for Clark to work for Lougheed. He was one of the original members of both an inner strategy committee and a policy group. His contribution to strategy was much more important than his policy work, Lougheed says.

After an initial meeting at Lougheed's Banff retreat in June the group met regularly for lunch at Calgary's

Holiday Inn. David Jenkins and Harold Veale, lawyers and former Clark colleagues at the University of Alberta, were there. They were joined by various others, including Ron Helmer, a Calgary oil consultant, Robert Dinkel, a Calgary lawyer, and Jim Edwards, an Edmonton radio man.

When they spoke to the Holiday Inn lunch circle Helmer and Clark tried to impress each other with their command of English. Clark would never hesitate to use a complicated word and Helmer maintained that Clark delighted in using words other members of the group would be unlikely to know. "Come on, Joe, what the hell does that mean?" Helmer would interject. He, too, was interested in words. Jenkins remembers Clark as the driving force behind every meeting, always prodding the group to do this or that.

One hot August day, Clark and I went together to room 959 of the Palliser Hotel for the organizing meeting of Lougheed's communications committee. After breakfast, Lougheed made some introductory remarks about the importance of organization. I made a note of his comment that "we need to get away from the one-man legislature that is a farce." He spoke in terms of a six- to ten-year program to achieve the goal.

His own strengths and weaknesses were discussed. He was young, a credible team leader, an outdoorsman, all supposedly in favourable contrast to the dour Ernest C. Manning. But Lougheed was a lawyer, an urbanite, rich, and intense and these were perceived by some present to be negative traits in Alberta.

Joe and his father Charles were appointed to the communications committee, but Joe channelled his talents through the strategy and policy committees. "I was clearly the most political person in Peter's entourage," Clark recalls, "but that was pretty limited expe-

rience. I was young. I had been in the Lazerte campaign
and with Kirby and had done political — though not
partisan — work at the Farmers Union of Alberta. Peter
put a lot of confidence in my judgment and ability. We
were quite close."

Lougheed acknowledges Clark's "very major role in
getting people".

Social Credit relied, not unnaturally for a party in
power thirty years, on old timers, often overconfident
workers. Clark and Lougheed went into the towns and
villages and found new, younger people. There was no
easy way. Only years of hard work could lead to power.
The work must begin at the constituency, every constituency, level. To be effective they must have a good
tactical feel for Alberta.

On one such outing Clark went to Okotoks to see a
prominent doctor, Morris Gibson. His daughter
Catriona met Clark at the door. Not expecting to find a
stranger at the door, she was clad only in a bath towel.
Their first embarrassment soon gave way to laughter.
Clark and Catriona Gibson became close friends and
spent a great deal of time together. They were out driving
on Highway 2 South in the fall of 1966 when news came
over the radio that Manning had called a byelection in
Pincher Creek-Crownsnest.

Clark pulled into a gas station at Nanton and called
Lougheed. Both were upset. They had not been expecting
the call so soon. Lougheed asked Clark to go to Pincher
Creek immediately.

It had already been decided that Lougheed would not
run himself. Pincher Creek was NDP territory and the
risk for the new leader was too great. The only known
Conservative declined to run. Lougheed and Clark
moved into the Turtle Mountain Inn, at nearby Frank.
They decided to put up the best show they could with an

able young candidate named Alex Wells, who lived in Blairmore. The leader and his assistant drove out along the main roads, nailing up their own election posters as they went, only to have them blown down by a strong west wind.

Garth Turcotte, the NDP candidate, won easily with Wells trailing a poor third. But that campaign was not nearly as negative as the bald results suggest. Lougheed and Clark learned from the NDP campaign tactics they would never forget. They copied and improved upon them.

"We were immensely impressed by them," says Clark, "we knew we were kids up against them." It was hard door-to-door campaigning that won for Turcotte and in Social Credit Alberta door-to-door campaigning was innovative, to say the least. Socred candidates had become accustomed to getting themselves elected simply by attending a few tea parties. The byelection in Pincher Creek served as a dress rehearsal in miniature for the general election of 1967.

Clark decided he needed more authority to carry out his organizational work for Lougheed. He ran for vice-president of the party and was elected at the annual meeting of 1966. Charles Clark was overheard to say at that convention that he was tired of being introduced to people as Joe Clark's father.

The twenty-seven-year-old vice-president was interviewed by the *Edmonton Journal*. "Mr. Clark says there is a danger, particularly for young people, that politics may become their whole life. And it seems certain that the danger, if it is a danger, has engulfed Joe Clark. He said people can't do anything well unless they are wrapped up in it, and it appears Joe is wrapped up in politics."

With the 1967 election less than a year away, Lougheed turned to the nitty-gritty of policy. He, Clark and David

Jenkins had heated disputes over the wording of policy statements and Clark and Jenkins found themselves ranged against Lougheed, the lawyer, arguing for clarity and simplicity. "That's how it's done in journalism, Peter," they would argue.

Clark sensed that the closeness of his relationship with Lougheed could not survive the election campaign. In any case, his organizing role had become redundant as the special campaign committee assumed control of strategy, and Clark wanted to run as a candidate himself. His natural preference was to run in Okotoks-High River, but Lougheed thought he was too young. They agreed that the constituency was one they could win and they should not jeopardize their chances with a new candidate when they already had a good prospect in Tom Hughes, a prominent rancher.

Clark agreed instead to take a shot at Calgary South, a riding held by the respected Speaker of the Legislature, Social Credit's Arthur Dixon. Nobody wanted the riding and its certain defeat. "Nobody gave him a snowball's chance in hell," Lougheed recalls.

David Jenkins got together with lawyers Douglas Korman and Bryan Targett to set up a managerial troika. I helped with a campaign flyer. Joe Clark, for all his activity, was not exactly a household word in Calgary. The paper was called, "What'sajoeclark?"

We took over a recently abandoned restaurant as campaign headquarters. It brought us unexpected dividends. Customers, unaware of the restaurant's demise, dropped in for their usual coffee, which they got, free, with an explanation of why they should vote for Joe Clark.

Clark, meanwhile, was really running — door to door. This was an effective refinement of the NDP techniques used in Pincher Creek. Both Clark and Lougheed tackled a block at a time, with workers going ahead, offering people a chance to meet the candidate. The candidate didn't waste time with empty houses or unrepentant Social Crediters.

Clark was not as athletic as Lougheed. When it came to running in an election the mind was willing but the flesh grew weak. With three days to go, Clark's knees began to puff and he was forced to stop campaigning.

The time could have made the difference between his defeat and a startling upset. Even his defeat was startling. Out of nowhere he came within 462 votes of beating Dixon. The results were Dixon, 5,401; Clark, 4,940; Jack Peters (NDP), 1,388; Willis O'Leary (L), 1,146. Dixon had won the previous election by 3,132 votes.

Lougheed won easily in Calgary West and took five others with him to form the first beachhead of the Conservative party in the Alberta legislature. His relationship with Clark would never be the same. Lougheed had now to look to his elected colleagues.

Clark was drawn to Alberta because under Lougheed he sensed that things were changing. He was also attracted to the man whose federal leadership campaign was then in the formative stages — Davie Fulton — and he considered his talents more suited to federal politics. When Fulton invited him to join his leadership campaign he accepted with pleasure.

He spent several months with Fulton, first in Alberta, later in Ottawa. "He felt the best thing he could do for me was to get a large Alberta delegation — and we won a majority of Alberta delegates," Fulton recollects. Later Clark did most of Fulton's speech writing, working with Fulton's executive assistant, Lowell Murray, and David Jenkins, both good friends, and others. One was Brian Mulroney, Fulton's Quebec fund-raiser. Clark and Mulroney had known each other since 1961 when Clark was national president of the Progressive Conservative Student Federation. They would see a lot more of each other.

7

WITH STANFIELD IN OTTAWA

CLARK was again at loose ends when Davie Fulton failed to win the Tory leadership in 1967. He wondered whether he should go back to Alberta. What were his chances of running there in 1968? He might as well pack his bags, he thought. There was nothing else to do. It was rather a letdown after the excitement of the leadership convention where Fulton was instrumental in electing Robert Stanfield.

The telephone rang. It was Robert Stanfield himself, who Clark had never got to know personally. Stanfield needed staff. Would Clark be interested in coming to his office as an assistant for three or four weeks to see them over a transitional period?

He had nothing else to do and there was always the possibility that something more permanent might turn up somewhere. Clark accepted, and joined Stanfield, then without a Commons seat, in his transition office on the third floor of Ottawa's Chateau Laurier. Although Stanfield didn't know Clark, Davie Fulton and Flora MacDonald, who had worked closely with him, had recommended him.

The three or four weeks became five or six. Clark helped Stanfield to persuade Lowell Murray to join the office as chief of staff. Murray, Fulton's campaign manager, was travelling in the Far East when Stanfield approached him and he agreed to join Stanfield's staff on his return. Clark was happy to stay as long as Stanfield wanted, although he knew now that, sooner or later, he wanted to be elected. Sooner meant the federal election, due in 1968, and to which the new leader and his assistants must turn their talents immediately. Clark thought about running in Rocky Mountain or in Jasper-Edson but Stanfield, having sized him up, decided he needed his speech-writing talents and urged him to stay.

After winning his Commons seat Stanfield moved to Suite 409S, the office in the Centre Block of the Parliament Buildings vacated by John Diefenbaker. The Opposition leader's oak-panelled corner office had been the office of prime ministers from Macdonald to Diefenbaker, but Lester Pearson decided not to use it after he won the 1963 general election when he tired of waiting for Diefenbaker to move. As Opposition leader's office it was even then too small, although Stanfield had only a small staff of three assistants. (By 1977, the office had doubled in staff and expanded to include a wing of offices in the nearby Confederation Building.) Clark took a small office in the Press Building, across from the Hill, but it proved too inconvenient to keep a speechwriter outside the main office. He then moved to a comfortable office, 444S, just down the corridor from Stanfield's suite and eventually into the main aide's office (later to be occupied by his own chief of staff, William Neville).

Clark's colleagues in the office considered him a good "idea man." Clark learned to master Stanfield's hesitant, drawling cadences. "You'd swear Stanfield had drawled it into the dictaphone himself," says Lowell Murray. But Clark did not find his job easy. During their first year together Murray sometimes rewrote his work, much to Clark's disgust, to bring out the Stanfield style. If work was difficult, Clark would indulge his passion for movies, just disappearing in mid-afternoon, leaving colleagues asking each other "where the hell is he?" Nevertheless colleagues considered him a perfectionist. On a particularly important speech he was known to work late into the night at home taking pains to get it just right. He would get up when he reached a sticking point and walk the two blocks to the grounds of Government House, the residence of the Governor-General, and return, polishing a phrase mentally.

He shared a furnished apartment in a new twelve-storey brick block at 80 Rideau Terrace with Murray and Graham Scott; Graham was a friend and supporter from university days who had also joined the Stanfield staff. The apartment was in east central Ottawa, a five-minute drive from Parliament Hill, just outside Rockcliffe village and within walking distance of Stanfield's official residence, the scene of frequent strategy talks.

Clark had a sense of humour that Stanfield sometimes rejected. Once on a CBC television profile of the leader, Clark alluded to his speech-writing frustrations. "What can you do with a guy who throws away some of your best lines?" he asked. Stanfield appreciated his frankness; straight talk is often lacking around a political leader. Stanfield remembers a closed meeting for the media at Toronto's Albany Club at which he and Dalton Camp spoke. Stanfield thought it had been a fair success and at the airport commented to Clark that they must establish more credibility among the media. "Well," replied Clark, "we sure didn't do it last night."

Indeed, Clark's strength in public relations came to the fore in Stanfield's office. He was often able to give advice, which was respected, on the morale of party organization in various parts of the country. He advised the leader where to go and what to do. He was the brains behind several schemes intended to bring Stanfield closer to specific interest groups, to get them to know him better and for him to learn their problems at first hand. This resulted in favourable national press coverage. On Clark's suggestion Stanfield spent four days on the livestock farm of Len Berg, at Sedgewick in northern Alberta, then moved down to another farm in grain country around Arrowood, seventy-five miles southeast of Calgary.

The idea for the trip was another indication of Clark's continuing interest in small communities. He had run provincially in the urban riding of Calgary-South rather than in his native High River out of a sense of party duty, but while he worked for Stanfield his mind turned back to the rural Canada he knew best. Cities invoked a sense of collectivism which repelled him. He had long discussions with colleagues, friends, academics and politicians about the inevitability of urbanization. The trend to the growth of cities was not inevitable, he argued. Studies of demographers and sociologists tended to be self-fulfilling prophecies, but he believed that the smaller community was worth preserving, and could be preserved, if government had the will and the strength of policy.

Clark and Stanfield could be quite self-deprecating at times, but they were different breeds, Clark aggressive, Stanfield deliberative. Clark's habit of speaking casually in articulate paragraphs was not congenial to Stanfield's temperament. Stanfield was not one to engage in office repartee, yet Clark's style forced him to do so, or he imagined it did, and at times he felt uncomfortable.

Stanfield had reservations about Clark. "I considered him too highly strung and nervous to be a practising politician. I thought he would probably return to Alberta eventually." This was contrary to what was actually in Clark's mind at the time.

Clark was aware of his marked personality differences with the leader, although he found them no more than he had experienced with Lougheed or Fulton.

It suited him temporarily to stay in Ottawa. He wanted to learn French. In Alberta it wouldn't be easy, but in Ottawa he was eligible for the newly established federal language courses. He achieved "bilingual status" by the time he left. Bilingual status didn't mean he was bilingual, as Clark readily acknowledged, but he worked at it, often sitting up late at night reading French novels.

At the same time he was aware of his total lack of physical exercise and resolved to do something about it. As a child, he had almost drowned when on a rare fishing trip with his father. He decided he would learn to swim. He phoned the Ottawa YMCA to inquire about lessons, time and cost. "How old is your lad, sir?" inquired a voice. Undaunted, he enrolled himself and went to classes with children. But he became bored soon and gave up.

Clark had a liberated view of women at that time, long before it became fashionable. When he was twenty-one he had regretted in a letter to a friend that a woman he knew had settled for the role of "cocktail wife." He got to know many women through their husbands, usually political colleagues. Clark didn't treat the wives of his friends in an off-hand way or as incidental to their husbands. He often made a point of getting to know them as well as he knew their husbands. He would engage them in serious conversation, remember a birthday, even write a letter to one of them if he had something to say of particular interest to them. Some of the couples he knew were David and Dreena Jenkins from his University of Alberta days, Davie and Pat Fulton from the early sixties, Norman and Anna Ruth Atkins, a little later. And he probably knew Mary Stanfield as well as he knew "R.L." as the staff called the leader.

By the time he went to work for Stanfield in 1967
Lowell Murray believed Clark was interested in marriage, although it wasn't his nature to say much about his
personal life. In his undergraduate days at the University
of Alberta and when he was at Dalhousie Law School, he
had taken out girls when the occasion demanded, among
them classmate Noella Brennan (now Noella Fisher, a
lawyer with the Nova Scotia Attorney-General's department) and Judith McMahon (now Judith Maxwell of the
C.D. Howe Institute in Montreal). At the University of
British Columbia, he cultivated the serious but short-
lived relationship with Liberal Penny Riordan. A year or
so later he met Catriona Gibson.

Friends in Alberta to whom he introduced Catriona
were aware that she and Joe were seeing as much of each
other as possible during 1965 and 1966.

Catriona took law at Queen's University, Kingston,
where she graduated at the top of her class in 1967. She
went on to article with a law firm in Calgary for a year.
Women were not easily accepted in law and the firm that
allowed her to article declined to let her practise law. She
took a job with the French oil firm, Aquitane, for a year,
then decided to return to university for a master's degree.
She chose Toronto's Osgoode Hall which, incidentally
(and likely it was no more than that), took her closer to
Clark, who had gone to work for Stanfield in 1967.
Friends assumed — hoped even — that they would
eventually marry.

During her first year at Osgoode, in the fall of 1969,
Clark took advantage of a party policy meeting in Peterborough, to arrange a meeting with Catriona afterwards
in Huntsville. She took one route back to Toronto, Clark
another to Ottawa. On the way home Catriona was killed
in a car accident. When Clark heard the news, two full
days later, he was shattered. He went to Okotoks, just

north of High River, for the funeral and shared the grief of Catriona's family.

A month before Catriona Gibson was killed my family had left Calgary for London, England, where I became a correspondent for FP Publications. At that time Clark was talking about travel; he was pretty sure he would visit us in London.

Back in Ottawa Lowell Murray was also getting restless and Clark, who admired Murray and liked working with him thought again, more seriously, about getting away altogether for a period of reflection. Stanfield tried to persuade both to stay, particularly Murray on whom he leaned heavily.

Murray's mind was made up. He quit at the end of February 1970, leaving Clark as both the principal speechwriter and assistant until he himself left at the end of May. Clark says, "The reason I left Stanfield — and I would have left anyone — was that I realized there were limits to what you can do in a staff job. A good staff member has to give advice to a leader that falls within the context of the initiatives of that leader. There were some things I wanted to do myself. I was interested in more than just being a staff person.

"I decided my usefulness to him was expiring and his to me. I wanted to be elected. I think my talents are greater in the front room. I have some in the back room but others are far more effective there than me."

Towards the end of May a letter arrived at our apartment on London's Putney Heath. Joe would arrive in a few days to take up our standing offer of a room as long as he needed it. I had to go to Rome to cover a NATO conference so I arranged to meet Joe in Paris on the way home. We reached Orly at eight o'clock in the evening and we put ourselves at the mercy of the accommodation bureau. They found us a room in a quaint little frame hotel on the Left Bank. There was no lobby, just a window on the left as you entered where the concierge sat. Clark's French was good enough to get us registered and to determine that we were on the sixth of seven floors. There were no elevators, so we humped our bags up the six flights of narrow stairs. Fatigued, we fell into the two single beds. We shared a common washroom, off the hall, with some other guests on the floor above. They played drums pretty well all night and kept Joe awake. We spent a couple of days as tourists, visiting the Louvre and cruising down the Seine. We also decided to see the Bastille and hopped off the Metro at the Place de la Bastille emerging into the square only to realize that it had been razed two hundred years before during the revolution. We were both clearly tired.

8

INTERLUDE IN ENGLAND

PUTNEY Heath rises like an oasis as you round the bend by the Green Man public house at the top of Putney Hill. And it is as welcome, after the congested traffic and acrid fumes of the high street and the hyperactivity of the city. The Green Man sits at a fork in the road. Most of the traffic bowls along, skirting the heath, in one direction towards Wimbledon or Guildford, in the other towards Kingston upon Thames. In between, running arrow-straight into the trees is Wildcroft Road. It is deserted but for the occasional car. It leads to a cricket pitch, a sort of village green, a cluster of expensive private homes, a compound of apartment buildings and, of course, a pub. On weekends the Roehampton cricket club from the neighbouring village plays on the green surrounded by magnificent hearty oaks, tall elms and plane trees.

The Telegraph Inn, a quarter of a mile from the Green Man, was in 1970 a small, sparsely furnished pub. Several pictures on the wall of the saloon bar showed what the pub had been like in its earlier days. It occupied the site of a semaphore signal station used to relay messages from the Admiralty to Portsmouth. Until the sixties the main road to Portsmouth ran outside; now it is diverted around the heath. On weekends an enterprising fish-monger set up a stand outside and sold cockles, mussels and shrimp to the customers who sat outside the pub, drinking their pints. It was a great family occasion outside the Telegraph Inn at noon every Sunday in fine weather. The owner complained that he lost two dozen pint glass mugs every Sunday, but the constant queue at the bar tempered one's sympathy.

It was to our flat near Putney Heath that Joe Clark came in June 1970. He lived with us for four months and also spent two months in France.

In an interview with Peter Desbarats of Global Television, Clark said he spent the summer sleeping by a cricket pitch in Putney. He did rather more than sleep. He arrived just in time for the British general election campaign which led to the defeat of Harold Wilson's government by the Tories under Edward Heath in 1970. He came to several of the election meetings I covered for FP Publications. His interest took him to Conservative Central Office, once for one of Heath's daily press conferences. On election night, he watched the returns on television in Trafalgar Square.

He had several other interests, apart from sleeping. He worked on his thesis about innovation in political conventions for a master's degree. He studied in the library of the Commonwealth Institute, on Northumberland Street near Trafalgar Square. He made a point of studying British politics closely; once the election was over, he waited for the autumn party conferences. He also availed himself of the cultural activities of London in their full range from the theatre to rock concerts.

The notion that he is a loner has gained currency because he is not "one of the boys" in an easy-going drinking sense. However, he has always enjoyed associating with friends. Even at this time when he was looking for change and rest in foreign countries he did not wish to be entirely on his own. Sometimes he would go with us to dinner, or the theatre. Once when I was

away on assignment he took Cecilia to a concert in the
Royal Festival Hall when the new prime minister,
Edward Heath, was in the audience. He sought out other
Canadians. One was Linda Anderson, a student in his
political science course at the University of Alberta in
1964, who was at the London School of Economics.
Another was Christine Forsyth, studying for her docto-
rate in English literature. They became close friends.

He was with Christine when they noticed the death of
Iain Macleod proclaimed on a poster outside a news-
agent's kiosk in Notting Hill Gate.

Macleod, leader of the progressive wing of the British
Conservative party, had a razor-sharp mind. He was an
eloquent debater in the House of Commons and had
become Chancellor of the Exchequer in Heath's government. I remember attending the first debate on economics in the new Parliament. Taunted by Harold Wilson,
Macleod had shot back caustically: "Look who's talking,
the walking wastepaper basket." It was a brilliant jab at
the time, alluding to Tory posters depicting Labour
campaign promises as scraps of paper in a wastepaper
basket. In Macleod's death, Clark thought, the Conservatives had lost a great man. He seemed to be
genuinely saddened. He told Christine Forsyth that
Macleod was the only man in the cabinet with the breadth
and sophistication to lead the Tory party as it should be.

Linda Anderson recalls that Clark showed her a
reference to Macleod in the *Economist* which said that
"he understood acutely the people in his party and in the
country that he represented. He did not despise what they
wanted. But he missed few chances of persuading them
that they might want something a little better." She
thought it pointed out rather well Clark's own political
philosophy.

He spent several weeks during the summer at the

university residence in Besançon, studying French. Besançon, a city of 100,000, was a good place to study because the University was a local industry and residents were sympathetic to students struggling with the language.

Clark wrote one letter to us from Besançon, containing observations on the state of his present well-being.

"If one were subject to depression, you could literally go bonkers studying a foreign language in a foreign environment. The advantage of immersion is that there is no opportunity to escape into the familiar. I have a limited competence, and can generally make myself understood — I even bought a coat-hanger — but some poor unilingual kid, dropped without a word of dialect into the centre of, say, India, could find despair just trying to get to the bathroom."

Joe returned to Britain for the autumn party conferences at Blackpool. He was particularly interested in the fringe meetings, organized by various groups within the parties, after the main daily conference session. He was impressed by the late Richard Crossman at the Labour conference and made a note of one of Crossman's comments. "In Britain we have a non partisan civil service but in Britain non partisan means Tory." Substituting Liberal for Tory, Clark paraphrased the comment during his leadership campaign. (Both he and Crossman were referring to the highest levels of the civil service.) At the Conservative party conference, he was particularly interested in the presentation of Lord Eccles, the minister for the arts. The discussion was about dissatisfaction in British society and the quality of life.

"If I ask myself why the British people are not now doing their best," Eccles said, "the answer must be that it is because their imagination and spirit have been starved in comparison with their growing intake of material things. The stomach can prosper while the heart grows faint." Eccles proposed to implement a vigorous program to bring artistic activities within reach of more people. "The quality of life," he said, "demands that we should support that which enhances the individual's understanding of himself and his society, and which arouses in him the desire and the capacity to use his own powers to the full." Fine words. Yet nothing much ever came of them. The Heath government's legacy to the arts was a system of charging admission to museums and art galleries which had traditionally been free.

Clark later arranged to interview Eccles for CBC radio — one of several times he tried his hand at interviewing. Christine Forsyth went along as an assistant and gave this account of the occasion in a letter to me.

"We decided that the only way to set the right tone was to take a taxi to the minister's house in Belgrave Square. We were admitted, after some questioning, to the minister's secretary, who remained and took notes throughout the interview. The minister was very sharp and responded quite critically at times to Joe's questions. My heart would sink to think Joe was not being taken seriously, but Joe told me afterward that it was the minister's prerogative to pounce on a bad question and berate the interviewer; he knew the interviewer would merely erase these criticisms later.

"Joe was very conscious, however of doing his homework and of asking the right questions, to win the interviewer's confidence, without presupposing answers in an obvious fashion. In the end the interview went quite well, nerves and all, with Joe getting Lord Eccles to speak on the government's role in the arts, how far, through subsidy and assistance, the government should go in deciding what the people should hear or see, what was good for them as opposed to giving the people what they thought they wanted. Obviously the questioning went deeper than the issue of government arts grants, and the minister trod the ground very warily; he did not allow anything to be imputed and was very rigorous with Joe.

"There was a moment when the minister took a phone call, was briefed by his secretary, and made some off-the-cuff derogatory remark about a London journalist's piece in that day's paper. Joe was adjusting rewinding and winding his tape recorder at the time. Later, on the stair way, the secretary cornered us and backed us into a little anteroom. She had noticed that my tape recorder had been running the whole time and demanded firmly that I find the spot on the tape with the remarks about the journalist and erase it, then replay it to her satisfaction. The erasure worked all too well and we left regretting somewhat that we hadn't got away with this little treason, but impressed with the thoroughness of the office."

London at the beginning of the seventies had lost some of the trendy glitter of the mid-sixties. Swinging London was only a shade of its former self, if you were interested in the Beatles, Carnaby Street and the King's Road. Yet culturally it remained as lively as ever and in specific fields, music for example, it had more than ever to offer. And Samuel Johnson's famous epigram still rang true: "A man who is tired of London is tired of life, for there is in London all that life can afford...." The West End stage offered the richest fare in the English-speaking world in both the playwrights (Simon Gray, Harold Pinter, Tom Stoppard, Christopher Hampton) and the performers (Alan Bates, Alec Guinness, Robert Morley, Maggie Smith, Glenda Jackson).

The most eminent conductor and composer of the age, Pierre Boulez, had become leader of the BBC Symphony; André Previn was at the helm of the London Symphony Orchestra; Colin Davis was music director at Convent

Garden, still unchallenged as the world capital of opera.

Joe enjoyed the theatre. He would come home to describe his delight in Christopher Hampton's *The Philanthropist* or Simon Gray's *Butley*. He usually accompanied Christine Forsyth on these outings. "I felt a little like a resource person for Joe in the arts," she commented. They went to see T.S. Eliot's *Murder in the Cathedral,* staged on location in Canterbury Cathedral, and happened to sit behind the Archbishop of Canterbury, Dr. Michael Ramsay and his wife.

Clark appeared to be making a conscious effort to catch up on what was new in the arts. He took every visit to a play seriously, in total contrast to his habit of dropping into movies good or bad for escape and light diversion. Here he made judgments about everything he saw or heard. His friends felt obliged to take a position in response to his views. It could be unsettling, even irritating. "I even sensed a kind of implied criticism in his tendency to judge," Christine Forsyth has said, "especially when I had recommended some entertainment or expedition. I now think it was a natural reflex in him to assess what these things were all about, how they occurred, what produced the phenomenon, and then on to a judgment, perhaps even a moral criticism, of whether they were good or bad in themselves, or indicated some good or bad trend in the host society."

Probably in the same spirit, Joe went with Christine to rock concerts. "He was keen on knowing what young people were up to," she says, "and we therefore presented ourselves at two or three concerts to observe young people in action in their natural habitat. We went to a successful evening of folk-rock music by the Fairport Convention at the Fairfield Halls, Croydon. We were a bit staidly dressed, sat in the dearer seats, and did not dance in the aisles as many did; but the music was pleasant enough, being a kind of electrified folk with a lively beat (almost Canadian). Another much less successful expedition was to an outdoor concert in a park in south London, where we sat on the grass among lolling, half-naked couples, empty pop bottles, pot fumes and besieged by dismal, wailing music (the promised main act never showed up). We left early. About a year later we went to a Frank Zappa concert at the Saddler's Wells Coliseum, sat in excellent seats and were generally surrounded by people like ourselves (not worth observing) while the real youth sat up with the hoi polloi in the gods."

Clark returned to France, this time to Paris, in the fall of 1970 for another course in speaking French. Before he left he made a "deal" with my daughter, also named Christine.

Christine, eight at the time, and her friends were playing a game with a lot of imagination that required them to "travel." In a casual manner Christine told Joe that she would be going to Paris. "Oh, that's good," he responded, "because I'm going to Paris, too." They "arranged" to meet under the Eiffel Tower at a given time. That was the end of it until Joe returned several weeks later. Upon seeing Christine, he demanded to know why she hadn't kept their date under the Tower. As she hadn't shown up, he said, he had brought something for her to mark the occasion. Whereupon he produced an ingenious magic kit. Christine had hours of fun with it; she cherishes it and occasionally brings it out for the benefit of company to this day.

As a bachelor in his early thirties, Joe took an unusual interest in children and they reciprocated. When Robert Scammell, his friend from the University of Alberta's *Gateway,* and his wife had a daughter, Joe wrote a long and humorous letter to their son about the problems and joys of having a little sister. And Joe suggested the name Chantelle for the daughter of his friends David and Dreena Jenkins.

Clark wrote good letters. In a way he had made his living by writing speeches, slogans and pamphlets. His stay in Europe was a kind of sabbatical and some of his best letters were written there. One of them came from Paris.

"My description won't do justice. But, tired tonight, buffeted by French fonctionnaires, I went to eat about eight, along a new street, and came to a restaurant called Don Quixote. No customers were there, two waitresses, one on each side of the bar, each with a drink. The room was a little larger than the one in your place where I slept, with seven tables spread around three walls, the bar along the fourth. Candle-lit, red table cloths, and three inexpert murals of the Don and his windmill. The menu offered a Dubonnet for nine francs, and I saw on the rack, beside my coat, a note that it would cost me two francs to get it back. Clip joint, but I was too tired to leave; and they had paella on the menu, which I dimly remembered as one of the dishes which won me, so briefly and so fully, to food in Spain. So I stayed to be clipped. Then the procession began.

"First, a couple intent on amour, he with a 1920s moustache, she with one of those constructed complexions you wouldn't want to wear in a storm. They settled a table away from me and started nuzzling; I read a magazine, in self-defence. Then three Negroes, a svelte sweatered girl, and two men. Then a taxi in front and out of that a rather regal woman, of what the French might call a certain size. She seemed to be the owner and, in her entry, dusted a few bottles and scrutinized the guests. Then she went behind the bar and asked where was Danielle. Danielle was out, but shortly came in, on a leash, leading a woman so English-looking she might have been Agatha Christie. Danielle is a poodle, and provided the first uproarious episode of the night. She sniffed, in proprietary fashion, around the feet of most of us; you get used to that in French restaurants. Then suddenly, one of the Negro men bolted up from his bench-style seat. He apparently was sitting in Danielle's corner, and had been preoccupied in conversation when suddenly this poodle muzzle pushed warmly along his backside. He stood, with a very remarkable dignity, staring down at intransigent Danielle, long enough for Madame the owner to put the poodle on a leash; Agatha was against that, obviously thinking the leash had a better occupant.

"At this stage there entered the Lady in Black, one of those striking women you see only at night, statuesque, strong, her bangs framing a pale and haughty face. This restaurant-bar is not far from Pigalle, and suddenly seemed more than just clip. The girl obviously had nothing to do, and did it with style, pouring my wine, bringing my bread, spooning out paella. We were even now, if you count Danielle, six customers, six with the house. Then came a man with two guitars. He played flamenco for a while, almost unobtrusively, then broke into a shouting tenor that transfixed the room. Next came a rough-looking fellow, in a white shirt, who kissed all but the customers on every cheek, put on a vest, and became the headwaiter. Finally a fruity-looking young man came, and kissed, and took the second guitar.

"He had a remarkable voice, of range and sensitivity, and where the first player had bullied us into silence, he had us almost in awe. I know virtually no Spanish but enough that when he said, in a song, 'nos camarades doloros,' I was not only affected by the atmosphere of that voice and theme and setting, but startled to see how cynical had been all my thoughts to that moment. The lady in black was clapping her hands in that staccato style of the Spanish accompanist; one of the waitresses had reappeared in a backless dress and colorful flamenco skirt, and castanets, and danced, with more determination than grace, but seriously. And it occurred to me that what happened was more than just a change in personal mood; I had moved, momentarily, and aided by the wine and music, out of my Anglo Saxon reserve, and into the romantic.

"Given the preoccupations of the hour — Trudeau is pictured looking distraught on the front of *L'Express* — and indeed the persistent, if subconscious, preoccupation of any Canadian who knows and fears our national fragility — I was reminded, again, that the talk of 'deux nations' extends well beyond one electoral campaign, beyond a discussion of the distribution of powers. It is the essence of Canada — that we have that unbridgeable and vital combination of Anglo-Saxon reserve and Latin romance, and that the cross-fertilization has been sufficient that I, from High River, can perceive that 'doloros' is much deeper than Anglo-Saxon sadness, much more basic, and that a René Levesque can be so determined to work within the rule of law. (It reminds me also that I don't consider Trudeau a representative Canadian; he is too much a rationalist to be French, too inflexible to be Anglo-Saxon; when he went to Harvard he followed his true instinct; he belongs in the modern Puritan society, where everything is coded and the code is everything. That is most alarming if one is worried about the various implications of 'continentalism' because if earlier prime ministers were continentalists by convenience, Trudeau is by conviction; he prefers the American value system more than that of France or Britain, more than that of Quebec or Ontario. And of course he presumes Alberta not to have one.)

"But, back at Don Quixote, as the wine wore off, and I began again to wonder if these celebrants were 'really sincere,' five (5!) more men came, carrying cases that could have been instruments, could, if you remember Al Capone, have been guns. Wanting to remain a citizen of 'deux nations,' I left with that in doubt. So that was Paris while you were in St. Malo — an indication of what could have been avoided if the 'Mariner' had never left there.

"I'm taking courses now in the Centre Censier, one of the sites and centres of what the enthusiasts choose to call 'The Second French Revolution,' that of May 68, and of intermittent skirmishes since. All over there are signs urging us to get into the streets, for one cause or another. Damn romantics."

The months in Europe were a welcome sabbatical. He used the break to think, to reflect on his career and to fix his own perspective on life. Christine Forsyth says political discussions with Joe usually fixed on pragmatic lines and on personalities. She thinks he appreciated the influence of character on political events.

Joe went to Europe with only the general idea that he wanted to run for election. While there he made the decision to seek nomination as soon as possible. He returned to Canada fully refreshed in mind and body. He went, not to the backrooms of Ottawa, as he had nine years before, but home to Alberta determined to win not only a nomination but an election. As he started on that task he wrote to us to say how much he missed England.

He had encountered a prospective constituent who had emigrated. They had discussed the critic Bernard Levin, who had been associated with the television satirical program "That Was The Week That Was" during the sixties. Clark wrote that he missed the quality of critics such as Levin, and, indeed, the entire British quality press. "But," he wrote, "Britain doesn't have the mountains or the wilderness and new things starting — our compensation for a pale press is the excitement of being on what Wallace Stegner calls the building end. During my first excursion to Europe (and it was an excursion to, not an incursion into) I realized that some people were of the old world and some of the new; I'm a little more able now to belong to both but my preference, when all is said, is here."

9
ELECTED IN ROCKY MOUNTAIN

BACK in Alberta, Clark was attracted by a most unattractive constituency. It was known as Rocky Mountain, a vast wedge-shaped area sprawling from the U.S. border, north five hundred miles to mining and timber country. It was forbidding because it had no north-south system of travel, except perhaps the Banff-Jasper Highway, snowbound in winter. It had not one single population centre, but many small towns. It contained prosperous ranches, poor farmland, oil and gas fields, three national parks, a pulp and paper industry and coal mining. No wonder the Alberta members of Parliament petitioned the Speaker of the House of Commons against the constituency when the Electoral Boundaries Commission proposed it in 1966.

Clark took an apartment in Calgary in the riding of Calgary Centre, which was being vacated by the veteran Conservative Douglas Harkness. He toyed with the thought of seeking the nomination there but rejected it. It was a Conservative seat and Clark wanted to gain one from the Liberals and only in "Rocky" could he do that. He would have preferred to run in his native High River but the town was in Crowfoot, held also by a Conservative, Jack Horner. The boundary of Rocky Mountain ran a few miles west of the town.

From his Calgary base Clark had easy access to the

part of Rocky Mountain that lay to the west and south of High River. He was less than an hour's drive from the Banff area. And if he chose to explore the northern end of the riding, he could get there by way of Edmonton. In the spring of 1971 he knew practically no one in the constituency he proposed to serve.

There was the additional obstacle that the sitting Liberal Allen Sulatycky had become a respected and popular member since he won the election of 1969 with a comfortable margin of 1,658 votes. He would be no pushover, particularly for an outsider.

From the point of view of Hugh Gourlay in Banff, Clark was not only an outsider but an opportunist. Gourlay, the official Conservative candidate, and Doug Caston, an independent, had split the Conservative vote in 1968. Here was Clark looking for a chance to come in and take the seat while Gourlay and Caston factions quarrelled. In the summer of 1971, however, there was no assurance of a split in the next election. If Clark's only goal was to get elected there were easier ways to do it.

He wrote to people he knew in the party, enclosing a list of the towns in Rocky Mountain, and asking for any names of persons who might help him. The replies yielded a slender list which proved to be the basis of his organization.

Although he was running for the nomination, he was also doing enough freelance work to pay the rent. Sulatycky thought Clark was paid eleven thousand dollars by the newly elected Conservative government in Alberta to prepare some promotion material for Premier Lougheed's planned visit to Japan. Pressed by Social Credit MLAs, the Alberta government would admit only that Clark was associated during the summer with a firm that did only seventeen hundred dollars' worth of work for the trip.

Armed only with his list and his grass roots political experience, Clark climbed into his car and drove off into the Rocky Mountain constituency. He went to one town after another where he didn't know a soul. Drayton Valley was typical of the snags he ran into; he couldn't even locate the one person whose name he had been given.

After scouting around the riding he decided to make his home in Edson, one of the largest towns and with the advantage of having good highway links with other centres. The prospective candidate had to set up organizations in towns he aspired to represent.

His first fight was for the nomination, as both Gourlay and Caston had declared their intention to seek it. Winning the nomination would be but a first step; the winner would then have to face a successful sitting member. After it became known that Clark had moved into the constituency, Sulatycky began to fly home from Ottawa every weekend, rather than every third weekend.

In the battle for the nomination, the location of the nomination meeting was important. A meeting in Banff could easily favour Gourlay on his home ground, as similarly, Jasper would favour Caston. On the other hand Turner Valley or Blairmore were potential Clark strongholds.

Clark and his supporters suggested that several nomination meetings be held in the main population centres, using the preferential ballot. Malvern Davies of Turner Valley, the constituency association president, was cool to both Clark and his ideas but Clark had a friend on the executive in Fred Bradley, now MLA for Pincher Creek. At a meeting held in November to select delegates to the next national convention he met two more important allies, Marilyn Maclean, the vice-president, and her husband Lloyd, mayor of Drayton

Valley and owner of a prosperous oil well servicing company.

The association agreed in principle to the idea of a series of nomination meetings at its annual meeting, which was held in conjunction with the provincial party convention in November. Several other executive meetings were held to discuss plans and set dates. It was decided that five meetings would be held on successive nights, with two days off followed by five more meetings.

Clark, meanwhile, was out campaigning. He awaited the executive's final decision in Edson where he was seeking out potential supporters. David Jenkins called him from Edmonton to say their proposals for a series of nomination meetings had been lost on all counts. As Clark groaned into the phone, Jenkins quickly ended the bad joke.

At this time Joe wrote to us in England. He was preparing for an election at any time.

"I'm feeling a little stir crazy," he wrote, "and maybe one relief is to write to people out of the stir. The weather here is atrocious — sixty-five below this morning in Athabasca — and for the first time since I was a paper boy, walking in it — the immobility of the winter is getting me down. It's beautiful — hoar frost, the sun, that frozen blue sky — but you have to warm a plugged-in car twenty minutes before you dare move it, and a two-block walk, however exhilarating, is bitter before it's over. This is a long spell — it was briefly interrupted ten days ago by two days of chinook, but then plunged again to relentless cold, and no break is in sight. Most things go on, sluggishly, and when you get word from Pekisko where the ranchers are snowed and settled in, you do realize that for most of us, technology has made quite a conquest of nature. But it isn't pleasant — and it isn't sure; by coincidence the air traffic controllers went on strike this week, and the cold and snow have closed rail and highway movement between British Columbia and the rest, so there is virtually no Canadian way to or from that coast, emphasizing the frailty of our control.

"Sometimes, even in France, certainly in Spain, I had the feeling I couldn't rely on the law. That is a feeling peculiar to Britons, Canadians and maybe Americans, who grow accustomed to assuming that, in some emergency, they will have the 'right to counsel,' or some other protection at home, and miss that security where the law is less regular. That may be our elemental claim to civilization. But winters like this remind that that kind of security isn't all-encompassing; it doesn't protect against a blizzard, which can be as random as a madman with an axe, and yet more frequent to more of us.

"My other problem, probably worse than the weather, is that this quest for the nomination stretches endlessly on. It's the sort of thing one should be able to be philosophic about: say it will happen and I will win or lose; but I can't do that. It is always on my mind, and in a territory so immense, there are always people you haven't seen, places you haven't been, and you know those oversights are invitations to your opponents. It is also a singular thing, uncommunicable to people who haven't driven home fifty miles at night from a sparsely attended meeting, or aren't haunted by the knowledge they haven't yet been to Grand Cache, and the other guy might get there first. It's ludicrous and I laugh at the condition, describing it, but that doesn't make it easier."

Nomination meetings were arranged in Blairmore, Turner Valley, Banff, Whitecourt, Jasper, Edson, Hinton, Swan Hills, Grande Cache and Drayton Valley. Davies was appointed returning officer; he and his brother Stan would take the ballot box around to five meetings, Marilyn Maclean to the other five. The box would travel a thousand miles in a sealed bag, with candidates and agents checking the seals before every meeting.

Three weeks before the meetings started, Davies announced he had a legal opinion that the association's constitution did not permit the use of a preferential ballot. Clark got a contrary opinion. Davies summoned an executive meeting to settle the matter; it met in Edmonton on a wintry February Sunday evening.

Heavy snow fell as Fred Bradley and George Waite, a pro-Clark constituency association director, left Blairmore at nine o'clock in the morning. They stopped in Calgary to pick up David Jenkins, now Clark's official agent. Visibility was about ten yards as they passed one trailer truck after another on the divided Highway 2 North from Calgary. They reached the Macdonald Hotel at six o'clock, nine hours for a drive of three hundred miles.

Jenkins presented the case for using a preferential form of ballot. Theoretically, two candidates can be tied with the same number of votes under the more usual simple choice ballot where the voter places an "X" beside the preferred candidate. All possibility of deadlock, however remote, must be avoided, Jenkins argued, when there would be ten separate nominating meetings. And the solution was the preferential ballot. He didn't add, but it was part of Clark's strategy, that the preferential ballot can help a candidate with strong second choice prospects. In view of the enmity Caston and Gourlay had stirred up during their 1968 campaign, it was unlikely that voters favouring one or the other as first choice would give second preference to the other. That was where Clark stood to gain substantially.

(On the first count of ballots only first choices, the number ones, are counted and if one candidate emerges with a majority, the election is decided. But if there is no winner, the last choice candidate is dropped from contention. The ballots for that candidate are then recounted and the votes for second choice on the ballot are added to those of the candidates still in the race.)

Conflicting legal opinions were presented. As the debate dragged on inconclusively, Roy Watson, national vice-president of the party, happened to come into the room, and both sides agreed to take his independent ruling. He favoured the preferential ballot. The meeting adjourned at 10 P.M.

As snow continued to fall — it turned out to be the heaviest snowfall of the winter at sixteen inches — Bradley, Jenkins and Waite again set out. They got back to Calgary at 6 A.M.

There was much more of the same weather. The meetings themselves were gruelling. Clark thought he needed heavy support in the south to compensate for opposition strength elsewhere. He hoped for about thirty-five supporters from the ranch country at Blairmore. One made it through the snow and he too late to vote.

Clark fared better at the meeting in Turner Valley because a family friend had the foresight to keep all roads plowed to the golf club where the meeting was held. But Clark foolishly agreed to amend the rules to allow persons who arrived late to mark ballots.

This precedent was used against him the very next night in Banff. There, on opponent Hugh Gourlay's home ground, an angry dispute broke out when Clark opposed Gourlay's efforts to allow late arrivals to vote. According to the rules, no ballots were to be distributed after the candidates began to speak. At one point in the heated debate on the floor lawyer Kenneth Harkness, son of Douglas Harkness, threatened, on behalf of Clark, to seek an injunction if the rules were violated. Harkness was one of several Calgary lawyers who came with Jenkins to protect Clark's interests. The Clark people feared Gourlay would add to his proven strength at home by packing the meeting with transients. Later they believed their suspicions were justified when mail sent to persons on the Banff mailing list was returned as undeliverable. The Banff meeting ended with Clark taking the advice of his lawyer friends and allowing late arrivals to vote provided they signed affidavits stating they arrived after the distribution of ballots had been completed or that they had not been told that they had to collect a ballot before the speeches began. A party worker expressed the bitter feelings the dispute was generating with the comment that it was turning people to the opposition. He seemed to be right. "For me it's Allen (Sulatycky) all the way," said one constituent.

The final meeting and the ballot counting took place on March 18 in the Frank Maddock High School Gymnasium at Drayton Valley, which had been a Sulatycky stronghold in 1968. Lloyd Maclean invested five hundred dollars of his own money to bring the Alpine band from Edmonton for dancing and celebrations after the counting. Clark drew the last speaking position. Gourlay and Caston started by attacking Clark before the crowd of three hundred. Clark countered his opponents' attacks with a quip, "You must admit, a fellow who can get Doug Caston and Hugh Gourlay working together must have something going for him.... They both think I need to serve a longer political apprenticeship. I answer they should be running for the Senate." He called for a more positive approach to politics. "The West has been so busy complaining it can't reach a positive conclusion. The future of Canada is not in Toronto or Montreal.... It's out here on the building end of Canada." Once again Clark had used the Wallace Stegner phrase, "the building end." It comes from Stegner's *Wolf Willow*, where he wrote: "History is a pontoon bridge. Every man walks and works at its building end, and has come as far as he has over the pontoons aided by others he may never have heard of."

The announcement of Clark's second ballot victory brought out a brave show of unity on stage and scenes of elation among the supporters. Joe's mother Grace, who practically had to be restrained during some of the earlier attacks on her son, was delighted. Gourlay said the campaign had cost him a lot of money and he'd better get back to Banff to earn some more. The new candidate went to bed, leaving the supporters to celebrate his success at the Ambassador Motel.

Clark's campaign to unseat Sulatycky began the very next morning. He asked Marilyn Maclean to be his campaign co-ordinator. She hesitated at first; her husband was already working for Clark and she questioned whether it was good to have so much involvement in one family. Eventually she was persuaded to take on the load and the Maclean house, overlooking their yard filled with heavy machinery on Fifty-fourth Street, became the Clark headquarters.

A general meeting was called for May in Jasper, as an election warm-up. Clark brought in his old friend Davie Fulton as guest speaker. He also proposed the defeated Caston as association president, despite objections from some supporters who were unwilling to forget the nomination battle so soon.

Clark took speaking engagements wherever he could find them. One of the most significant turned out to be an address to the annual meeting of the Banff-Lake Louise Chamber of Commerce.

The president of the chamber that year was W.S. (Bill)

Herron, from a prominent Banff family, owner of the Mount Norquay ski lifts. Herron, unlike most Banff people, had not been impressed with Sulatycky and was looking for an alternative. He had never before been politically active.

Driving home from that meeting, Herron and his wife Carol agreed Clark was their man. "We can not only vote." for him, we can help him get elected." Their home became Clark's Banff headquarters.

Clark hoped to get away for a holiday with us in England. He wrote on June 6, 1972, to ask whether we would be home if he came and whether he could give our telephone number to his constituency people, just in case an election were called.

"I very much doubt that anything will happen here — Trudeau has literally guaranteed there would be no summer election, although he left open an escape hatch concerning those familiar 'unforeseen circumstances' — but I would feel more comfortable if my people could keep in touch with me. It puts quite a crimp in a campaign when you can't find the candidate.

"The delay in the election date is probably working to my electoral advantage, although it may send me to Parliament a bankrupt. CBC, with a little prompting from the local Grits, has got very high-hat about work being done by nominated candidates, so that source of income is closed. I am thus doing some public relations writing, which seems less soul-destroying when it pays your bills. Most of my time, however, is spent on the campaign, and I'm finding my travels most interesting. The other Sunday I visited two Ukrainian farmers, separately, and with an interpreter: one spoke quite active English, and read a lot in our language; the other, older, had only a few words, and I of course have none of his. The older man's house, or living room, was quite beautifully done, by himself, in those ornate patterns and bright colours you find on the Ukrainian Easter egg. He brought out a bottle of his special Scotch, unsheathed only on extraordinary occasions, and both language and breeding forbade me from declining. I sat and swallowed a kitchen-glass-full of the stuff, and have little recollection of my drive home; but it's a certain thing that to have refused would have hurt him quite severely. God knows how much of that I'll encounter. But it is fascinating to encounter the variety of lives, traditions and attitudes in a stretch of country that is not only large, but relatively unhomogenized; a relatively low proportion of my constituents take their styles from the city or the media, some because their English is fragile, some because television doesn't reach them, some because they're too busy. Anyway, it has been a sufficiently fascinating experience that election will be but a bonus, rather than the only value of the exercise.

"I think we probably will win, although it is far from being certain. Allen Sulatycky, the Liberal incumbent, and parliamentary secretary to Jean Chrétien, is intelligent, personable, and has worked hard. His name is much better known, even yet, than mine, although the election delay gives me a chance to reduce the gap."

He wrote again on June 25 to say that he almost certainly could not come to England. He had to be in Priddis, near High River, on July 9 and in Edson for a rodeo on July 19 so he would not be able to take advantage of the excursion fare. Again he gave us an entertaining excerpt from his campaign.

"If you're interested in the occasional diaries of an exhausted candidate, this weekend has been rained on, but not out. Friday night, I flew from Calgary to Edmonton, expecting to find a rented car; it wasn't there, presumably because the days of downpour had sufficiently dispirited the local rental agent that he quit that night. I called the manager, who was born to manage but not to dispense and he, after being unable to find any staff who knew the practical aspects of his business, came down himself to their downtown office, at midnight, to try to extricate my promised car. First, he couldn't get into the garage where his fleet was; then, he got in, and couldn't get out; mercifully, he was then able to roust an employee, who sprung both my car and his master. I drove to Spruce Grove, until the rain got me down, then checked into something called the Ambassador Motel. A freight train runs down the corridor every twenty minutes, and the walls were not only paper-thin but that night separated me, on my right, from a loud snorer and, on my left, from a relentlessly insatiable amorous couple. (It was, if you care to think of it that way, a counterpoint of fundamental human sounds, covering the extremes, if not the range, from peace to passion.) I got up early, naturally, to drive to Whitecourt, where they had been unable to arrange my mount for the parade, so I watched. I then drove to Fox Creek, a town of fifteen hundred which you perhaps have never heard of, since it wasn't there when you last were permanently here, for a barbecue, under canvas. It was a ball, not least because of the visiting band, the Bonnyville Bruisers, whose drummer is eight years old. I stayed that night with quiet friends, but got up at 7 A.M. anyway to return to Whitecourt, for the pancake breakfast in the street, which was rained out when I got there. What saved the day was that I went to Mass, and there met seven sisters, of the order of who knows what, who came from St. Boniface and, of course, knew the Lonergans [Cecilia Humphreys' family]. (Well... we knew of the Lonergans. They are a family one knows of.) Having thus established my bona fides, as a friend of yours, they bequeathed me a drunken

Indian who had become so disappointed at the raining-out of the rodeo that he had commenced a tear which landed him first in jail, then in the hospital, then in the care of the sisters, and then in my car, to be transported back to his home in Blue Ridge, because I was going that way, and because I know the Lonergans.

"If you think there is any fiction here, I assure you there is none. That is why I am going to take a holiday *some*where, and also why there is some substance to the suspicion that Rocky Mountain is not yet ready for a candidate who holidays on the continent.

"The other evening I had occasion to speak to the Catholic Women's League of Hinton (Alta!), many of whose members are French, some unilingually so. So I naturally dusted off my own proficiency, portions of which follow:

" 'Quand je parle français, les anglais comprennent toujours, mais les français ne comprennent jamais. De temps en temps, j'ai des problèmes avec mes mots. Une fois, j'étais à la Messe à Ottawa, et je me suis meler les mots "pêche" et "pêcher". J'ai demandé pardon pour mes poissons.

" 'Pouvez-vous croire que ma mère enseigne le français à High River? Il y avait un prêtre qui s'appellait Trudeau, et il connaisait que, chez moi, nous sommes Conservateurs. Toujours quand il téléphonait, il disait: 'Bonjour, c'est Père Trudeau.' Vous comprenez que ce n'est pas Pierre Trudeau qui parle ce soir. J'ai plus de cheveux sur ma tête.'

"The CWL vote is beginning to look solid. In Hinton."

Early on in the campaign, Jenkins went into Jasper on a futile fund-raising campaign. He recalled later that he got "the royal run-around" and no money. Each person he approached had some excuse and the name of someone else he might try.

Lloyd Maclean introduced Clark to the oil companies with offices in Drayton Valley. Clark took Maclean's advice to stand when the company executives were seated. He had noticed that a speaker usually came across more impressively by not joining the seated group. It was a learning experience for Clark and he did most of the questioning.

The October 30 general election was called on September 1. The Clark team assembled in the Maclean's living room over the Labour Day holiday for a two-day strategy planning session. They paused only long enough to send out for Chinese food.

Sitting around the dining room table, the group cut the unwieldy constituency up into twelve zones, each with an appointed campaign manager in charge of a corps of poll captains. Bradley agreed to take over as driver-manager. Jenkins was in his accustomed role of agent and fund raiser.

The group found themselves faced with a task not unlike the one that had faced Clark in Calgary South in 1967. A little-known candidate was running against a popular established opponent. Now a one-time loser, he really couldn't afford to lose again.

After the nomination Clark had arranged for a recognition factor survey, which turned out to be surprisingly encouraging. True, he was recognized by only 15 percent of the respondents, but Sulatycky fared little better, with 21 percent.

Marilyn Maclean was disturbed when people asked her if the thirty-three-year-old candidate was a homosexual. She feared a whispering campaign that would be difficult to handle. All she could say was that she had no reason to think so. At this stage the voters of Rocky Mountain did not know their candidate well enough to know that he had cultivated close friendships with several women and casual friendships with many others during the last decade.

Fortunately the questions died; the campaign was entirely clean.

Clark knew he had to run hard. He and Bradley embarked on an exhausting driving tour of seventeen-hour days. They applied the old methods of personal approach and knocking on doors.

On one such outing, in Bushtown on the outskirts of Coleman, Clark was surprised to find residents who said they liked him but couldn't vote. After a few of these polite rebuffs he began to ask questions. He asked if they were recent immigrants. On the contrary, he discovered they were immigrants all right, but they had lived here half a century.

After he won the election Clark took up the cause of six Polish immigrants and won for them the Canadian citizenship they had been denied over the years. He wrote about them in a weekly column for newspapers in his constituency.

"Some of them have lived and worked in Canada for more than sixty years — and worked hard, mining underground for coal. However, until April 3, 1974, they had been denied the right to become citizens of the country they helped build.

"As older Albertans would remember, the 1930s were particularly difficult and turbulent in the Crowsnest Pass. Unemployment was high and labour-management relations bitter. The Communist Party became so strong that, for a while, Blairmore's main street was renamed 'Tim Buck Avenue,' after the Canadian Communist leader. There were strikes, some violence, some damage to property.

"The police, trying to keep order, noted the names of people who were suspected of breaching the peace.

Inevitably, in the circumstances, they sometimes made mistakes, and noted the names of innocent people.

"But all those names — of the innocent, the guilty, and the people who lost their tempers and threw one rock in a lifetime — went into files that found their way to Ottawa.

"Years later, when people who had been brushed by that violence applied for Canadian citizenship, the files came up again.

"The Canadian Citizenship Act allows the minister to reject certain applications for citizenship 'in the public interest,' without giving reason. Usually the reason is that a government file contains evidence of crime, sedition, or some other undesirable activity.

"Sometimes those files are wrong. Since they are secret, they are difficult to challenge; and right or wrong, they are a minister's only guide in judging suitability for citizenship.

"Some people in the Pass were denied citizenship on the basis of a word — or an action — or a suspicion that occurred some forty years ago."

The Conservative candidate in the Bushtown poll in the 1966 general election had won eight or nine votes. The highest for a Conservative previously was eighteen. Bushtown gave Clark a hundred and fifty votes in the election of 1974.

On election day the Maclean home took on the characteristics of a Clark family reunion. Joe's father and mother, Charles and Grace Clark, and his brother and sister-in-law Peter and Marcia Clark came up from High River and Calgary. Jenkins was on hand in case of legal problems. This time the living room became election central.

During the evening workers took returns by phone from polling stations throughout the constituency. They pinned the results to a big board, with every polling station on it, in the Macleans' living room.

Clark won convincingly, polling 12,983 votes to Sulatycky's 7,975. In Drayton Valley, Clark reversed a Liberal majority, winning 58 percent of the vote, compared to Sulatycky's 24.5 percent. Workers and well-wishers flocked to the Scout Hall for a victory celebration.

The reasons for Clark's success are not hard to find. It seems probable that Sulatycky underestimated him. The word from Liberals who knew Clark in Ottawa was that he was aloof and arrogant. Sulatycky says the main reason for his defeat was the strong tide running against the Liberals in that election campaign.

10
MAUREEN

MAUREEN McTeer had just about had it with the Conservatives. She had been fired from the parliamentary research staff. She was fed up. With only a few days remaining in the 1972 federal election campaign she was without a job.

Money was important to her. Her family could not afford to finance university careers for six children.

Her political interests had first led Maureen to work as a research assistant in the Tories' parliamentary research office during the summers of 1971 and 1972. She still had one year left to complete her bachelor of arts degree at the University of Ottawa, but she decided to stay on at the research office through the election campaign to save for her return to university the following year to take up law studies.

Her problem, it seemed, was an over-abundance of enthusiasm for causes. She would work all day (except — according to Geoffrey Molyneux, her boss — for her long lunch hours) at the research office on Sparks Street. Then she was off to work until the early hours for Ottawa area candidates. Molyneux expected his staff to work day and night with him. Maureen's zeal for the party won her no marks in his books. Nor did her enthusiasm for "women's lib" causes. She was one of several young women who talked a lot, a little too much, perhaps, about women's issues. And she was one of several let go. Her extra-curricular enthusiasms rather than her lack of diligence or ability led to the parting of the ways. Her colleagues of the day are unstinting in their praise. Molyneux himself says, "She was very highly motivated and it showed up in her work." In fact he thought sufficiently highly of her to send her before the election was called on some advance work in Ontario centres where Leader Robert Stanfield planned to speak. At one point there were plans for this twenty-one-year-old to do some extensive advance work during the election campaign itself. And during her routine day she was frequently called upon to prepare material for Mr. Stanfield and others to use during the daily Question Period in the House of Commons.

Her first reaction upon being fired was to fight. She complained strongly to Tom Sloan, Stanfield's principal assistant. Sloan called Molyneux to discuss the issue and inquired whether there was anything, even then, that could be done about it. As there were only a few days left in the campaign, he wondered if perhaps Molyneux might reconsider. Molyneux stuck to his guns.

For Maureen it was the low point in five years of enthusiastic work for the Conservatives, countless hours of door-knocking for Bert Lawrence, the provincial candidate in Carleton East, speeches, membership drives, fund-raising parties. Perhaps she would just bide her time, she thought in November 1972, until the next fall. Then she would enter law school. If she could just get a job to see her through the winter....

After the election a friend mentioned that a young Alberta freshman member of Parliament was looking for help. His name was Joe Clark. Maureen wasn't too sure she wanted to work for an Albertan. "I figured, what the heck, I'll give him a try — he's new, he's young and he sounds pretty able." Molyneux assured Clark when he called to check Maureen out that there were no problems apart from what he already knew. She went to work in Clark's office as a research assistant early in 1973.

She had been an even more precocious political child than her new boss. True, his whole life since the age of seventeen had been politics and journalism, mostly politics. But Maureen had been travelling and thumping political drums since the tender age of twelve. Her father, John McTeer, had been a grass roots politician in eastern Ontario since before Maureen was born. When Joe Clark, as vice-president of the Alberta Conservative party, was building a machine for Peter Lougheed, Maureen McTeer was bumping along the dust roads of Cumberland Township, helping her dad run for municipal office. He lost and she was shattered. "She cried and cried and cried," her mother recalls. "She was the only one who cried." When her father was campaign manager for Albert Belanger, the successful provincial Tory candidate in Prescott and Russell, she became interested in Ontario politics. At the age of fifteen she thought of Premier John Robarts as a father figure. At the age of sixteen Joe Clark had not been elected to anything outside his school. Maureen at sixteen was the president of the Prescott-Russell Young Progressive Conservative (YPC) branch. "We were taught as we were growing up that we had a responsibility to be involved in the political process and that you lost your right to complain if you didn't vote and didn't participate. We all have a stake in the future: that was my father's teaching. I took it seriously. It's something that gets into your blood," Maureen says.

The second oldest of six children, Maureen went to a one-room school. She enjoyed the rustic tranquillity of her father's farm near the banks of the Ottawa River, outside the village of Cumberland, twenty-five miles east of Ottawa.

Her first three years of education were in French at the small local separate school. Most parents in the area sent their children to the larger English public school. The McTeers were Roman Catholics and they saw the French school as a good opportunity to set their children along the road to bilingualism. After the third year, some classes were in French, others in English, an ideal bilingual combination seldom available and rarely taken by parents with children growing up in the late fifties.

Rivalry was strong among the McTeer children — you had to be sharp and enthusiastic to hold your own, at work or at play. In studies, Maureen would compete for good marks with her older sister, Colleen. Her mother Bea says she would set a goal of equalling the marks of a girl ahead of her in class. She had to work for her success, particularly later when she went to Ottawa's Notre Dame High School.

John McTeer at various times farmed, raised turkeys and fine horses and ran a moving business. Mrs. McTeer stayed at home with the children for fourteen years, but when Maureen was a teenager her mother went to work for an insurance firm in Ottawa. In 1967 the family undertook the building of a new house. Maureen, by then fifteen, was expected to stay home and cook for the family and the hired carpenter. "She didn't like it one bit," her mother says. Nevertheless, she was a great success, according to the carpenter, who said he didn't know how anyone so young could bake such fine pies.

For recreation the McTeer family rode horses, walked in the scenic countryside, tossed a football around, or played baseball or hockey with the local boys. John McTeer remembers talking to Maureen about a career — about law and politics. At about fourteen, he says, Maureen was expressing an interest in both. Law, he thought, might be a natural for his daughter in Cumberland. "I hoped to groom her for politics out here," he says, adding with a wry smile, "now she has a much bigger responsibility."

Maureen says she thought first of being a doctor but soon dismissed it because her chemistry and physics marks weren't good enough.

She applied for nursing at Ottawa's Civic Hospital but soon dropped the idea when she realized she couldn't stand the sight of blood. "I'm not your nurse, mother," she said at the time. The family nurse turned out to be her sister Pamela.

She was attracted to politics. And she had observed during what she now calls "my gung-ho period in politics" that many politicians were lawyers. "It always occurred to me that I seemed to be training myself for a political career. I had that feeling from quite early on. I thought of myself as a young, energetic and bilingual woman having a fair amount of knowlege at a fairly young age of what politics was all about. I thought inevitably it was going to lead somewhere in politics. It was always my thought that I'd run against John Turner and I thought I'd show him [chuckling]. I thought if we [the Conservatives] had a bilingual woman in her mid-thirties who could speak out on issues affecting Ottawa-Carleton, John Turner wouldn't have a snowball's hope in hell." But she had another reason, which she explains as a determination to see whether the profession was as cliquish as it appeared — "whether they were really such a bunch of old fogies, or whether they would let women in." She also thought it would be nice to know what her rights were.

In preparation for law she went through a three-year bachelor of arts program at the University of Ottawa. There she was every bit as politically involved as Joe

Clark had been twelve years earlier at the University of Alberta. In high school, Maureen had won two debating scholarships and, recognizing the importance to politics of public debating, she closely identified with the University of Ottawa-*Ottawa Journal* annual debating scholarship program. Naturally, she was a member of the university PC club and served a term on the executive of the Eastern Ontario YPCs and another term as vice-president of the provincial organization.

"The training I received in debates has been the best possible for developing a logical approach to solving problems," she says. "I learned how to stand on my own feet and defend my thoughts and opinions — such ability is proving a terrific asset in campaign work for Joe; it will be invaluable in a court of law."

John Grace, *Ottawa Journal* editorial editor, was impressed by Maureen McTeer. As chairman of the final judging panel during her two years in the debating program, Grace commented, "I've never seen anyone before or since who impressed me so much with her ease and ability to think on her feet."

Maureen was a strong supporter of Bert Lawrence during the 1971 Ontario leadership campaign and convention. She "starred" in a film made by journalism students at Ottawa's Carleton University. She is shown escorting federal leader Stanfield around, introducing him to various people. She appears downhearted when Mr. Lawrence is forced out of the race on the second ballot. "I felt lost," she says in the film "I went into the committee room and had a good cry."

Of the prospect of voting for front-runners William Davis or Allan Lawrence, she says, "I was unable to bring myself to vote for what I believed was the decaying establishment." And she was far from overjoyed when Mr. Davis won. The theme of the convention was "a new wave." Commented Maureen McTeer, "It seemed to be such a good chance for a new wave and it seems to have ended in such a little ripple."

The McTeer family's support for Bert Lawrence ran strongly right up to the Ottawa Carleton federal byelection in the autumn of 1976. John McTeer had been associated with Lawrence campaigns since 1963. Even as early as the leadership campaign convention in February, the McTeers were making no secret of their campaign to get Bert Lawrence the nomination. John McTeer always regarded Lawrence as the straightest politician he knew. He was the kind of person who would say plainly that he couldn't solve a problem, or that he could; you knew exactly where you stood with him. Others said the same thing about Joe Clark. No doubt Clark told the McTeers he couldn't go along with them. While officially neutral in the contest for the nomination between Lawrence and Jean Pigott, an Ottawa businesswoman, Clark was not displeased when Mrs. Pigott won.

When Maureen went to work in Clark's office towards the end of 1972, he was thirty-three, she not yet twenty-one. Their relationship was still formal and professional. Maureen worried that the job might not last. She was still attempting to finish her last year in arts at university, managing to take all but one course at night. She would turn up in Clark's office late in the morning, making up time on weekends and occasionally at night. She was not a typist. "I would have made a lousy secretary," she says. She found that Clark often did his own research and wrote his own speeches. His secretary was a recently arrived refugee from Uganda. While she was a good typist she could not be expected to understand the political side of the office. Maureen concentrated mainly on Clark's constituency matters.

She was prepared for the worst when he invited her out

to dinner one cold March night. Perhaps, she thought, he was taking the least painful way of firing her. They went to the Cafe Louis IX, a first class restaurant in Hull, much patronized by Ottawa political and bureaucratic circles. "Joe was very ill at ease, and I was too," she recalled. The wine waiter didn't help. He was one of those characters fond of displaying superior airs and a little intimidating to patrons not thoroughly conversant with wine lists.

"He acted as though we were a couple of hicks from the woods. He did intimidate us into buying a full bottle of wine." They both drank rather more than was their custom. Even so, over steaks, on this their first date they found conversation difficult. When they left the restaurant, matters were not improved when they lost their way home. Noticing the Alberta licence plates on Clark's Capri, an RCMP officer followed them for blocks and eventually stopped them. When the officer, who had been recently posted from Alberta, discovered Clark was an Alberta MP he did his best to direct the couple back to the highway leading across the river to Ottawa.

In spite of that inauspicious beginning, the night was the first event of a whirlwind romance. Movies, more dinners, and visits to the McTeer farm followed regularly. For her twenty-first birthday her new boss gave Maureen twenty-one roses. "I knew he liked me."

Just before Easter 1973, after an interruption of several months, Joe and I resumed our correspondence. Clark's first letter didn't mention Maureen. It was his usual compendium of good humour and comment on the political scene and, for my benefit, the press. His parents were well. His brother and sister-in-law were expecting a child in early October. The letter contained much personal trivia.

He began by chiding me for my complaint about his failure to correspond with friends. "The intimation of

"THE SHOP"
The High River Times Building, built in 1927. Joe Clark worked in his father's shop as a teen ager.

JOE CLARK'S HOME
The family home in High River, built by Joe Clark's grandfather in 1909.

HIGH RIVER COUNTRY
Joe Clark's father took this photograph of High River country. Clark took it with him to Ottawa and hung it in Stornoway, the official residence of the leader of the Opposition.

A SMALL TOWN IN WINTER
Railway Street looking east across High River's business district.

A FAMILY HOLIDAY
Joe Clark, left, with his mother Grace and brother Peter
on a family holiday in 1949.

A FAMILY GROUP
Joe Clark with his
mother, grandfather
Charles Clark, and
aunt Bessie Burke in a
grain field near his
home in High River.

CHARLES CLARK

JOHN VANDERMEULEN

JOE'S FIRST PICTURE
Joe Clark at three weeks.

CONTACTS
Friend John Vandermeulen took this picture of his university roommate telephoning a political friend.

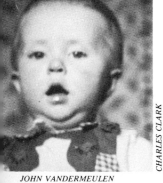

CHARLES CLARK

JOHN VANDERMEULEN

THE BUDDING POLITICIAN
Clark as a child, holding forth in his playpen.

AT THE WEDDING OF FRIENDS
Joe Clark gives the toast to the bride at the wedding of friends Gail and John Vandermeulen.

CHUCK STOODY, OTTAWA JOURNAL

THE CANDIDATES

Clark, left, joins fellow candidates Brian Mulroney, Flora MacDonald, Pat Nowlan, Paul Hellyer, Heward Grafftey, Claude Wagner and John Fraser before the voting.

CLARK WITH FLORA MACDONALD

Clark and Flora MacDonald wear each other's colours after her withdrawal after the second ballot in Clark's favour.

RUSSELL MANT, OTTAWA JOURNAL

WITH "THE CHIEF"
Former Prime Minister John Diefenbaker congratulates Joe Clark in a committee room at Ottawa's Civic Centre minutes after Clark won the leadership on February 22, 1976.

POLICE ESCORT VICTORIOUS CLARK
A "flying wedge" of Ottawa policemen carry the victorious Clark and Maureen to the stage of the Ottawa Civic Centre after Clark won the leadership of the Progressive Conservative party, February 22, 1976.

WITH RIDING WORKERS
Joe Clark talks with riding workers on a charter aircraft between Edmonton and Banff, 1977.

A COOKOUT
Dancing in a tent with a member of his riding at a cookout near Banff.

IN BANFF
Talking with townspeople on the street in Banff.

CATHERINE
Joe Clark gives his daughter a ride on his shoulders, 1978.

MAUREEN AND CATHERINE
Maureen McTeer and her daughter, aged eight months, 1977.

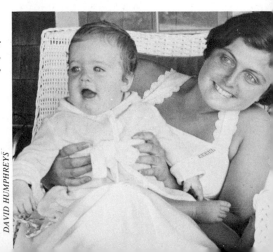

snobbery in your last letter was quite uncalled for (although it has achieved its purpose, and evoked a response), and simply serves to illustrate again how little you journalists comprehend the burdens and demands of running a country. Single-handed.

"In fact I have felt very pushed and busy, particularly since January, and have been failing in my obligations towards too many friends. One becomes aware that that obligation is, in fact, not towards friends but to oneself, because there truly is the danger of becoming locked in here, isolated from a more personal world. I am of course enjoying myself immensely. The House itself was a strangely disquieting place in the early days. Little things unnerved me. For example, there is a tradition that a member, leaving his seat or coming to it, bows to the Speaker before sitting or leaving. My first day there, I realized I didn't know how deeply one bows, and so sat there stupidly until some old hand got up, bent a ritual inch or two in Lamoureux's direction, and thus tipped me off. I had real trouble speaking there, still do.

"The first few weeks, even when I had supplemental questions prepared, and written before me, I had trouble getting them out. It sounds self-conscious, but one in fact is aware that this is the place where Diefenbaker, Laurier and Macdonald and others spoke, and that knowledge is inhibiting. I am more at ease in Question Period now, but still have to develop a natural speaking style.

"I've spoken five times, twice on youth-related matters (RLS has made me chairman of a special, and minor [no pun intended] caucus committee on youth) once on the failure of housing legislation to serve the towns and last week on aboriginal rights.... My method is still — as it is for speeches to other bodies — to prepare a fairly full text, and that isn't the way to proceed in the

House. You get locked into the text. Yet I am still sufficiently in awe of the place that I don't feel ready to get up with just headnotes. I must do that soon, because I'm sure I can, and the important trick is to do it once."

He alluded to the present state of the nation ruled by a minority Liberal government. "My impression is that the country perceives itself to be at the cross-roads — different regions and different commentators will disagree as to what roads, precisely, are intersecting; but there is a general air of being in an important time — and short-term legislation will not be regarded as adequate. It may be that our best bet is to help make Parliament work, and thus reveal the weakness of whatever the present government, with its preoccupation naturally upon what went wrong October 30, brings in."

We were coming back to Ottawa in the summer and Clark offered us the use of his apartment. Still no hint of any forthcoming marriage. There were two extra bedrooms, he said, and we could share them. If the House was recessed, we would be alone there for three or four weeks because he would be in the riding.

He concluded, "Now I must go and finish some correspondence with constituents. My life these days is full of unemployment insurance claims, inquiries about airports and other problems that might seem petty on a sweeping stage, but are of immense importance to the people who raise them. People who are also electors. Of mine."

I duly accepted the invitation to stay at his apartment at 300 Cooper Street in Centre Town Ottawa and in a reply written on June 17, Clark confirmed the arrangements. He wrote about some CBC radio interview he had heard, then passed on information about the apartment. He closed with this: "One change in my own circumstance

— which serves only to make my invitation to you all the warmer — is that I am getting married June 30, to Maureen McTeer of Ottawa. This is information to be guarded until after the fact. We are having a very small wedding, thirty or forty people, almost entirely family. This is partly because I would have particular problems knowing who *not* to invite, particularly in a season when so many of my supporters are taking holidays and could come. Our solution has been to not invite almost everybody.

"And the only way we can make that work is to not tell almost everybody. So I hope you will respect the confidence until the thirtieth is past. Maureen wants me to emphasize that our invitation stands — we have planned our summer and fall on the assumption you will be with us, for as long as you need. Maureen will be with me in the riding in the summer, and is going to law school at the U of Ottawa in the fall, so will not be in your way nor consider you in hers."

That indeed proved to be the case. We arrived when the newlyweds were touring the constituency. We still felt self-conscious, moving into an apartment in which the bride had never lived and which was filled with freshly opened and unopened wedding presents.

Maureen still intended to finish law school and had every intention of practising. There, incidentally, she differed from her husband, who had also gone into law because it was a profession closely related to politics, but who could never see himself practising law. Explaining why she kept her own name after their marriage, Maureen said that as she was going to be the only lawyer in the McTeer family, "I thought it would be nice to practise in my own name and have a McTeer on a law firm door somewhere — something my parents could be proud of." Before the leadership campaign she made arrangements to article with a Calgary law firm and meanwhile, she became a familiar sight on Parliament Hill. After classes she would join Joe for dinner in the Parliamentary restaurant. As he spoke in the House, she watched from the members' gallery.

They were married during a period of political uncertainty and tension. After the 1972 election which elected Clark for the first time, the Liberals formed a minority government and concentrated on keeping themselves in power. "My assumption," Maureen says, "was that there would be an election soon — that we would win and that Joe would be in the cabinet. He was young and able and shared many views with R.L. (Stanfield). It never occurred to me that we would not win."

Clark wasn't talking about his ambitions. He may have joked with high school colleagues in High River about being prime minister, but from university days onwards, friends had to draw their own conclusions about his personal ambitions not from anything he said, but from observing his total immersion in and dedication to politics. John McTeer himself said it best. "He had a definite political goal in life, which was to go up."

Working, arguing, speaking, reading, Clark had been learning politics for fifteen years when he entered the Commons. It isn't surprising, therefore, that from the very beginning his speeches in the Commons were highly political in content and were delivered with wit and obvious relish.

Joe's last letter to us reflected a growing enthusiasm for the House of Commons.

"This is a red-letter day, of sorts, for me, in which I can almost call Hansard my own. I'm in it three times, once on a question, once on a speech I knew I had to make, and once because a matter came up before our speakers were in the House, and I had to pitch in. The speech I had to make was great fun. We are discussing a very important bill limiting election expenses — the abuse it neglects to limit is the capacity of a party in power to use government prerogatives for its own purposes. I took particular satisfaction in listing the flagrant abuses of the NDP government of Manitoba, since the NDP have been preaching so sanctimoniously about the bad practice of others. My suggestion was that the only effect they have had on bad practice was to make it worse, and that their motive for chasing the money-lenders out of the Temple was to take over the action. It actually got Stanley Knowles exercised, which I thought would happen only in case of a fire. At one point, as I was cataloguing the sins of the Liberals, the Speaker wondered if I was in order, and I replied, in parliamentary language, that it was necessary for the House to understand that, with Liberals, sneakiness is a habit, not an accident. I wonder, in retrospect, if I went a little far, but it enlivened the evening, and added spirit to a debate that has heretofore been too polite."

A fellow freshman but much older member, Allan McKinnon of Victoria, says his first reaction was that Clark should stop insulting all those cabinet ministers with his heckling. He was abrasive in the House. He was also abrasive in caucus. This was one of the reasons that only a few members of caucus supported his bid for the leadership in 1976. McKinnon says it wasn't long before he realized that Clark was well informed on all topics he raised. "It quickly became apparent that he was the best heckler by far on our side of the House."

11
THE LEADERSHIP RACE

CLARK swept to victory in the general election held on June 18, 1974. He captured Rocky Mountain for the second time by winning 9,812 more votes than his Liberal opponent. This win, one of the most convincing achieved by any candidate, consolidated his position in the party and in Parliament. No longer was he the freshman member in a shaky, minority Parliament.

He spent election night in Drayton Valley at the home of Marilyn Maclean, his campaign manager. Next morning he set out with Maureen and his father for the Clark home in High River and a few days of rest and thought. Although Clark's own position was solid, the party had failed disappointingly to persuade voters to accept its proposals for wage and price controls as a means of controlling inflation, running at a rate of 12 percent annually in May 1974. Still, Clark could look forward to four years in which to establish himself as an Opposition critic and debater in the House.

Robert Stanfield had lost his third consecutive election as leader and almost immediately press speculation arose over his future and possible successors. Such prospects did not please Clark, one of Stanfield's staunchest supporters in the caucus until the leader resigned.

The rest in High River was brief. After a few days Clark visited David Jenkins, then general manager of Nu West

Development Corporation, in Edmonton's industrial west end. Besides being one of Clark's oldest and most trusted friends, Jenkins had just come through his third campaign as helpful expediter. Jenkins was aggressive and optimistic. He had an infectious enthusiasm.

"Now you should think seriously about the leadership," Jenkins said, quite unexpectedly. The suggestion took Clark by surprise. He had come to discuss the housekeeping details of his own election, not the leadership.

Back in Ottawa the victorious members of caucus assembled to discuss the future. Stanfield lost no time in making his own decision. He announced on August 5 that he would resign, staying in office only until a leadership convention could be convened.

He said it might be good for the party to have a French-Canadian leader from Quebec, "but I'm not saying my successor should be chosen from there."

The caucus the previous day had endorsed Stanfield's plans with some dissension. Jack Horner, the Alberta MP for Crowfoot, said he might leave the party as a result of the caucus's endorsation of Stanfield's plan.

Clark frequently visited Banff, one of the main population centres of his constituency. Later in the summer, he dropped in to see his old comrade Peter Lougheed in the premier's retreat home. They had met there nine years before to discuss their assault on the Social Credit bastion. This time Clark came with a specific question: would Lougheed run for the leadership? Lougheed's name had been kicked around in several post-election post-mortems in the press as a strong prospect for the leadership. He and Clark talked for three hours, during which time Lougheed assured Clark that he would not run. Clark knew that Lougheed believed he had a job to do in Alberta and that he felt more at ease in provincial politics than he would in Ottawa. He would also soon be facing his second election in Alberta, which would mean a second full term as premier of the province.

On the question of Clark's own suitability for leadership office, there were no neutrals among those who knew him well. Nobody thought he was totally unsuited to the task and that he should never consider it. Broadly there were four viewpoints.

Jenkins' view was in a class by itself. He had described himself as a devoted disciple of Clark's. He would walk through broken glass for him. It was only a matter of time before others would see the quality and Clark would make it to the top.

Others, like Graham Scott, who worked for Clark as a student politician, thought he was too young. They advised him to wait for next time.

Some refused to believe that Lougheed would not run and preferred him to Clark. Calgary Centre MP Harvie Andre was among them.

The fourth viewpoint belonged to the recent acquaintances who had been so impressed by Clark in a short time that they were prepared to encourage him to run. One was Jim Hawkes, a psychology professor at the University of Calgary. He had known Clark since the fall of 1971 when Hawkes joined a policy committee set up by Harvie Andre in Calgary Centre. He had encouraged Clark to run, even in 1973, when the two met occasionally in Ottawa. Another was Allan McKinnon, the Victoria MP, who came to Parliament for the first time with Clark in the election of 1972.

"You'd better think about running, Joe," McKinnon told him as they met in the corridors of Parliament one day in the autumn of 1974. Clark asked McKinnon if he was serious. Assured he was, Clark said he would be thinking about it.

Steve Paproski, the member for Edmonton Centre, similarly offered encouragement. By the end of 1974 Clark was beginning to seriously consider running for the leadership. By deciding to holiday with Maureen and Jenkins and his wife Dreena in Martinique over the Christmas period, Clark set himself up for more of the Jenkins' no-so-gentle persuasion. And he got it.

In February Clark went out to help Fred Bradley campaign in the Alberta provincial riding, Pincher Creek, which takes in some of Clark's federal Rocky Mountain constituency. Bradley too, was encouraging. Harold Veale, the Edmonton lawyer and former university debating colleague, telephoned to urge him to run, regardless of Lougheed's plans.

In Ottawa during the winter Maureen worked hard at her studies in second year law at the University of Ottawa. One of her professors, Mark Krasnick, also urged Joe to seek the leadership. Krasnick provided a link to academic policy discussions. He belonged to a small discussion group which included Professor Sandy Borins of Carleton University's school of public administration and his wife Carole Uhlaner, a graduate student. Both of them had worked for George McGovern in the 1972 U.S. presidential race. Another member of the group was Ian McKinnon, Allan McKinnon's son and a graduate student in political science. Clark met them informally several times. He discussed his decentralization ideas, they argued and made their comments. Later they were to draft Clark's policy papers in the leadership campaign.

In April, Clark went to see Jim Foster, the lanky, youthful-looking attorney-general of Alberta who had marched with him as a student fifteen years before. When Foster practised law, before becoming attorney-general, Clark used to drop in to his home with a girl friend for dinner and they had kept in touch since that time. Now Clark wanted to know whether Foster could confirm his own belief about Lougheed's intentions. Joining them were David Jenkins, Harvie Andre and Peter Jenner, Foster's executive assistant. Foster said the next leader must be fully bilingual, whereupon Clark uttered two sentences in French. Nobody in the office understood their literal meaning but the message was clear. Lougheed was not bilingual and had little hope of becoming so, as they all well knew. But Foster thought Lougheed might still be persuaded to change his mind.

"You know, Jim, if Peter doesn't run, I might have to," Clark told Foster.

"Joe, if Peter doesn't run, you have no alternative. You have an obligation to run."

Clark returned to see Foster in May. Again Foster encouraged him, with a cautionary note that he must run to win. In June, Lloyd Maclean cornered him during a visit to Drayton Valley to advise him "to get in there and get the nomination." The forcefulness of Maclean's advice surprised Clark. His wife Marilyn was a litte more cautious.

Clark and Maureen then went again to see Lougheed in his Legislative Building office in Edmonton. But he assured them he stood by his position of the previous summer. Now he had fought his election, giving voters an undertaking that he would complete his term as premier.

On June 19, Clark and Maureen went to dinner at the Oakville home of former Halton MP Terry O'Connor. During the meal and afterwards, driving to the Stratford Festival, Clark discussed his prospects for a leadership campaign. For the first time he said what he was to repeat many times in the campaign. He wanted to run and he would run to win. It would be a this-time campaign, not a token effort to establish his credentials for another race.

O'Connor said unequivocally he would support Clark. He agreed to attend a feasibility meeting on July 30 in Toronto.

Clark made two calls. One was to Tim Woolstencroft, brother of an old college friend, Peter Woolstencroft, and asked him to organize some youth clubs in the party's student wing to support his candidacy. He called another friend, George Cooper from his class at Dalhousie Law School, to organize a meeting in Halifax.

On July 30, a group of friends joined Clark and Maureen for sandwiches and coffee in the Mayfair Room of the Bristol Place Hotel, near Malton airport. They were pessimistic about Clark's prospects. In fact the vote in the group was ten to four against his candidacy. Only MPs Harvie Andre (Calgary Centre) and Allan Mc-Kinnon (Victoria) joined Clark and Maureen in favour. At this meeting Terry O'Connor was urging Clark to throw in his lot with Flora MacDonald, whose organization was already impressive.

Michel Cogger, Clark's roommate when he was associate national director of the party in Ottawa, made it clear he would support Mulroney if he ran. James Balfour, the former MP, who knew Clark well, was committed already to candidate James Gillies. Jean Bazin, a Quebec organizer who had known Clark since student days, was there. He later backed Mulroney. Other Quebec Conservatives at the meeting were Jean Peloquin and Yvonne Sirois, both of whom went with Clark.

The main item on the agenda at the feasibility meeting was a survey of other candidates and their prospects. The group compiled a list of twenty-two possible candidates. The first column gave the group's rating of each candidate's ability (not desirability) to win the convention on a scale of one to ten. The second gave the consensus of the meeting of the candidate's ability to win an election and the third gave an opinion of whether the candidate would run. ("U" means undecided.)

John Fraser	4	No	Yes
John Reynolds	4	No	U
Peter Lougheed	10	Yes	U
Jack Horner	4	No	Yes
John Diefenbaker	2	No	U
Jim Gillies	5	Yes	Yes
Flora MacDonald	8	Yes	Yes
Sinclair Stevens	6	Yes	Yes
Allan Lawrence	2	No	U
Walter Baker	2	No	U
David Crombie	5	No	U
Bill Davis	8	Yes	Yes
or			
D'Arcy McKeough	7	Yes	Yes
Claude Wagner	8	Yes	Yes
Heward Grafftey	3	No	Yes
Brian Mulroney	4	No	U
Leonard Jones	1	No	U
James McGrath	3	No	Yes
Pat Nowlan	2	No	U
Robert Coates	1	No	U
David MacDonald	1	No	U
Elmer McKay	2	No	U

This was mid-summer 1975, before the Ontario election that reduced the Davis government to a minority position. Any discussion about the leadership naturally included speculation that either Davis or McKeough, the provincial treasurer, might run and be a strong candidate. Next to Lougheed, who was given top rating, this group gave the Davis-McKeough combination the highest rating. (Of those who actually did run for the leadership, the group gave the top rating to Claude Wagner and Flora MacDonald, both in terms of ability to win the convention and to win an election.)

Clark, of course, believed Lougheed would not run. There was also considerable doubt about Davis or McKeough. That left Wagner and MacDonald at the top. Clark was close to MacDonald on many policy questions and he regarded her as a friend; this did not influence his decision to run himself. He proceeded to outline his strengths to the group. He had proven effective as a debater in the House of Commons. He had support in several regions and strong youth appeal, because of his work in the party and his age. He had some Quebec strength, though not much. And he had good contacts from coast to coast. Flora MacDonald could qualify on most of the same counts. Clark was better in the House; MacDonald had more contacts. But Clark had the trump card — he could give interviews and speeches in French. His only disadvantage, he said, was his youth; he might have trouble being taken seriously at first. He emphasized that if he ran it would be only in a serious attempt to win; there would be no question of running simply to establish credentials for the next time. He added that he thought enough money could be raised to pay for a national tour to survey his prospects.

After the Toronto meeting, Clark telephoned Fred Bradley in Blairmore to ask him to arrange several meetings in his constituency for himself and Richard Gwyn, the *Toronto Star* columnist, who had expressed an interest in visiting that part of the country. Clark and Maureen then left for France where Clark took immersion courses in French at Royan, near Bordeaux.

Clark believed that his command of French would be a strong factor in the leadership race and he says he did improve his French with this short course. The improvement, though, was not enough to avoid confusion at the barbershop just before he returned to Canada. He asked for a trim but not a crew cut. The barber heard crew cut and that's what he got — returning to the campaign with a haircut that made him look even younger than he was.

Rested and refreshed, Clark plunged into serious preparations for his campaign. He arranged a breakfast meeting at Calgary's Palliser Hotel on the morning of September 15. Present were his brother Peter, now practising law in Calgary, the Calgary Centre MP Harvie Andre, Jim Hawkes, Michael Robison, president of Calgary South PC Association, and John Rookes, president of Calgary Centre.

Again, Lougheed was the first choice of the meeting. One favoured Liberal John Turner, whose name had been proposed in the press, because he thought Turner could beat Trudeau. Hawkes, a psychologist, came out unequivocally for Clark. He would choose Clark over Lougheed even if the premier ran, he said, and he announced then and there that he was ready to work for Clark (which he immediately did, starting right after the meeting).

Hawkes was to be important to Clark's campaign. He was as close as Clark ever came to having a working effective campaign director. In fact, Clark was his own director, both nominally and effectively throughout the campaign, but when that proved to be administratively impossible, and as dangerous gaps became apparent, it was Hawkes who quickly stepped in. In September, he was the first off the fence and into Clark's campaign. In November, he took over as co-ordinator for the whole of western Canada. In mid-January, when Clark's national headquarters was foundering for lack of direction, he flew to Ottawa to harness the mass of youthful enthusiasm.

Hawkes was forty-one — a quiet man with a casual manner about him that put people at their ease.

He had grown up in Calgary, the son of a switcher for the Canadian National Railways. His father was killed in 1950 while Jim, then aged fifteen, was in Britain as the YMCA's Boy of the Year.

The family scrambled for two years. His mother went out to work for eighty-five dollars a month, and Jim worked weekends at the YMCA from midnight to eight in the morning for fifty cents an hour, sleeping when he could on a desk top. He stayed with the YMCA and became youth secretary in the Montreal Westmount branch. In 1959 he returned to Calgary to set up two community branches for the Calgary YMCA. Hawkes's Y experience made him an expert in volunteer work. It taught him that a paid organizer's goal was to do himself out of a job; he should do nothing that he could find a volunteer to do. In 1961 he left the YMCA to become dean of students at Mount Royal Junior College during that institution's transition from private to public financing.

He later decided to go into psychology and went first to the University of Calgary and then on to Colorado State University where he took his doctorate in experimental psychology.

Working with disadvantaged people in Denver, Hawkes found that government was getting in the way. Regulations were seldom if ever thought out for their impact on society; they were usually there for financial reasons. Hawkes' experience coincided with the violent period on U.S. campuses during the late sixties. He watched and was appalled as a campus building was burned to the ground. When Hawkes returned to Canada in 1970, it was with a strong sense of the power that governments have and the importance of how they use that power.

With a colleague, Bill Gabbert, he established a research organization, Hawkes, Gabbert and Associates. One of his first commissions was a study for the Calgary Social Planning Council. It was there that he met Harvie Andre, who was then a member of the task force set up to examine the Council's work; their political relationship began from that association. When Hawkes later volunteered his services to Andre, Andre asked him to chair a policy committee on welfare. Joe Clark was at some of the early policy meetings.

As a delegate to the party's policy convention in Ottawa, Hawkes really saw Clark in action, masterminding policy exercises, getting Calgary resolutions on to the floor of the convention, telling the delegates to be here and to be there. As a result, the Hawkes-Clark link was firmly in place.

Hawkes went to Ottawa several times a year. He had been appointed to the welfare grants committee of the department of national health and welfare, which met three times a year. He also managed a federal contract from manpower and immigration for the University of Calgary to evaluate the Local Improvement Program, the system of federal grants available for specific local projects. That was a five-month undertaking that took Hawkes from Newfoundland to Vancouver Island adding to the depth of his own perception of Canada and the federal government.

When he was in Ottawa, Hawkes usually dropped in to see Clark at the apartment he shared with Harvie Andre on Cooper Street. They talked politics, Hawkes' LIP work in particular, and the leadership of the Conservative party. Even before the 1974 election, Hawkes had urged Clark to consider running himself. When he did run, it was no coincidence that one of his central campaign themes was the excessive intervention in the work of local voluntary agencies by the federal government.

By the fall of 1975, Clark and Hawkes knew each other well. Their interests had already converged. Both had demonstrated capacities to motivate young people, both believed in encouraging the small against the large, whether in business, government, or community and both believed in individual initiative and free enterprise. After that inconclusive meeting in the Palliser Hotel on September 15, Clark and Hawkes had a brief private talk.

Clark told Hawkes that he felt his weakest policy field was economics. Hawkes managed to arrange, for that very afternoon, a one-and-a-half hour briefing for Clark by Robert Wright, a University of Calgary economics professor. This was typical of Hawkes' approach, and his quick and efficient tackling of problems became a constant source of help to Clark throughout his campaign for the leadership and after.

Clark went next to Toronto, where his friend from Dalhousie, lawyer Peter Hayden, organized a get-acquainted meeting in his home. This was at the time Toronto Tories were asking, "Who the hell is Joe Clark?" Having met him, some of those at Hayden's home declined to work for him. Only Hayden and Ralph Hedlin, the organizer who had hired Clark for the Kirby campaign in 1959, now a private consultant, agreed to set up the framework of an Ontario organization. In Edmonton, meanwhile, David Jenkins and Harold Veale organized a meeting at the Royal Glenora Club to appeal for funds. At this stage they were asking friends to donate a hundred dollars because they were friends, rather than as a commitment to Clark.

The byelection for the Montreal constituency of Hochelaga was called at this time — the election to be held on October 14. Conservative prospects did not look promising. Their candidate, thirty-three-year-old radiology technician Jacques Lavoie, faced the federal Communications Minister Pierre Juneau, who had resigned as head of the Canadian Radio and Television Commission to take the appointment. Clark decided to go door-knocking for Lavoie. He wanted the French experience and he needed to meet people in Quebec. His natural allies, Michel Cogger and Jean Bazin, were favouring Mulroney. "I wasn't very welcome," Clark recalled, "they didn't have much for me to do." He spent much of his time in party headquarters helping Lavoie give interviews.

He arranged a meeting of his own at the Sherbrooke Street Holiday Inn on the evening of September 25. A small group of uncommitted party activists showed up. The most important person Clark met that night was Dr. Gaston Rivard, a party organizer for northwestern Quebec who was looking around for a candidate to support. He did not believe that Claude Wagner could win an election. Quebec was so divided between Wagner and Mulroney that Rivard thought an outsider would be preferable, but he would have to be French-speaking and young.

Rivard was beginning to think of supporting Mulroney and told a friend to ask Mulroney to telephone him if he was serious about running. Even though Mulroney did not call, Rivard phoned about a hundred party people to sound them out about him. When Clark won over Rivard to his cause at the reception, Rivard offered to call his list of names again to drum up their support for Clark.

In the early hours of the morning Rivard called on Claude Boiselle and told him, "I think we have our candidate." Boiselle was the advance man for Robert Stanfield in Quebec during the 1974 election campaign. He had known Clark since 1973 when he supported and

Clark directed the campaign of Michael Meighen for the party presidency. Boiselle was interested, even enthusiastic as he and Rivard talked through most of the night. Next morning Clark called to thank Boiselle for agreeing to work for him. Rivard had phoned to volunteer both their names and also to caution that he didn't expect to be able to do much in Quebec. Wagner had a lot of delegates and it looked as though Mulroney would run, taking many more. Rivard talked about a modest goal of fifty of Quebec's six hundred delegates.

Clark got a mixed reaction on his first water-testing visit to the Maritimes. George Cooper, his Dalhousie classmate, committed to his support since July, arranged a full itinerary for September 25 — the day Clark was there. He brought together about thirty-five party workers for lunch at their own expense in the Board of Trade Club in downtown Scotia Square. Uncharacteristically Clark was nervous as he explained why he would run. The audience was friendly but a little patronizing. We like you, Joe, they seemed to say, but you're too young.

Former attorney-general and health minister of Nova Scotia, R.A. Donahue, told him a story. Roland A. Ritchie, when he was a Halifax lawyer in 1956 had brought Davie Fulton to town for an assessment of his leadership chances. Ritchie took Fulton to see Donahue. Did he want to hear the truth or did he want to be flattered? Donahue asked Fulton. The truth was that Diefenbaker would win the convention and Fulton didn't have a chance. That was where Clark was today.

Clark was more comfortable in his alma mater, the Dalhousie Law School, where he held the stage the next afternoon for about an hour. He cracked jokes at the expense of former professors, some in his audience. The students appreciated his frankness; for example, his comment that there was little difference in philosophy between Conservatives and Liberals was considered disarmingly straight. Similarly, he said that as a politician he could not presume to speak as an expert on economics.

George Cooper discussed the visit with colleagues in Halifax. In his summing-up letter to Clark he commented, "Your problem is youth. As a result, the feeling is that you should wear three-piece suits, not light coloured two-piece suits with flared trousers. Everybody knows you are young; don't emphasize it by wearing youthful clothes.

"Try to speak without too much activity with your hands, which are long and skinny and convey something of a Diefenbaker impression. This might mean you should speak from behind a lectern or table, or otherwise keep your hands out of the way."

Clark's Dalhousie classmate from Newfoundland, Edward Poole, had not seen Clark since 1962 and it was a little difficult for him to see Clark as a leadership candidate, until, that is, he saw him perform at Dalhousie. Poole, a former provincial party president, knew all the right people and introduced Clark to as many as possible.

Still concerned about his lack of depth in some policy areas, Clark visited Sandy Borins and Carole Uhlaner in Ottawa in early October. He told them he had made up his mind to run and needed help on some of the "hard" issues, particularly the economy and energy. Borins agreed to put together an economic brief and to arrange for various other policy sessions in Ottawa.

Clark had not yet announced his candidacy for the leadership but his criss-crossing of the country was giving him the feel of the depth of support he might expect. But friends and committed supporters were anxious for a definite announcement.

David Jenkins, Harold Veale and David King gained the impression that a meeting on the night of Wednesday, October 8 in Jenkins living room signified the real beginning of the Clark campaign, although the official announcement was more than a month away.

Clark arrived at Jenkins' capacious home in Edmonton's posh Valleyview Crescent late and tired. Jenkins, Veale and King had met a few days earlier with Jim Foster in his Legislative Building office, and they all agreed that Clark must be pressured to commit himself. It was tough raising money for a question mark candidate.

These four waited for Clark's arrival. With them were Jenkins' wife, Dreena, Yvonne Johnson, an experienced Red Deer organizer, Dave Hancock and Rolly Cook of the Young Conservatives, and Fred Bradley, MLA for Pincher Creek. They left dramatically vacant a soft easy chair to which they ushered Clark when he arrived. He flopped into the welcoming chair, which soon turned into a hot seat for a grilling from the fresh supporters gathered around it. They questioned him one after another. Jenkins thought Clark was prevaricating. It was left to Veale, the courtroom lawyer, to deliver the coup de grace.

"Do you have the nucleus of a team across Canada ready to help?"

"Yes."

"Do you feel that you are better than the other candidates?"

(Cautiously) "Yes."

"Do you agree we must act immediately or forget it?"

"Yes."

"Joe, this means you're a candidate."

Cheers went up as everyone jumped around and danced in celebration of the candidate's declaration.

"I cross-examined him into being a candidate," Veale said.

In fact, given the work Clark had done and the impressions he had gained, and in spite of the considerable negative advice he had been given, it is hardly likely that his answer that night could have been No. That, at least, is his own impression.

"I don't think there are points where decisions are finally taken," he says. "They got me to articulate a decision, then there were no arguments put. I had the sense that there was enough strength around to get people together and mount a campaign."

Having said his formal Yes, Clark went to bed, the bed in Jenkins' basement where he had so often slept and which was reserved for him.

Jenkins, King, Woolstencroft and Bradley accompanied Clark to the British Columbia provincial convention that weekend in Vancouver. Jenkins and Clark shared a hotel room in the Holiday Inn to economize. The others circulated among the delegates, button-holing them to visit Clark's room. They offered nothing to drink, not even coffee or sandwiches, just questions and answers. Clark was no stranger here; he had lived and worked in Vancouver for his year at law school and the Fulton provincial campaign. A key person in his campaign on the Mainland was former Albertan Mac D. Campbell. Campbell, who was vice-president of the Alberta Young Progressive Conservatives in 1967, had been at the University of Alberta with Clark. He had only just moved to Vancouver from Toronto, as treasurer of the Daon Corporation, a big builder. Campbell kept the Clark flag flying in British Columbia. MP Allan McKinnon also supported Clark — he was the only MP to support him at this stage — but he was necessarily in Ottawa a lot and, in any case, his strength lay mainly in Vancouver Island. Expectations for the weekend were not high. This was John Fraser's home territory and Clark's foray was as successful as could be expected under the circumstances.

Jenkins, King and Foster started to meet every week at noon. Their first meeting was in Foster's office on Wednesday, October 15, when they decided to send appeals for support to all Alberta MLAs and to all constituency presidents. They began to draw up a list of people they could ask to donate a hundred dollars each.

The weekend of October 18 and 19 was another watershed in Clark's campaign. Out of it came all his campaign strategy and organization.

Maureen McTeer called Gaston Rivard in Montreal on the preceding Monday, asking him to book space for a national planning conclave on the following weekend. Clark was in New York on an MPs visit to the United Nations.

Jenkins, Veale and King flew to Ottawa on the Friday. They spent most of Saturday in Clark's Confederation Building fifth floor office making long distance phone calls. Clark spent part of the day with them and then went out to see Harvie Andre and Douglas Roche, member for Edmonton-Strathcona, to ask for their support. Andre, already with him in spirit, couldn't believe that Lougheed would not run; he associated himself at the time with the draft-Lougheed movement. His wife Joan was already committed to Clark and was working hard scheduling his itinerary. That Saturday afternoon, Andre declined to declare publicly for Clark but agreed to continue his private support. Not so the other MP, Douglas Roche. He told Clark he believed the country and the party needed a French-Canadian leader. Clark had gone out of his way to encourage Roche, when he was editor of the *Western Catholic Reporter,* to enter federal politics. Now Roche's attitude disturbed the young candidate. David King told him there would be many more setbacks during the campaign and if Clark couldn't accept them his mettle was not of leadership calibre.

In Clark's office, Jenkins found himself fielding a thirty-minute harangue from a disgruntled Clark constituent from Canmore. The caller complained about Indians letting their livestock loose on roads, putting the public at risk. Who would want to be prime minister, with the country's worries as close as the telephone, Jenkins thought.

The group gathered for discussion over dinner in Clark's newly purchased house at 36 Rockcliffe Way in the central Ottawa community of Linden Lea. The street, as the name suggests, leads into the wealthy village of Rockcliffe but is a few streets away. The Clarks had moved from an apartment a short walk from Parliament Hill to an apartment in Linden Lea the previous year. When their lease fell due in June 1975 they decided to buy a house. They bought the Rockcliffe Way house in August for fifty-four thousand dollars and sold it the following spring (after Clark won the leadership) for fifty-six thousand. They actually lost a thousand dollars on the transaction because out of the selling price they had to pay a three thousand dollar commission. Clark's brother Peter advised holding the property as an investment but Clark demurred on grounds that it might be difficult for the leader of the Opposition to be a landlord.

When the Clarks took possession in August, 36 Rockcliffe Way could best be described as a house with potential. It was small, on a small lot, and badly in need of redecoration and improvements. The dining room was on the right as you entered the house, stairs to two-and-a-half bedrooms on the left. A self-contained kitchen came next on the right, and, at the end of the hall, an addition to the original First World War building, a cosy living

room focused on a fireplace. Maureen had been busy
with the help of her mother wall-papering and repainting
from top to bottom. They had finished just in time to
welcome Clark's political associates as first guests for this
mid-October dinner. It was served buffet style, roast beef
and blueberry pie Maureen made from her mother's
recipe. The guests sat around the fire in the living room.

The good-humoured conversation served mainly to
cheer Clark. The stated purpose was to compile a list of
his qualities that could strengthen his public image. It was
a frustrating experience. Politics was Clark's life. He
read. He went to movies, good and bad. Occasionally he
rode a bicycle. Maureen had got him on to the tennis
courts a few times. The list of the human side of Joe
Clark:

> He watches television, particularly "Mannix."
> He cross-country skis — occasionally.
> He reads mystery novels. Likes Ross MacDonald
> and John Le Carré.
> He likes violent movies.
> He's a Coke addict. He also has one bottle of
> beer sometimes.
> He's a horseman (rejected — too western).

Any thought of getting a football angle fizzled when
Clark asked who Norm Kimball (the Edmonton Eskimos
general manager) was.

The discussion was out of character to the strategy of
Clark's campaign. He intended to win the leadership by
focusing on issues and the delegates, not by crafting an
image. Except for having Clark photographed raking
leaves and shovelling snow, the campaign was to pay little
attention to questions of image.

The serious business of the evening was the date and
manner of his formal announcement. Clark wanted to go
further than a straight announcement in Edmonton.

Somebody suggested chasing the sun across the country, putting down in every province. It might be imaginative enough to attract media attention, but it was too expensive. Clark wanted to follow his Edmonton announcement with one immediately afterwards in Quebec. November 10 was suggested for Edmonton with a repeat performance the next day in Montreal, with as many prominent supporters at a press conference in each city as could be rounded up.

Sunday's meeting in Montreal started shortly after noon. Seated around the table at the Montreal Airport Hilton were Jenkins, Montreal lawyer Pierre Bouchard, Gaston Rivard, Clark, student Rolly Cook, Jim Hawkes, John McTeer, Andre, King, Claude Boiselle, Ralph Hedlin, Peter Hayden, Maureen, Veale, Allan McKinnon, George Cooper and Gilles Pratte.

Clark called the meeting to order at 2 P.M. and for the rest of the time proved he was a master chairman. Crisply he called on one after another to comment on his credibility as a candidate and the fund-raising prospects in each region represented.

The result was a consensus that Clark had as strong a chance as anyone else in the absence of Lougheed. Andre and some others thought the spectre of Lougheed remained. When would it disappear? If he had not declared by November 15, it was agreed, he could be safely ruled out. As a result of that feeling the announcement dates were set for November 18 in Edmonton, November 19 in Montreal.

Veale agreed to take on the job of acting national finance chairman. Jenkins was the natural choice for the acting national comptroller's job. King agreed to be acting national campaign co-ordinator. All took the jobs on an "acting" basis because they assumed big names would later take over. Of course, "Mr. Big" never materialized.

Rivard and his Quebec colleagues strongly objected to waiting a month for the official announcement. How could they run a campaign without a declared candidate? It looked as though the meeting would degenerate into a dispute over the date. Clark stepped in. He understood Quebec's concern, he said and knew there were problems of money. He would meet the Quebecers afterwards and he was confident that among them they could resolve their dilemma. The meeting moved on to the next item, strategy. The campaign would be based on face-to-face meetings with the delegates, starting far afield and working into Ontario later. It would be strictly a positive campaign; no attacks would be made on other candidates. If Clark finished in the top five, they thought, he would have a good shot at the leadership.

Clark was extremely cautious on the question of money. Veale agreed to investigate the legality of making donations income tax deductible, through the party's PC Canada fund. Clark stressed the need for financial frugality. "We don't have an abundance of personal wealth to draw on," he said — a classic understatement for a man living entirely on an MP's salary of $18,000 plus $6,000 expenses.

In the meeting he projected brisk confidence. Hawkes, though committed to supporting Clark since the September meeting in Calgary, confessed to having had some reservations about him as prime minister until that day. "There was a toughness in him I had no reason to suspect, or to see," he said. "He ran a first rate meeting."

"I knew the implications of saying, you're in," Clark said later. "They were financial. They involved impositions on your friends and they involved media. I didn't want to say I was in until I was sure we had a chance of being in. I recognized the Quebec position. They could neither organize nor raise funds for a candidate who was only a possibility."

Outside in the washroom, he felt a twinge of self-doubt. Turning to Cooper as they stood at the urinals, Clark said, "You know, George, it's a long shot."

A week later, I sat on my front porch in brilliant sunshine waiting for Joe and Maureen to pick me up at one o'clock. They were late and it was a quarter after when their brown Capri rolled around the corner. Maureen had been delayed. They were off to a reception, arranged by Claude Boiselle, in Montreal and they invited me along for the drive. The reception was to start at three o'clock. First we sped to the Confederation Building to pick up some publicity files. We searched through every filing cabinet and desk drawer without finding them. All we could find was a photograph that showed Clark with a five-o'clock shadow. Clark was irritated and we were even later. As we sped along newly completed Highway 417 at eighty miles an hour, (we would have been very late had we been forced to take the old two-lane Highway 17) I thought about a remark of Joe's brother Peter, about Joe and speed limits. Peter had recalled how furious Joe had been when the RCMP once stopped him for speeding in Alberta. He had reacted as though speed limits were obstacles deliberately put between him and his destination and the officer who tried to enforce them brought down Clark's full wrath upon his head. I hoped police patrols were mercifully infrequent on this new highway.

During the drive, I said I would do anything I could to help in the campaign, as long as it remained private. I agreed with the suggestion that I should produce a tabloid paper, to run several times during the campaign and daily during the leadership convention. We arrived at the reception, near downtown Place Dupuis, about twenty minutes late. I left to visit a friend and we agreed to meet later for dinner and the drive home.

Attendance was poor at the next national organization meeting, held at the Bristol Place Hotel in Toronto. George Cooper, Harold Veale and David Jenkins compiled what they called a "first ballot guesstimate" of support for Clark and nine other candidates. They gave Clark 450 votes broken down by provinces: Newfoundland 17; Nova Scotia 15; New Brunswick 30; Prince Edward Island 8; Quebec 50; Ontario 90; Manitoba 30; Saskatchewan 50; Alberta 125 and British Columbia 35. Their total first ballot guesses for the others were: MacDonald 405; Stevens 259; Wagner 395; Mulroney 445; Nowlan 63; Grafftey 90; Fraser 100; Horner 110 (50 from Alberta); Yewchuk 22. Clark's group listened to a roll call of refusals, province after province, name after name (some prominent), of people who declined to work for Clark. The meeting coincided with one of Brian Mulroney's in the same hotel and the Clark people resolved never to let that happen again. There was some good-natured banter in the bar afterwards. Noting their candidate's late arrival for a drink, one of Mulroney's supporters said, "Brian's late because it takes so long for him to adjust his chin before he goes out in public."

Jack Horner kept the Lougheed myth alive the following Sunday on the CTV program, "Question Period," the program that would soon be a landmark in Clark's campaign. Horner said he thought Lougheed would win the convention, defeating Horner and the others if he got into the race "relatively soon." Asked about other candidates, Horner said, "I don't consider Joe Clark a suitable choice for me."

Clark's official announcement was made on Tuesday November 18 in the Edmonton Plaza Hotel. He introduced Pierre Bouchard from Quebec, James Foster, attorney-general of Alberta and Allan McKinnon from British Columbia. They personified his claim to have good people from all regions working for him. Others were to be announced next day in Montreal. He also introduced three basic themes. He picked economics first, calling for national standards of discipline and restraint. Besides abolishing waste, government must establish and follow means to measure the productivity of government spending, Clark said. His second point was what he called "the national political habit" — one-party government. The Liberals were the architects of most programs that proved inadequate today and, entrenched in power, the party would not reassess them. He then turned to the nature of Canada and the strength of its diversity. "Canada is too big for any one identity or ideology, and the attempts to make us all the same serve only to frustrate and divide. We should recognize that a respect for diversity is itself a form of Canadian identity. Let us build a sense of community rather than the central bureaucracy," he said. He closed with the reminder that only hard work would win an election; he would ask MPs to spend at least a weekend every month in the constituencies that had to be won.

It was a good start. His press conference was well attended by the Edmonton media and the story was picked up by national television and press.

Clark's Montreal announcement at the Salon au Courant at the Holiday Inn, Place Dupuis, was timed for eleven-thirty the next morning because his French was noticeably sharper in the morning than in the evening when he was more tired. His claim to fluency in the other official language would rest on the ease with which he might handle the inevitable questions. He received mixed notices. The headline in *Journal de Montreal* read, "Mr.

Clark is bilingual — mostly in English." The small Quebec group had made a big point about Clark's bilingual capacity, probably raising too high expectations among the press. He was no Trudeau, but neither was he a Stanfield. Clark could handle himself, with just a little help from the more thoroughly fluent Maureen. On this and other platforms she didn't hesitate to help with the mot juste, prompting *Vancouver Sun* columnist Allan Fotheringham to note that she had the audacity to correct her husband's French before the entire nation on television. If some commentators saw that as a negative quality, Clark did not — he felt that Maureen's French helped him on every foray into Quebec.

In his French text, Clark fashioned his diversity theme into the Quebec mould. "Mr. Trudeau grew up under a strong premier in Quebec — a premier he didn't like — and now he seems to believe that every premier is going to be a Maurice Duplessis, so he tries to take to Ottawa powers or revenues that should stay with the provinces." He said his party must become a home to the millions of Quebecers who believe in Canada but who no longer believe in the Liberal party.

Even as Clark spoke in Montreal, newspapers were reporting that several MPs had travelled to Edmonton to persuade Lougheed to declare. They were unsuccessful but refused to accept his refusal. "Wait a month or a month-and-a-half — it's too early yet," was their response when asked if Lougheed would be seeking the leadership.

In Edmonton two days later, four days after Clark's announcement there, Lougheed again refused. "I feel committed to my obligation to the people of Alberta," he said. Lougheed followed with another No during a weekend meeting with Sean O'Sullivan, the member for Hamilton-Wentworth. Through a statement issued on the Monday by O'Sullivan, he said it again: "Mr. Lougheed described the leadership question as a closed door."

Finally, Lougheed issued a formal declaration on Wednesday November 26: "I consider myself fully committed to completing the job I was elected to do — to guide Alberta, as premier, through the difficult transition period of the seventies."

Still the caucus would not believe him. If only enough Albertans would make Lougheed aware of their wish that he go national, there was still time. However Heath Macquarrie, the member for Hillsborough, P.E.I., who was leading the caucus draft movement, sadly accepted his word this time as a categorical refusal. Said Macquarrie: "I believe this splendid man has missed the opportunity of becoming prime minister of Canada and the country may be losing the services of a most able national leader."

12
RUNNING HARD

CLARK began his formal campaign with an intensive three-day swing through the Maritimes. After making his announcement in Montreal he flew directly to Fredericton where George Cooper met him on the evening of November 19. Ahead were four days of receptions, lunches and interviews. He lunched with the New Brunswick PC caucus on the Thursday. Gone was the nervousness which had been noticed everywhere he went during his September visit. Premier Richard Hatfield introduced him as "my good friend, Joe Clark". It was a cordial reception, without any question of commitments.

In St. John, he encountered the current leading issues of New Brunswick politics, capital punishment and Leonard Jones. Clark was against both. At lunch with about thirty potential delegates, those issues were raised in one question after another.

Driving with Cooper to Jones' hometown of Moncton, Clark joked that he thought he had the answer, "We combine both issues and hang Len Jones." Jones, the former mayor of Moncton, had been denied party endorsement by Robert Stanfield because he opposed the leader's position in support of a federal bilingual policy. Now he himself was trying to run for the leadership. Both English and French language papers in Moncton interviewed Clark and chose to feature his opposition to Jones.

Maureen joined her husband in Moncton for the weekend, and they went on to P.E.I., to the Charlotte-town Hotel where they talked to about fifty people, who showed interest — but no commitment.

At dawn they awoke to a raging storm. No commercial airlines were flying, so they arranged for a light Navajo plane to take them to Sydney. Maureen was sick all the way across the Northumberland Strait. "I've been flying for twelve years," their pilot remarked when they landed safely, but shaken, at Sydney, "but I've never seen it as bad as this." They made their way to the Isle Royal Hotel for an early afternoon meeting.

The capital punishment issue returned to haunt Clark during a reception Cooper had arranged for that evening in Halifax. Questions about the death penalty and about crime put him on the defensive. They took up time he would rather (and better) have spent on his own issues. As he stood there nervously fiddling with his ring in the Nova Scotian hotel, the scene was reminiscent of his September visit.

Clark turned next to the home of the Big Blue Machine — Toronto. But he looked, not to the several establish-ment Tories he knew in Toronto, but to a Dalhousie Law School contemporary, Peter Hayden. Hayden comes from an old Conservative family in Peterborough but he began to take his politics seriously only in his third year at Dalhousie. He had worked for several Toronto candi-dates, including Dalton Camp, and he finished working for Roy McMurtry, the Ontario attorney-general, just as the Clark campaign was being put together.

"I started to work for Joe first because he was a friend, but he was young and good and I wanted to see him as leader," Hayden said. Clark's main campaign themes appealed to Hayden, a lawyer in his thirties, who had made a name for himself in foreign investment law and was the author of a technical book on the subject. In the fall of 1975 Peter Hayden was disturbed about several aspects of government. In his work, he had encountered many laws which allowed excessive discretion to boards and tribunals and to ministerial interpretation.

He was disturbed by the size and complexity of government. And Clark was telling his audiences that central government was becoming too strong and insensitive; that power was being excessively concentrated in the hands of the public service élite, which was seeking to impose its values on a distant, diversified country. Above all, Clark was a pragmatist and Hayden didn't believe government could be anything else. "I don't think Joe Clark is left wing, or right wing," he said. Hayden claimed he knew of no position taken by Clark that bothered him.

Hayden was important to Clark. Ontario had nearly a third of the convention's delegates, and Metro Toronto nearly a third again of the Ontario total. Rings of friendship, Clark's then Hayden's, came together to form a ramshackle campaign organization. Hayden was a friend of another Conservative lawyer, Eleanor Richardson. Although she favoured Brian Mulroney's candidacy, she arranged Clark's first reception on November 25 at the Granite Club. It was a cool occasion both for the freezing rain that kept many delegates at home and for the sceptical reception those who came gave to Clark. Eleanor Richardson herself did not support Clark, but her close friend, Barbara Drucker, later became his chief Toronto organizer, working closely with Hayden, as Metro chairman.

Barbara Drucker was the link to a third ring, which included Brian Turnbull, a Waterloo, Ontario lawyer and alderman. Turnbull was a prominent Conservative, a former candidate in Waterloo. Turnbull knew Clark and was impressed by him. "Before you get all hepped up about Brian Mulroney," he told Barbara Drucker, "you should take a look at Clark." First they had a good look at Mulroney. Turnbull accompanied Mrs. Drucker, her husband Thomas and Eleanor Richardson to a Mulroney appearance at the Hotel Toronto. "He fell apart," Barbara Drucker said. He was testy with delegates' questions and his inexperience showed on policy matters. The meeting was so poorly organized that people at the back of the room couldn't see or hear him.

They went back to Mrs. Drucker's home and talked until three in the morning. "Maybe instead of a winner, we should go with someone we can support," said Turnbull. They agreed that Clark was a candidate they would be proud to work for and Turnbull said he would arrange for Barbara Drucker to meet him. The first opportunity came during Clark's second visit to Toronto, on December 3. Clark had still made virtually no impact in Toronto, while Mulroney had become the darling of the media and the bandwagons of Sinclair Stevens, James Gillies and Flora MacDonald were beginning to roll. Clark's Granite Club appearance on November 25 had been disappointing. Clark had spent most of his time assuring the sceptical audience that Lougheed would not run and Hayden had wondered whether it was worth the candidate's time to return to Toronto. His one achievement had been an appearance on CFTO television with political reporter Fraser Kelly.

Barbara Drucker was waiting for Clark at Toronto City Hall on December 3. Turnbull had told her to expect a tall, erect, dignified person. "I expected a kid — judging from that *Time* picture," she said. When no one of the description appeared she approached a man waiting nearby, and asked if he, too, were waiting for Clark. "I *am* Joe Clark," he said.

While he might not have looked much like the candidate she was expecting, Clark immediately demonstrated his ability. Mrs. Drucker accompanied him to an interview with CITY-TV, which he had to do without the benefit of an interviewer. The station had sent along a crew with instructions to do a Clark interview but no interviewer showed up. According to Mrs. Drucker, Clark, unfazed, took the microphone and delivered a fifteen minute monologue, making it all sound as if it were in response to questions. But he was not amused.

"I didn't like that," he snapped as they strode out of City Hall, "I don't want that to happen again." Mrs. Drucker assured him she had nothing to do with it as they went on to a meeting with Hayden, Turnbull and Eleanor Richardson.

Before long Barbara Drucker told Clark she would work full-time for him on his Ontario campaign. Her decision gave Clark a significant working arm in a key centre. Married to an international lawyer, Thomas Drucker, Barbara Drucker was assistant operations manager in the University of Toronto's office of statistics and records. Now she quit her job, a move she had been considering anyway, to work for Clark. Her kitchen became his Toronto action central with four phones, and a photocopier in the basement.

Clark's second assault on the consciousness of Toronto met only modest success. Only eighteen persons turned up for a meeting Hayden had arranged in the evening for eastern Metro constituencies. At the time Hayden was gloomy. Was it all worth the time and the effort? Only three members of the Ontario legislature turned up to a meeting arranged by the deputy whip Albert Belanger. Maureen McTeer's father, John McTeer, had worked for

Belanger in Prescott-Russell provincial constituency and Maureen had spoken at Belanger's first campaign meeting in Hawkesbury back in 1967.

Belanger said later he chose the Wednesday for the meeting with Clark because the legislature was not sitting; however, because the government had just been returned with a minority of the seats, many members had to attend committee meetings that day. At least half the members who attended asked Belanger who Clark was. Afterwards, they said his presentation was good but he seemed to be rather young to be seeking the nomination. There were no commitments.

Clark did much better later in the members' dining room. He had an animated conversation with nine members. Hayden, at least, was impressed. Later in the afternoon Clark appealed directly to Dennis Timbrell, then Ontario energy minister, who told him, correctly, that Premier William Davis had ordered all ministers to remain aloof from the federal leadership campaigns. Here was an Alberta candidate, who favoured raising oil prices toward international levels, appealing to the provincial minister who was trying to keep prices down. Timbrell was the only known Ontario minister to vote for Clark's opponent Claude Wagner, on the fourth ballot in the convention.

With a nucleus of organization now in place in Toronto, Clark switched his attention to Saskatchewan. There he had no friends to count upon. He decided the provincial party's annual convention, in Regina, December 6 and 7, would be a good place to begin. Jim Hawkes, his Calgary organizer, had agreed at the end of November to take on campaign responsibility for all of western Canada. Hawkes joined Clark in Regina, along with the Alberta MLAs, David King, Fred Bradley, and Gordon Stromberg, and university students Tim Woolstencroft,

David Hancock and Rolly Cook. It was the strongest
delegation he had yet mustered; it had to face the power
of the whole Horner family, promoting Jack.

Jack Horner's campaign appeared to be in command
of the Regina Inn when the Clark entourage arrived on
Friday night. Next morning the others left Clark alone in
his room with a supply of coffee and went to buttonhole
delegates at the convention. At first they couldn't find
anyone who wanted to accept their invitation to go up to
talk to Clark. Instead, they decided to bring Clark to the
delegates. He spent most of the day circulating and
talking to anyone who would listen. For the rest of the
weekend delegates were brought to Clark's room. "If we
could get people in with him for more than an hour, they
were volunteering to help," said Hawkes. Indeed, one of
the strengths of the campaign lay in its weakness. The
moment anybody became committed to the candidate, he
was a somebody, transformed instantly into a key
worker, with some particular responsibility. Richard
Hobson phoned his sister Stephanie Campbell in Ottawa
to suggest she might help Clark. She phoned headquarters and found herself in charge of the hospitality
suites during the convention.

In a similar way, Robert Andrews, a lawyer from
Kindersley, became Clark's Saskatchewan chairman.
Now, campaign leaders recall the weekend in Regina
mainly as "the time Bob Andrews came aboard." They
had gone to Regina with no chairman for Saskatchewan.

Andrews had been open-minded on the leadership
question but leaning towards Mulroney; the party needed
a new face. Andrews knew the Horners. He had worked
for Jack's brother Norval in the 1974 election. When
Andrews met Jack Horner at Regina, he mentioned
Clark's candidacy. Horner said Clark was a front for
Dalton Camp and that he thought Clark was really

running for next time. His theory was that Clark, Flora MacDonald and John Fraser would pull first ballot votes that would flow later to Mulroney. Then Andrews had a long talk with Alberta MLA Bradley, who introduced him to Clark. Three days after Regina, Hawkes called to ask Andrews if he would take on Saskatchewan and found that the face-to-face private meeting in Clark's suite had produced a devoted supporter. Andrews was to take nearly two months away from his law practice to organize an itinerary that would take Clark into every one of the province's thirteen constituencies. The Horner support turned out to be less solid than first impressions suggested and Clark left Regina with ten firm offers of support.

Clark also lacked a base in Manitoba. During the late fall the province's Conservatives were preoccupied with a rather bitter contest for the leadership between Sterling Lyon, a former attorney-general, and Sydney Spivak, a former industry minister, in the Roblin government. Clark decided to stay out of Manitoba until that score was settled. (Lyon won and later became premier.) Unlike some candidates, Clark made no approach to the provincial convention, held on the same weekend as the Saskatchewan meeting. But he was the first candidate in afterwards, arriving with Hawkes on the following Thursday, December 11. The welcome was muted. Len Domino, a past president of the Progressive Conservative Youth Federation, who supported Gillies, arranged a reception at party headquarters in Winnipeg. A typical comment to Hawkes was: "It was sure nice of you to come. We enjoyed meeting Joe Clark. We have just finished our own leadership contest and we're all going on holidays till after Christmas."

Before they left, Hawkes called his old college friend Bruce McFarlane, extension director at Brandon University. McFarlane gave him the name of Lee Clark, a well-known local Tory. A month later Lee Clark took on responsibility for Clark's campaign in Manitoba.

While Clark's travels seemed successful in gaining much needed support and workers, his absence in Ottawa showed the need for leadership in the central campaign office. Although Morag Oracheski, a former secretary of Clark's, had competently taken charge of the office, she was not in a position to make major decisions. The campaign was quietly being run out of Clark's office in the Confederation Building where several students were assisting Mrs. Oracheski. Joan Andre, wife of MP Harvie Andre, took charge of Clark's travel plans.

The tabloid paper for which I was responsible was born in confusion. Clark suggested the name *Eye-Opener* as a snappy title, evoking the family's newspaper heritage, and appropriate for a sheet to be slipped under hotel doors before daybreak during the convention. While Clark was away campaigning, Claude Boiselle, Montreal public relations man, produced an ornate design of a key with a slogan, Clark is the Key. Maureen didn't like the design. Others complained that *Eye-Opener* wasn't bilingual. Ralph Hedlin, nominally national campaign chairman, said the *Eye-Opener* was too complicated and favoured the *Joe Clark News*. In the welter of conflicting advice the first edition went to press with a simplified key design, drawn by a Grade 9 student, using Clark's name in black over a yellow background.

Yellow and black became Clark's effective convention colours and there are various stories about how they came to be used. They appeared first in the tabloid simply because they formed an appealing colour combination. In a conversation before Christmas Maureen suggested the colours should be used more widely. Harvie Andre, Clark's convention chairman, said he took the colours from a package of Matinee cigarettes, which he smokes, during a mid-January planning meeting. Andre and his associates were looking for distinctive ways to create visual impact as a substitute for costly public relations. Barbara Drucker of Toronto says she picked the colours up from a previous Ontario campaign run for candidate Alan Eagleson. Finally, Marilyn Maclean, Clark's campaign manager in Rocky Mountain, produced some yellow and black cards left over from his 1972 election campaign. Whoever started it, what is important is that everyone agreed on the effectiveness of the colours — they served their purpose.

During the pre-Christmas period the campaign *was* Joe Clark. He still had no effective organization at this time, when other name candidates already had central offices and impressive staffs. David King had agreed to run the Ottawa central office but his arrival was still some time away. A candidate with a good reputation for organization and strategy was running with a makeshift organization and his personal strategy.

Clark's ability to write well on the run — learned in his newspaper days — stood him in good stead at this time. Some of the main theme stories for the paper would come to me in almost publishable note form, dictated by Clark during a brief stopover. He would call instructions to his office and later to headquarters from far flung points on his itinerary, sometimes ordering his staff to do routine things, as for instance the call from Regina asking that a speech be copied and sent to the parliamentary press gallery.

He set his basic theme in speeches wherever he went. "In practical terms," he was saying, "that means a turn away from inappropriate centralization; we must vest the provinces with the fiscal and political power to nurture vital regional and provincial and local interests, thus encouraging a regionalism that is cheerfully committed to one nation." On the economy, the hardest of all the issues after federal wage and price controls, Clark knew he needed depth. His instinctive reaction was to call for national discipline, led by government, and a new means to measure the productivity of government spending.

In spite of his efforts, many of his speeches and comments went unread and unremarked. There was a lack of any effective attempt to communicate directly to members of the press. This contributed to the media's slow start in taking the Clark candidacy seriously.

Similarly, organizational faults were responsible for a misunderstanding which led Clark's people to prepare not one policy paper for the convention, but four. Clark had no representative at the meeting called by the convention organizers to discuss details of the convention, including the preparation of the policy contributions papers. Somehow, Clark's people were left with the impression that they must prepare four policy papers for inclusion in the convention book.

Clark had followed up his October meetings with Sandy Borins and Carole Uhlaner in Ottawa and had suggested as broad themes for his campaign diversity, creativity and community — which became known as the "holy trilogy."

In December Borins and Uhlaner agreed to co-ordinate all Clark's policy papers. By this time Borins and his colleagues had been talking to Clark informally for more than a year and they now set to work to distil from those talks the four policy papers they believed were required. Borins himself wrote the paper on economic policy, Ian McKinnon did the resources, external affairs and defence paper, Mark Krasnick wrote papers on social justice and parliamentary structures. By early January, first drafts were complete and two weeks later

Clark approved them, while hopping with Borins in a light aircraft along the north shore of New Brunswick.

It was only then, after the papers were completed that they found they had made a mistake.

Morag Oracheski found that one statement ran a little over the stipulated two thousand words and phoned Chester Bert at party headquarters to ask if it mattered. What did she mean? Bert replied, only one statement was required.

"I nearly dropped the phone," Mrs. Oracheski recalled later, "I couldn't believe it." She thought of the hours of patient work that had been done — the hounding of Clark to read and edit the papers and of Claude Boiselle to translate them into French. All that effort could not be wasted. The decision was made to print all four policy papers anyway. The error in fact turned out to be an advantage. Clark was the only candidate able to distribute such a complete policy statement during the convention, and at the policy sessions, with the four drafts in his hands, he was able to draw freely from both the English and French texts as he spoke.

During December Clark's problems on his home ground in Alberta began to show. Although Foster, Jenkins, King and Veale were spearheading the fund-raising from Edmonton, they also had to spend a great deal of time on the national campaign. Jack Horner shook them during the second week of December with his announcement that thirty-three of Alberta's sixty-five MLAs supported him. The claim raised questions, well-founded as it turned out, about whether Clark could carry his own home province.

Nationally there were still no front-runners in the leadership race when Clark went back to Toronto to look at his Ontario organization. He took the overnight flight from Edmonton International Airport on Thursday,

December 18. Tim Woolstencroft saw him off. Clark's eyes were red from lack of sleep and strain.

The main item on the next day's agenda in Toronto was a meeting with the editorial board of the *Globe and Mail,* the paper Clark had often scoffed at for its pretensions as a national newspaper. Clark made enough impression on members of the board that he was one of the three candidates that they endorsed. The others were Flora MacDonald and Brian Mulroney.

The next morning, which turned out to be the day of Toronto's worst snowfall of the season, Clark met with his supporters in Hayden's law office. Brian Turnbull and Richard Hobson were there from Kitchener-Waterloo, together with Peter Hayden, Ralph Hedlin and Barbara Drucker. Maureen McTeer had accompanied her husband.

Clark described the way he thought the organization should be carried out. He assured the others that Lougheed would not run. He expressed some hope that Hal Jackman, the prominent Tory who was leading the draft-Lougheed movement in Toronto, would back him once he realized the futility of his efforts. And he won over Hobson to his cause. The Waterloo lawyer had come only because Turnbull had persuaded him to. "I'll be proud to say I worked for him no matter what happens," Hobson said after the meeting. The glaring weakness in Clark's Ontario campaign could be seen in the responsibility that Hobson carried away with him. He was asked to take on thirty-six constituencies stretching from Windsor to Owen Sound.

Barbara Drucker took Clark back to her home for a scheduled interview with the Toronto *Sun*. They found themselves locked out of the house in heavy weather. They argued on the steps about which one of them should climb through the milk box to open the door. "Joe, you

can't conduct an interview if you're stuck in a milk box,"
Mrs. Drucker said when Clark wanted to squeeze
through. He allowed good sense to triumph over chivalry
and let her open the door. She forgot a pile of garbage
inside, below the milk box, and knocked it over,
spreading it all over the floor. Clark tiptoed through the
garbage and was busy talking to the *Sun* while Mrs.
Drucker cleaned up the mess.

There was a short break for the Christmas holiday.
First, Clark and Maureen went to High River to be with
his parents, then they flew to Phoenix for some rest at
nearby Scottsdale. Campaigning resumed on New Year's
Day at Vancouver with Clark's appearance on an open-
line show. Chuck Cook, a fellow candidate in Calgary
during the 1967 Alberta election, was now host of an
open-line show in Vancouver, and he was delighted to
have Clark as his guest on New Year's Day.

Next morning Clark was already talking to eight or
nine leadership convention delegates he had arranged to
meet over breakfast when Allan McKinnon, his British
Columbia chairman, arrived at the Mexicana Inn in
Comox. McKinnon had arisen at five o'clock for the
three-hour drive, picking up a speeding ticket near
Duncan when, he said, he and the officer were the only
traffic on the road. They went back to Nanaimo for lunch
with a few more delegates, and on to Victoria for a press
conference at nightfall in the Empress Hotel. Only two
reporters showed up, one of whom was there only
because McKinnon had run into him in the elevator and
asked him to come. "We just sat there for a while being
embarrassed," McKinnon said.

Most of Greater Vancouver's delegates were invited to
receptions on January 3, in the morning at the Harbour
Side Holiday Inn and in the evening at a hotel in
Richmond. After the first reception, McKinnon said,

"Well, Joe, we're not making any enemies. People are listening." About fifty delegates turned out to each meeting. In between, Clark's party drove the forty-five miles to Abbotsford to meet half a dozen delegates in a hotel room. It was one of those times that left them wondering whether the effort was worthwhile. Back in Vancouver, Clark used a press conference to step up his attack on centralization in Ottawa. Prime Minister Trudeau, he said, "is the most dangerous centralist" in Canadian history. Afterwards Clark and Maureen flew to Kamloops to be ready for another round of the same early next day.

In Calgary, with its fiercely free enterprise oil industry, organizers kept running into rumours that Clark was a Communist. The rumours were always elusive and were nothing more than an embellishment of the nationally known Red Tory designation, used by the press to describe Tories with left of centre views. (As Peter Hayden said, "Red Tory was an attempt by the feeble-minded to categorize things that could not be categorized.") "Some pretty good people were very worried about that," Hawkes recalled. One was lawyer Carol Conrad, who agreed to become a provincial co-ordinator of the campaign while nervous about the rumours. Another was lawyer Barry Sullivan, who encountered them everywhere he went in his fund-raising drive. "It cropped up so often we began to ask ourselves, 'are we really supporting a Red?' because that's certainly not what we wanted." Further complicating their task was the spectre of Brian Mulroney, whose fund-raisers had several friends in the oil industry.

Clark himself didn't help matters by delivering the wrong speech to a fund-raising meeting of the Independent Petroleum Association of Canada in their downtown Calgary offices. He extolled the virtues of small companies, not realizing that his audience consisted of representatives of the multinationals. Not surprisingly, he was questioned about why big companies could not do some things better than smaller ones. The occasion wasn't a disaster but it would have raised more money if Clark had known his audience. During the campaign the fund-raisers were able to raise only a paltry three thousand dollars from the industry, though much more was to flow after Clark's victory. Sullivan said the money was raised by going around to friends and clients and demanding a hundred dollars for Clark strictly on the basis of their own friendship. "We were the hundred dollar boys."

Clark's people were worried about his lack of national television coverage. They were delighted with his successful appearance on the CTV Ottawa program, "Question Period." In retrospect Clark considers his appearance on January 3 one of the best strokes of luck of the entire campaign.

"Out of the blue one day Max Keeping (news director of CJOH Ottawa) called me and said they had an opening on 'Question Period' if I'd be prepared to go on," says Clark. "We cancelled a trip so that I could go on. I really think 'Question Period' was highly important because, first of all, I was good on it and seen to be good and, secondly, I think that a lot of journalists had — in their own schedules — decided personally to take seriously the leadership race come the first of the year and the first thing that happened was Clark on 'Question Period.' My most important national performance coincided precisely with journalistic interest and I think that on a variety of levels journalists began to take me seriously at that point. It was one of a series of pieces of good luck."

According to Keeping, Clark got his break only by going out of his way to take up his offer. Keeping and host Bruce Phillips knew they couldn't possibly fit all candidates into their weekly schedule. They decided to give priority to candidates who had not appeared on the program, ranking them according to their own judgment of the candidates' news interest. In order of priority their list included Wagner, MacDonald, Clark and Fraser. Wagner and MacDonald declined to accept the proposed dates. Had Clark not dropped other plans to accept, Keeping says, he would not have had another chance.

The panel on January 3 was made up of Charles Lynch of Southam News Services, Douglas Fisher of the Toronto *Sun* and Michael McCourt of CTV news. Just how unknown Clark still was came through in Phillips' assumption that he could not speak French.

"Oh, yes, I speak French," Clark told him.

"You do? Is that an acquired skill since coming here?"

"It's an acquired skill and, you know, I don't fool anybody about it. I'm not absolutely bilingual but I'm bilingual enough that I was able to campaign door to door in the Hochelaga byelection."

The opening line of questioning from all the panelists suggested a combination of the sceptical and the uninformed. Charles Lynch thought the name "Joe" would never do for a prime minister.

"I hope I can change that attitude," Clark said: "but —."

"You haven't got a middle name or something that would—."

"Joe is my middle name. My first name is Charles but—."

"Oh, that's great!"

Besides setting the record straight about his language ability and his name, he offered some (in retrospect) shrewd calculations about the convention. And he availed himself of the opportunity to outline his views about decentralization. Here is the most pertinent excerpt. Michael McCourt asked him how many delegates were supporting him at that time.

CLARK: Well, we think we have between a hundred and fifty and two hundred delegates committed at this stage and we're targetting to double that before we go into the first ballot, and I think that my position as a candidate is that I've got a much better chance of gaining subsequent ballots than anyone else in the race has. I think I can —

MCCOURT: Why do you say that?

CLARK: Well, because I think I can draw them from across the range. I think I can draw — when Sinc Stevens goes out — those people who are supporting Sinc because of his House of Commons effectiveness, I think many of them will switch to me. When Flora goes out, a lot of the people who have been supporting Flora will come to me because we've been friends, we've worked together. Even when Jack goes out, there is going to be some western Canadian support there and I think I'm in a position to claim that sort of support across the board that other people who are in the race are not. Now you'll want to verify that yourself but that's — I've been involved in organization for a long time. I'm an organization person. I think that you start in a thing like this by developing a base and of course I was relatively anonymous, still am, less anonymous now than I was several months ago on the delegate level, and that's because I've been able to go out and get people who are able to put me in touch with delegates and we've been crossing the country and will be continually until the convention date.

CHARLES LYNCH: You've been saying a lot of things in your speeches and the thing that I think is most distinctive is your views on provincial rights and decentralization. What reception are you getting to this? You've virtually said let's let the belt out a notch and give much more autonomy to the provinces and the regions. Is

this going over well with the delegates you're talking to?
CLARK: It seem to be. It goes over particularly well in regions that feel they have suffered from too much centralization.
LYNCH: How does it go over in Toronto though?
CLARK: It has not been negatively received in Toronto. The areas where there is a particular interest in this approach, Quebec, Western Canada and the Atlantic region, and to a lesser degree in Ontario, but certainly there doesn't seem to be any particular apprehension about it as I would judge delegate response.
LYNCH: You really believe in this as a philosophy?
CLARK: We're a federal country. We have to be. We're too diverse to be run by one government. You know, Macdonald tried to have one government. That was his hope when he founded the country and he's a pragmatist, he realized that you can't run everything from one place.
LYNCH: Do you agree with Lougheed's theory of provincial dynamics, that the real centres of action are going to be the provincial governments rather than the federal government in the future?
CLARK: I think that they are going to be more centres of action than they have been in the past. I think that Ottawa will remain a very important place and a very important government, and not simply in a static way, not simply as an administrative place, but I'd go lower than just provinces. You know, in the 1960s we went through a period in this country and in the States when we sort of gave up on localities. We thought that local communities couldn't do things so we mounted national programs to do things where we thought the local communities had failed. Now clearly those national programs by and large have failed. Urban renewal didn't work. It created bureaucracies but it didn't really create new neighbourhoods, and the war on poverty, mounted

as a national war, didn't work very effectively. We suffered seriously, I think, by setting up things like the Company of Young Canadians, even Local Initiatives which were supposed to take the place of genuine small *l* local initiative. I think that the centres of action in the country in the future, I certainly hope, they're going to be on local community levels, and that means there has to be some transfer of resources, I mean revenues, back to the provinces for redistribution among the cities, and not just cities but local communities.

The "Question Period" appearance had a tremendous effect on the morale of Clark's workers. No longer was Clark an unknown quantity. For the first time people across the country who had never met or even heard of him thought he had said something important and said it well. John McTeer, Clark's father-in-law, said, "People came up to me and said they would support Joe after his performance on 'Question Period.' That's when the campaign caught fire."

In Saskatchewan, Robert Andrews' strategy was to take Clark into distant areas. Anybody could come to Regina or Saskatoon and invite delegates to a reception. The cities would stay on the fence until the last minute anyway, he said. Clark would go where no other candidates went and impress the forgotten delegates. He would, for example, go to Hudson Bay, Saskatchewan, 175 miles northeast of Saskatoon.

In Clark's own words: "It was cold — fifty below zero, and I was very pleased to see some blankets. I had asked the pilot if we had blankets and he said, 'Sure, of course we do.' It was a short flight, about forty-five minutes, but I got pretty cold after about ten minutes in the air. I asked if I could have one of the blankets. He said, 'They're not for you, they're for the engines. When we land in this kind of weather we have to keep the heat in the engines, so we put the blankets around them'".

The next day Clark flew to only slightly warmer weather in Winnipeg where he delivered an address at noon to students and faculty of the University of Manitoba. His speech developed further the central theme of his campaign. "We have an obligation — an opportunity — to begin to redefine the relation between government and citizens of Canada. We are at the end of an age of too much faith in government, and are faced with two extreme responses. One extreme is represented by the prime minister, who has given up on a free society, and wants more regulation from the centre. The other extreme is represented by those politicians who are preoccupied with grievances about the past and who are not proposing positive contemporary solutions." He offered a third option, one that required redefining the roles of the various levels of government and the private citizen. As a means of restoring vigour to the parliamentary system, he suggested giving parliamentary committees the right to initiate inquiries without the government's permission; to give them the time and the expertise to make their inquiries substantial. Prime Minister Trudeau's answer to the power of multinational corporations and international unions had been increased intervention by Big Government, Clark said. "Mr. Trudeau ignores entirely the better option of resisting the big guys by encouraging the little guys." Incentives must be given to the small entrepreneurs of Canada. Ottawa must recognize that the provinces were more capable than it of determining policies for cities and towns and for a whole range of activities that require a responsiveness to local conditions. Government programs of the sixties, Clark said, such as LIP and OFY, delivered far less than they had promised. "Canadians were misled as to the limitations of government action, and now, when those limitations are evident in the failure or malfunction of programs that were far too ambitious we are sceptical about the capacity of government to do anything at all."

Later that day Clark and Fred Bradley met Hawkes and rented a car to drive to Brandon for an evening reception. As Clark wrote notes for his speech he began to feel unwell. They called ahead to warn Lee Clark and to ask him to arrange for a typist at the Red Oak Inn to prepare the speech for distribution. At dusk, they reached Brandon and Clark went directly to bed. The speech was ready to be copied five minutes before the eight o'clock meeting. Hawkes jimmied the lock on the Xerox machine and made copies, just in time.

What followed, according to Hawkes and Bradley, was Clark's finest hour of the campaign. Still unwell, he appeared at the reception wearing a casual jacket and sweater. The prepared text served only as a springboard for the rest of his speech. Both aides reported later that he held his audience of about forty-five people spellbound. "You could hear a pin drop" as Clark spoke about the future of the West, about why he was running, about wanting his party to be a home for all kinds of disenfranchised Canadians. He spoke with joy about the smaller towns becoming more attractive places to live in. Government, he said, is never neutral. Its every action, from approval of freight rates, to extension of a pension to exemption from a tax, is biased against some individual or group, and in favour of another. The question Canadians must ask is whether public policy is biased the way the public wants it. It was a statesmanlike speech and it brought the audience to its feet with enthusiastic applause when he finished.

Bradley was ecstatic. "I thought he gave one of the greatest speeches I'd ever heard. I couldn't believe the rapport he had with his audience. It reinforced everything I'd ever thought about Joe Clark — there was the prime minister of Canada." Hawkes, too, said the Brandon speech was the one that supported his own feeling that he was working for a future leader. As important, Lee Clark was so impressed that he agreed to become Clark's Manitoba chairman.

Because he was still unwell, Clark cancelled an appearance in Thunder Bay and flew back to Ottawa. Hawkes accompanied him as far as Toronto, where he had to be at a national planning conference on the weekend.

In Toronto, sitting around Peter Hayden's dining room table and later at the Airport Hilton, Clark's key people for the first time faced up to some hard truths. Jenkins, Veale and King were there from Edmonton to talk tough about money. All the key Ontario staff came, and George Cooper from Halifax, Barry Sullivan from Calgary, Pierre Bouchard from Montreal.

"We might as well quit looking for Mr. Big," Jenkins said. He had worked on the Fulton campaign during the 1967 leadership campaign and the Fulton people had pursued an elusive Mr. Big without any success, he said.

Clark had wanted to recruit a big name to lend his campaign credibility. He wanted to be convincing as a serious candidate, running to win rather than merely to establish his name for another time. It followed that a nationally known name would also help persuade other delegates to back Clark. And it would be useful for fund-raisers. But Jenkins, the chief fund-raiser, now said the thing to do was to settle down to an aggressive campaign based on small donations.

Furthermore, Clark's Ontario campaign's request for nineteen thousand dollars from central funds was out of the question. Jenkins cut it back to three thousand.

Jenkins had a mandate from Clark to keep him out of debt and he took his job seriously. Jenkins' attitude at many meetings instilled a sense of frugality in all campaign staff. The Ontario people were proud after the campaign to hand back eighteen hundred dollars to the central fund. The biggest expense in Toronto was six hundred dollars for telephones and copying. Hobson and Turnbull were forced to be self-supporting in southwestern Ontario, raising twelve hundred dollars to cover their own costs.

Jenkins' bombshell was the announcement that $120,000 had been committed to the national campaign. Most of those present assumed there would be about $250,000. Cash was not the only subject on the agenda. The group made an assessment of delegate support from across the country. It makes interesting reading in retrospect. As the estimates were marked down, this picture emerged:

Northwest Territories	4
British Columbia	30
Alberta	100
Saskatchewan	35
Manitoba	14
Ontario	28
Quebec	45
New Brunswick	15
Nova Scotia	25
Newfoundland	12
Prince Edward Island	4
TOTAL	312

Viewed in the light of the 277 first ballot votes Clark was actually to receive at the convention, those figures are interesting. They may have been coincidental, however, rather than a true reflection of the support

Clark had at this time — more than a month before the convention. There is much evidence to show that Clark's win was achieved late in the campaign and early in the convention. Also his system for making the estimates was much looser than the others': it was simply a question of assessments by provincial chairmen using all their contacts and their intuition. Flora MacDonald, on the other hand, had a representative in every riding reporting to a central control desk.

Luck or shrewd analysis, the national picture presented on January 9 was surprisingly in accord with the results, with the exceptions of Alberta and Ontario. Alberta gave Clark far less than a hundred on the first ballot, possibly as low as twenty-five. Ontario likely produced more than the estimated twenty-eight.

Clark phoned me the next week to dictate the following quotation for his tabloid newspaper: "Joe Clark seems to have a parliamentary edge over all the others, largely because he's younger and clearly the most articulate." It was taken from columnist Douglas Fisher's assessment of all candidates. Clark liked the quotation and asked me to be sure to include it in a digest of press comment in the tabloid campaign paper. It was a typical example of the way Clark personally attended to details, even at the height of the campaign.

Clark began to attract attention on his fourth visit to Toronto. It came just over a week after his performance on "Question Period." This time 150 delegates turned out to hear him speak to the Junior Board of Trade. He commented particularly on the quality of government programs. They should all be reviewed, he said. "That a program was appropriate and necessary five, ten and fifteen years ago does not in itself justify its continued existence. That as a nation, we could afford a program ten or fifteen years ago does not imply that we can afford it now. One key focus of such a review should be the reconciliation of conflicting policies. In some areas we now work at cross-purposes; for example, we actively pursue job creation and manpower training, yet we have introduced strong disincentives to work, such as the unemployment insurance program which encourages some people to work only eight weeks twice a year."

He also appeared on the Morton Shulman program on CITY-TV with Jack Horner. Clark did well there, perhaps as much because of Horner's performance as anything else. Horner apparently thought he was to appear alone with Shulman. During the interview he looked down and to his right, a characteristic some observers have noticed when he is angry. The program took place just a week after Horner had called an extraordinary press conference to attack almost all his fellow candidates. He had called Clark a college dropout who had never run a business. These remarks had prompted columnist Douglas Fisher to write Horner's chances off; perhaps they also strengthened Clark's.

On January 17 when Clark's convention committee gathered in its Ottawa campaign headquarters for its first, most important meeting, one thing was certain. No candidate would go to the convention with victory in the bag.

Certainly not Clark. On that Saturday his prospects, viewed from Ottawa, were gloomy. He might have been building up support personally, but his organization was not able to cope with the demands of a national campaign. Material was not going out to delegates, or it was going out late. Decisions were not being made. Harvie Andre, Clark's convention committee chairman was a greenhorn. He commanded an efficient machine, inherited from Douglas Harkness in Calgary, but he had no leadership convention experience. He also had a very low budget to work with.

Andre was fully aware of this as he called his committee to order. They were themselves as diverse as the country: Ralph Hedlin, the Toronto consultant, John McTeer, the eastern Ontario horse breeder, Jim Hawkes, the professional psychologist, Morag Oracheski, the office manager. And a score of enthusiastic university students. Andre told them they had little money so they would have to rely on ingenuity.

The Clark hospitality theme at the convention would be food products of Canada, and the food would be solicited. There would be no alcohol served; it clashed with Clark's image and it was too expensive anyway. Clark's Dairy of Ottawa would be asked to supply milk because of the name.

Andre concentrated on the convention centre itself. He knew that what happened in the Civic Centre during the three days before the voting could have a decisive bearing on the outcome. He decided to pursue the Clark colour theme. The committee agreed enthusiastically to invest in the offbeat yellow colour. They agreed to order two thousand scarves at seventy-five cents each. They also went in for square Joe Clark badges, just to be different, and, against all professional advice, posters with C-l-a-r-k spelled vertically.

By this time Clark was becoming exasperated with the Lougheed question. When United Press International approached him for comment about Lougheed's umpteenth denial on January 16, he was sharp and revealing. "I think the realists in the party know that Messiahs don't happen. That age is over in politics. Even if Peter were to come, which he's made clear he won't, he wouldn't be a Messiah." There was just the hint of a suggestion in that comment that Joe Clark thought he was the better candidate of the two men in any case. If pressed privately he would admit that he considered himself the better qualified for the country. Lougheed was not bilingual and there were doubts that he would master the language. As he himself realized, he was irrevocably identified with the Alberta interest and at odds with the government of Ontario. He was first and foremost an Albertan, who had not, unlike Clark, lived in and learned about other regions.

The turning point in the campaign came around this time, mid-January. For as Clark told the UPI and as all reasonable people realized, it was now too late for Lougheed. He would not be unmindful of Premier Duff Roblin's experience in his bid for the leadership in 1967. Roblin left himself five weeks to campaign and found it insufficient.

The press was beginning to take Clark seriously as he headed into the provincial convention of the Nova Scotia party on the weekend of January 24. Geoffrey Stevens of the *Globe and Mail* described him as a solid candidate in his column on January 23. "He is the sort of Tory who could make the party an attractive alternative for many middle-of-the-road voters."

Peter Thomson wrote in the *Montreal Star:* "The significant point is that Mr. Clark appears to have exhibited significant upward momentum. If he can continue that process he could be a force to contend with by voting day."

Delegates arriving at the venerable Lord Nelson Hotel in Halifax were sceptical, however, as George Cooper insisted that this man had a serious chance. But when they left many of them had been converted. In the dark-panelled ballroom of the hotel that Saturday afternoon Clark proved for the first time, and with all the other serious candidates present, that he was a heavyweight.

Media front-runners Brian Mulroney and Claude Wagner put on the biggest public relations displays at the Lord Nelson. Their organizers moved in early to sew up all the main hospitality rooms. Clark's men had to put up directional signs to guide people to a modest room upstairs. Yet Clark outdistanced them in the speaking stakes. His old Alberta university friend John Vandermeulen had booked Clark and Maureen into a quieter hotel, the Nova Scotia, the night before. Clark was rested and refreshed and at his wittiest on the Saturday.

After well-received speeches by favourite son Patrick Nowlan and Flora MacDonald, Clark bounced onto the big stage, strode to the microphone to announce that he was "the real Joe Clark," an allusion to a namesake in the office of the Nova Scotia PC leader. He leaned heavily on his themes of decentralization and the virtues of preserving Canada's small communities.

Claude Arpin, reporting in the *Montreal Star,* wrote that Wagner and Mulroney received only polite applause. "Sinclair Stevens and Joe Clark were loudly cheered, however." Watching Clark speak and hearing some of their own thoughts enunciated for the first time were his policy stalwarts, Sandy Borins and Carole Uhlaner.

Clark was among the few candidates to stay at the convention after all the candidates' speeches. He attended a bear-pit session sponsored by the Young Conservatives in the evening and talked to as many delegates personally as possible. Afterwards he followed up with a signed letter to every delegate.

The case of John Lohnes, a delegate from Lunenberg, illustrated the striking effect of Clark's open and direct approach. Lohnes, a truck driver, was an ordinary rank and file delegate. He had met none of the candidates and didn't expect to. John Vandermeulen saw him in the hotel lobby and struck up a conversation. Had he met Clark? Of course not. Vandermeulen promptly brought Clark over and introduced them. Clark took a few minutes to chat about questions raised by Lohnes. By nightfall

Lohnes was committed but he doubted whether he could afford to attend the federal leadership convention. Vandermeulen arranged for travel and a room, shared with another delegate. (It is typical of Clark's approach that when he saw Lohnes on the Ottawa convention floor a few weeks later, he spoke to him again, effectively impressing this one delegate.) There were many such cases where Clark "got through" to delegates quietly and personally. He talked to and got to know and recognize by name, hundreds of other ordinary delegates across the country.

Policy advisers Sandy Borins and Carole Uhlaner accompanied Clark on his trip to the Maritimes for the Nova Scotia provincial convention. It was the only payment they received for their untold hours of patient work. They came back with three main impressions. Clark was masterful in ad libbing on the themes they had helped prepare. He stood up well against travel fatigue, constantly hopping in and out of small aircraft. (It was almost impossible for a candidate to have a decent meal, they concluded, after telling people Clark was on an urgent call to Ottawa so that he could eat a steak alone in his room.) Both he and Maureen seemed to know a lot of names and family backgrounds.

Carole Uhlaner went on with Clark to St. John's for a dialogue with Memorial University students and four cabinet ministers. The ministers were intensely sceptical as Clark launched into his decentralization theme. Fine, they said, people have been saying that for years. What have you got to make it work? He may not have won them around but when he finished there was at least a meeting of minds and a melting of scepticism.

In Kitchener, on January 29, Clark delivered a speech that was right out of his Alberta days. Peter Lougheed had said the same thing, almost word for word. For

example, "Voters are not interested in what we are
against; they want to know what we are for — what
changes, in people, in policy, in approach, we will bring
as a government." He said the party must become
identified not as the Opposition but as "the alternative
government," another Lougheed favourite phrase. After
the convention, Clark said, the new leader must establish
three concurrent programs: to build a detailed, extensive
policy program; to move MPs around the country to give
them a broader understanding of the country they will
govern; to recruit capable men and women to come to
Ottawa as senior advisers "to help us give effect to the
reforms we are elected to achieve."

Clark's Toronto organization planned a big weekend
for the end of January — a reception for Metro delegates
on Friday evening, January 29 and a press conference for
"big name" Alberta supporters on the Saturday, followed
by a fund-raising dinner at $125 a plate. Late in the week
the weekend shaped up as a disaster. "Names," to the
Torontonians, apart from Lougheed himself were
Alberta cabinet ministers Don Getty, Merv Leitch and
Jim Foster. Lougheed was out of the question and neither
Getty nor Leitch could make the trip to Toronto. Even
Foster had an important meeting scheduled for the
weekend, but for Clark he cancelled his schedule at the
last minute. David Jenkins, who once worked for
Mannix Co. Ltd., arranged for the parent company
(Loram International Ltd.) to lend its jet to make the
return trip to Toronto.

Aboard were Foster, and MLAs Fred Bradley and
John Walker, unknown in Toronto. Their task was to
give the impression in Toronto that Alberta was behind
Clark. A press conference was called for Foster just
before the fund-raising dinner in the Plaza Two hotel.
The previous night's reception for delegates had been a

success. More than 180 attended and responded warmly to Clark. "We could sense that people were looking at him," Barbara Drucker said. "Two weeks before most of them wouldn't even have come out. That evening left us with a sense that we were moving."

The evening began badly when not one reporter showed up for the Foster press conference after his flight from Edmonton. He arrived waving a piece of paper containing the signatures of seventeen Alberta MLAs including six ministers who were backing Clark. Since the press conference was a non-event, the press release prepared for it was never sent out. For the record, it claimed a "solid majority of Alberta delegates" were supporting Clark. "Since it has become clear that Premier Lougheed is not a candidate there is little doubt that the support of western delegates is flowing very strongly toward Joe Clark." It was an unrealistic claim, never substantiated.

Fortunately the dinner that night restored morale. Clark spoke for twenty minutes. Harvie Andre and Allan McKinnon, watching backstage, observed the number of heads nodding in approval. "You don't suppose he could win, do you?" McKinnon asked and both came down with a bout of giggles. Afterwards, heading for the airport in a taxi, both felt for the first time that Clark could indeed win. Toronto Conservatives remained unsure right up until the convention.

Clark's last and best performance in Toronto came at the second of two Metro forums for all candidates. He was scheduled for the first but changed to the second so he could appear on the same platform as Brian Mulroney. Peter Hayden and Barbara Drucker were confident Clark would be the more impressive, and he was. Clark didn't get as many questions yet his answers were highly articulate and witty. Afterwards, Barbara Drucker commented, "He was dynamite, but so what?

He's a westerner in a town where the local boys are running. They don't see him as a winner." Clark agreed. He felt
there was no enthusiasm for him, but neither was there
for any of the others. Toronto was where the delegates
refused to be impressed. In all, during his campaign,
Clark made six two-day forays into Toronto and in the
opinion of organizer Peter Hayden he was overscheduled
to the point of irritation. He was meeting people
constantly, including the so-called Tory names: Hal
Jackman, the draft-Lougheed leader; Paul Clark, a
Metro Tory volunteer; Mayor David Crombie; Metro
Chairman Paul Godfrey; Warren Armstrong of the
Rosedale constituency association and Ted Rogers of
Rogers Cablevision.

By February 9, even Toronto delegates were talking
about Clark, not as a winner but as one candidate who
must be taken seriously. His four months' hard slog along
the campaign trail yielded a fair harvest of press attention
during the first two weeks of February. Jim Poling of the
Canadian Press wrote a well backgrounded interview
that was used by many papers. "I took an early decision
to go to the people who will be at the convention," Clark
said. "I don't think the (press) gallery realizes the support
I have as a candidate."

Marjorie Nichols wrote in her column in the
Vancouver Sun on January 28 that Clark was picking up
a bit of support all across the country. She quoted a
Conservative party insider as saying, "He's the pepper
shaker in this race." In Nichols' opinion Clark's
ascendancy was hurting Flora MacDonald's candidacy.

At the end of the month, Douglas Fisher the Toronto
Sun columnist, picked Clark, along with Mulroney and
Stevens, as one of the finalists at the convention. The
Kitchener-Waterloo Record quoted approvingly from
one of his speeches that said the voters were not interested

in what the candidates were against but what they were for. And, the *Record* said, Clark had a serious, positive image.

On a similar note, Harold Shea, Canadian Affairs editor of the *Halifax Chronicle-Herald*, writing on February 5, said, "People have begun to discover that, while he is young, he has spent half his lifetime in politics. His fluency in English and French has earned him broad acceptance. His approach to the problems of national development and national unity have enlarged his following. He now comes through as a man who deserves a second look."

More important than all these notices was the coverage given to a Clark fund-raising dinner in Edmonton on February 4. This was the dinner Jenkins and Veale had cooked up in mid-January when they realized their fund-raising was running far behind schedule. The dinner was a success in every way. Hal Veale said it was the single most important thing that happened during the campaign and few will argue with him. The dinner itself raised twenty thousand dollars, but about the same amount again was raised from the dinner organization in donations from people who couldn't attend but agreed to contribute a hundred dollars each.

Veale had called Carole Uhlaner who was working in Ottawa on Clark's speech for the dinner to say that Clark should attack Prime Minister Trudeau head-on because sentiment against him was running strongly in Edmonton. Clark was in good form when he arrived at the Edmonton Plaza hotel. It was not necessary for him to deliver any special attack on the prime minister; he was attacking him by name in almost every speech he made anyway. The Edmonton speech was a variation of the theme speech he was delivering everywhere. The *Edmonton Journal* reported it in these words:

"The dinner guests heard the thirty-six-year-old candidate lash out at Prime Minister Trudeau and press home the issue of decentralization. He blasted the notion that big business and big labour be counterbalanced by big government. Big government, Mr. Clark said, 'is more dangerous than the other giants.' Only government, he said, can bypass the regulations imposed on other bodies, and he cited Ottawa's overruling of the anti-inflation board on the postal settlement. However, Mr. Clark warned that the prime minister, with his centralist approach, 'may well be tempting us to become the defenders of unregulated big business.' The Liberals may support government, the NDP may support labour, but the Conservatives are not the voice of unregulated big business. Rather, the Conservatives have a wider mandate — a mandate to all Canadians. 'We must pay attention to Canadians whom other parties, other groups ignore.' "

The speech had the ring of Diefenbaker at the time he first impressed Clark in 1957. An aide said it was the best speech Clark had made. When it was reported nationally on the CTV news, the reporter described Clark as "a Brian Mulroney with brains and experience," a reference which delighted all Clark's key people from coast to coast. It strengthened their morale for the run-up to the convention. Ahead lay one last tour of Ontario ridings, and a speech in Montreal which led to some favourable comment in the daily newspaper *Montreal-Matin.*

The tour of southwest Ontario, from February 6 to 10, according to Clark, "almost did us in." On Saturday, February 7, he and Maureen were scheduled to fly from Chatham to Wiarton, near Owen Sound, in a light aircraft.

In describing the incident, Clark said: "There were snowdrifts on the runway, one of which we got stuck in.

People had to come out of the airport and push us out of the snowdrift. The weather was clearing but then another front came in after we took off. We hit something called a wind sheer — when two conflicting winds meet — and we just dropped, caught in the middle. The pilot righted the plane but we were very concerned. Then we were told we couldn't land at Wiarton because the weather had closed in there but we could land at Collingwood if we hurried. It would be closed, too, soon. We did land there finally in bad winds on an icy runway and we nearly hit another snowbank as we came down. Then we rented a car and drove through rough roads to our meeting, arriving three hours late. But most people had waited for us."

Clark spoke in Montreal on February 10, just two weeks before the convention. He would have preferred a larger audience but he had to settle for the Maisonneuve Optimist Club. The theme of his speech again dwelt on federal power:

"There have always been cycles to Canadian federalism, in some periods the central government would grow stronger, at other periods the provinces, to maintain a balance over time. We have clearly reached a point where the strength of the central government has broken the balance."

"Ottawa's desire for control has frozen progress on cablevision, forced provinces to follow social and development priorities they would not have chosen freely, and attempted to dilute traditional provincial jurisdiction in fields like resource development. Moreover, we have seen the failure of centralized programs like the war on poverty in Canada, and the Great Society programs in the United States and we know now that decisions are often taken more effectively by governments closer to the people affected."

The message went almost unreported next day in the

Quebec press but what comment there was was favourable. Jean V. Dufresne's article in *Montreal-Matin* was headed, "Joe Clark — bilingual for real." He wrote that Clark spoke French with ease and conversation never failed whether the subject was cablevision or oil. "A language is mastered only if you have something to say, and those who search for words are most often searching for ideas at the same time. In this respect the member of Parliament for Rocky Mountain is clearly the most interesting to listen to of all those running for the leadership."

Clark ended the campaign where it had started, in the Maritimes with George Cooper. He had a good meeting in Fredericton on February 11 with all members of the New Brunswick PC caucus. Cooper said he was relaxed and witty. Afterwards several delegates known to be supporters of Mulroney came up to Cooper and said, "You may think we're supporting Brian Mulroney but we want you to know that now we're with Joe Clark."

Our doorbell rang just after ten o'clock on Friday, February 13, as we prepared to go to bed. I went down in my pajamas to find Joe and Maureen on the doorstep. They thought they would stop by for a nightcap if it wouldn't keep us up unduly. I poured them each a Dubonnet, one of their favourite drinks, the only one apart from an occasional sherry or wine, or, in Joe's case, a beer. He was more relaxed than at any time since the previous summer. "I'm confident that we've done a good job and we have a good chance," he said. "It may not be won, but I know it isn't lost."

13
HEADQUARTERS

IT was a nondescript red brick pile of a building with a fancy entrance. It might have been a warehouse but the façade over the door suggested something special, like a bank. Etched in the concrete above the heavy doors were the words, "Bell Telephone Company of Canada," and, below them, the number 200. Number 200 was vacant when Rolly Cook happened by one day in December. He noticed the "for rent" sign. One does notice those signs when one has been looking for space to rent for days without any success. Cook was one of the university students working for Clark. Like half a dozen others who left their studies, he had given up his year in law at the University of Alberta. He was getting restless and a little tired of working on a campaign without headquarters. Two hundred First Avenue looked promising so he telephoned the real estate agent and arranged to see it.

The building was well situated, about half way between the Civic Centre where the convention would be held and downtown Ottawa. It was just off Bank Street, one of Ottawa's main thoroughfares, although too far away to offer any publicity advantages itself. When you entered you went up a small flight of stairs, which opened on the right to one huge room. An ideal working area.

On the left a door opened on to an area suitable for

offices. To the rear was another, smaller room, that might be used either for meetings or a workshop. Upstairs the entire floor surface was open. Cook discovered that it was possible to rent just the main room on the ground floor. At a price of five hundred dollars for three months, he doubted that they would find anything more suitable, so he signed a lease that afternoon, without checking with Clark, or John McTeer, who was in charge of finding a place. He got a reprimand for his bold initiative and a bus ticket to Alberta, but he had found a home. Cook was sent to Alberta to organize youth groups for Clark. He soon talked his way back into favour and work at the headquarters he had found.

The campaign organization needed it. Some of the arrangements were being made in Clark's office on the fifth floor of the Confederation Building. The organization consisted of Morag Oracheski and two or three students. Mrs. Oracheski, had agreed to return to work for Clark. At a meeting on December 10, he advised her to stop thinking as a secretary and begin to think as an executive. She would be required to make decisions as the campaign office manager. Mrs. Oracheski and the students worked out of Clark's MP office until they moved into 200 First Avenue on Sunday January 4.

Joan Andre, who had made Clark's travel arrangements from her house, joined the office. On the weekend of the move, Clark and his wife were campaigning in British Columbia.

David King had accepted the job of campaign co-ordinator on an acting basis (until Mr. Big came along), at the planning meeting on October 19 in Montreal. As soon as the office was established, the need for the campaign co-ordinator to be in the office was clear. King flew down from Edmonton on the following Tuesday, January 6, and stayed until the next Friday. Mr. Big was still nowhere in sight.

King found a bunch of enthusiastic students looking for direction. He felt it was important for all the staff to know what each was doing, so one of his first decisions was to hold a daily staff meeting in the big room. At one of his first meetings, King surveyed the group of young faces and commented, "I feel like getting a sign made for the wall, saying 'This is the crusade of the children.' " After his first visit John McTeer said, "I feel like a senior citizen." In fact the "children" were a group of bright and mature university students who had given up their studies to work on Clark's campaign for a top salary of $275 a month.

Besides Rolly Cook, there was Michael Ede from the University of Calgary. David Hancock had left first year law at the University of Alberta. Ken Hughes, whose parents ranched near High River, came from the University of Guelph. Hamilton Greenwood came from Queen's University. Peter Bennett gave up part of a year at Guelph University.

In addition, Tim Woolstencroft took leave from his job as research assistant to the Conservative caucus in Edmonton and Ted Foley and Robert Baxter took time away from jobs in Ottawa and Calgary. None was older than twenty-three. Most had worked in Michael Meighen's successful campaign for the party presidency in 1974, for which Clark had been campaign manager. After a few days the group worked well together. They began earlier and finished later than the staffs of rival candidates.

They were once described by Ottawa's *Le Droit* as "the young revolutionaries." And in reference to their life-style the description was reasonable. They bedded down in a rented room which became known in headquarters parlance as "the hovel." It was at the corner of St.

Andrew and Dalhousie streets in Ottawa's French speaking Lower Town. For the last three weeks of the campaign one of them slept in the office to provide a round-the-clock watch over the convention preparations.

The students gave Clark's campaign a dependable, constant work force that became essential. With some exceptions they were organized even when there was a lack of direction. And the problem of direction arose a few days after the office opened. David King was the member of the Alberta legislature for Edmonton Highlands; he was also legislative assistant to Premier Peter Lougheed. When the legislature was sitting, as it was during January, he was in demand. Now the premier called. It was a problem that neither King nor Clark had faced up to when King had assumed the job of national co-ordinator on an acting basis.

By the third week of January problems were building at First Avenue. Key decisions were being put off. Morale fell. The staff lacked direction after King returned to Edmonton. And sometimes they lacked money. Jenkins and Veale, the national comptroller and finance chairman, respectively, were in Edmonton. Jenkins, under Clark's orders to watch spending, had made it clear that any unauthorized expenditures over fifty dollars would come out of the spender's own pocket.

Regional workers soon realized all wasn't well at headquarters. In Toronto Barbara Drucker said she was called by four different people about the same thing. Once she called to complain that in the first edition of the Clark tabloid, Ontario Attorney General Roy McMurtry's name had been spelled McMurphy. The Toronto staff were still trying to persuade McMurtry to support Clark, yet when Mrs. Drucker called to express understandable dismay, she said the reaction was, So what? "I told them to screw off." In Waterloo, Richard Hobson said, "My impression was that it simply wasn't working."

Other mixups demoralized the staff. In mid-January the first mailing of campaign literature was sent mistakenly with third class postage. A month later, some delegates received their second mailing before the first had arrived. Clark himself showed up to be briefed by King only to discover that King had returned to Edmonton. On an important speech about inflation the office sent out a press release based on a first draft that was quite different from the second draft which was the one Clark used.

The campaign letterhead, which should have been ready in December, finally arrived on January 8 — with the wrong telephone number. An attempt to overprint was unsuccessful and volunteers had to cross it out by hand. Tim Woolstencroft described January 19 as "the ultimate depressing day." Maureen phoned all the way from Calgary to tell them they could borrow some coffee urns from Loblaws. "We told Maureen, we'll worry about those things, you worry about votes." At times, Woolstencroft said, "We felt almost alone. We felt the people who were supposed to be directing the campaign weren't." That was also the day Mrs. Oracheski commented that the place was as dirty as a pigsty. "Can't the janitor clean it up," asked Peter Bennett the student who became quarter-master for the convention supplies. He had just arrived and his comment reflected his lack of understanding of the situation. "Okay, Peter, you're the janitor," Mrs. Oracheski replied. In fact every second night all staff rolled up their sleeves and scrubbed the floors and emptied the wastepaper baskets.

If the low point was January 19, happier times were just around the corner. By that time King had realized he would not be able to be in Ottawa for the month when he was most needed. He phoned Jim Hawkes in Calgary on the night of January 20 to point out the crisis in Ottawa. Could Hawkes go? Next morning Hawkes requested permission to be absent from campus three days a week for the next month. He was warned he might have to arrange for compensation to the university but meanwhile he could take the first three days off while the dean got a ruling.

Hawkes then phoned Jenkins in Edmonton to get permission to buy a round-trip excursion air fare to Ottawa, explaining that by so doing he could save a hundred dollars. On the evening of Wednesday, January 21, Hawkes held his Social Work 435 class and then caught the midnight flight out of Calgary. He took a room in the downtown Bytown Hotel, appropriately for Hawkes, the old Ottawa YMCA building.

Both Hawkes' personality and his training now came into play. He is a quiet, deliberate person and he can exist on little sleep without losing his equanimity. He simply walked into 200 First Avenue and asked everyone to tell him about their jobs. He soon found out about their concerns and some specific problems. For example, the first tabloid paper was printed outside Ottawa because of cost. However, the printer was unable to deliver copies in Ottawa to meet the demanding schedule that would be required during the convention. And prices obtained from city printers for overnight production were too high. Now it fell to Hawkes to make a decision. Eventually he arranged for a reasonable price from *Le Droit*, the Ottawa French daily, as part of a total package printing price.

On his first night in Ottawa Hawkes met Clark and several campaign people in Harvie Andre's office for an evaluation. Hawkes said there were too many Indians, not enough chiefs. As a consequence the organization was having trouble setting priorities.

At that meeting, Pierre Bouchard, the Quebec chairman, told Maureen she would need two high fashion outfits for each day of the convention. She must not wear the same outfit twice. He thought this was essential if they wanted to add any votes from Quebec. "Nobody is going to tell me how to dress," was Maureen's reply. In fact her dress during the convention drew nothing but praise and it was probably not far from Bouchard's recommendation.

Hawkes stayed in Ottawa until January 27, working nineteen hours a day at First Avenue. Back in Calgary he took his classes on the Tuesday and Wednesday, January 27 and 28. The dean said he could continue the shuttle service but he should do it as quietly as possible. He arranged for a colleague to be on call to his students should they need help during his away days. The dean said no official record would be kept of Hawkes' absence. On the aircraft, flying back to Ottawa on the Thursday, Hawkes began to analyze jobs and available staff on a piece of foolscap. The basic problem was a serious manpower shortage, he thought. During his second visit he would devote himself to expanding the work force.

He called a staff meeting on Friday morning to tell everyone to carry on with what they were doing. He would be preoccupied for a few days getting them help. He called on John McTeer and Maureen to give him all the names of Ottawa people who might help and to specify their abilities. He then called all the Ottawa people he knew. By next morning he had a stream of people coming in to see him about volunteer work. He challenged all to find someone else; the ripple mentality, he called it.

Before he flew back to Calgary on the following Tuesday, February 3, Hawkes had enlisted the help of sixty new volunteers. (Clark's organization had four hundred by convention time.) On his next trip he assigned them to specific tasks. King hired a full-time press secretary, Hazel Strouts, at three hundred dollars a week and Hawkes hired a reporter for the tabloid paper, Paul McLaughlin, at a hundred a week.

Now the morale problem arose again, for almost the reverse reason. As the volunteers streamed in, the students, the original faithful, had to be persuaded to turn over their jobs to the newcomers. The students were delegates; they were needed to lobby and to vote at the convention. King returned with Hawkes on February 12, the Thursday before the convention. He put a big chart on the wall, with new Ottawa volunteer names slotted into jobs previously done by the students. Inevitably they felt resentment. They questioned the loyalty of some of the newcomers. Hawkes, King, and Morag Oracheski, all spent two or three hours a day trying to maintain morale. Quietly they said they understood how the students felt. While they might not like the dislocation, it was being done strictly in Joe's interests.

But by the time Clark and Maureen returned from their long weekend holiday in Bermuda on February 17, the Tuesday of convention week, staff at headquarters were tired and morale had slipped. They weren't in a party mood for the end of campaign celebration.

Ralph Hedlin held the title of national chairman but he didn't go to headquarters until the closing days of the campaign. The young staff neither knew nor trusted him. They responded flatly when he stood on a chair and delivered a pep talk. There was a total lack of rapport.

John McTeer tried to change the atmosphere. "Are you happy?" he called out. Response was less than reassuring. Many of the four hundred volunteers were fatigued and discouraged as they headed into the convention.

14
CONVENTION

CONVENTION chairman Harvie Andre picked up the telephone in Clark headquarters on February 10, the Tuesday before convention week, and placed an urgent call to national comptroller David Jenkins in Edmonton. "The hotels are on our backs," he reported, "we have to get some money *now*." A month had passed since Andre had asked five Ottawa hotels to reserve about twenty rooms for hospitality suites and committee rooms. Poster and information space had been booked in their lobbies. Now they wanted cash deposits.

Although Andre's call came within a week of the Edmonton dinner that raised forty thousand dollars, Jenkins had no ready cash to send. The dinner had merely bailed the campaign out of some of its debt. Joe and Maureen had been criss-crossing the country on the strength of their Air Canada credit card. Enormous bills for air fares, hotel rooms, advertising and printing demanded attention. Of course, the arduous travel schedule had paid off. Clark had established a private rapport between himself and hundreds of delegates everywhere which, if it did not result in open first-ballot support, had at least left goodwill to be further culti-vated at the convention. But the media, with one or two brief exceptions, were not traipsing around with him. There was no media build-up of Clark as a front-running candidate. Consequently, funds were scarce. Without media coverage donors had no way to measure Clark's progress. And most donors like to feel they are contributing to a candidate with a chance of winning.

Jenkins called his colleagues and arranged a meeting for noon next day in the offices of Alberta Attorney-General Jim Foster. Harold Veale, national finance chairman (the man who had been sitting in until Mr. Big came along), was there along with Robert Lloyd, Alberta finance chairman, and Donald Mackenzie, another key Edmonton supporter. The five decided in short order that the bank was their only recourse. They jumped into two cars and headed for the Toronto-Dominion bank's main branch in Edmonton Centre. On the strength of their five signatures the bank advanced a short-term loan of forty-thousand dollars. They paid off the twenty thousand dollar loan they had raised from the same bank in October and sent most of the remainder to Andre.

The bank kept their note with five names holding liability for twenty thousand and issued a copy to which other names could be added. When Veale and Jenkins went to Ottawa on Sunday February 15, they took the copy with them, adding, within a few days, fifteen names, thus reducing the liability to a thousand dollars each. Later the bank sent copies to the original five inscribed: "Commemoration. This is one of a series of five copies of what will no doubt become a historical document."

Jenkins and Veale went to the convention with a direct personal stake in the campaign. Clark himself had made it clear that he didn't want spending to outstrip revenues. Both he and Jenkins had learned lessons from the Davie Fulton campaign of 1967 when Fulton, as a losing candidate, was saddled with a debt which had to be paid off later. "We wanted Joe to be free and clear, win, lose or draw," Jenkins says. To accomplish this Jenkins and

Veale teamed up with Toronto fund-raisers Brad Sumner and Jeff Lyons for a telephone blitz. They called prospective donors from one end of the country to the other. Starting about 9 A.M. they would phone the Maritimes, where the time was an hour ahead of Ottawa. As the day wore on, they shifted their calls westward with the sun. When they finished about 8 P.M., offices were closing for the day in Vancouver. John McTeer provided lists of Ottawa and area merchants who could be considered potential donors. When they won a verbal commitment, ranging usually from twenty-five to a hundred dollars somebody jumped into a taxi to go and pick it up.

Topped off with this aggressive style, the fund-raising campaign cleared $169,135.60 for Clark. It consisted entirely of 1,118 small donations (an average donation of $151.21), allowing Jenkins to assert stoutly, "Nobody owns Joe Clark — he's his own man." Jenkins had insisted on a pay-as-you go policy throughout the campaign. "I think we were the only ones who wouldn't let anyone spend a cent unless we had the money," he says. Clark's campaign turned out to be one of the most modest of all candidates. Horner spent $278,383.44, Stevens $294,106.58, and Wagner $266,530.00.

The campaign ended on Friday February 13, and Clark called in Ralph Hedlin, Jim Hawkes, Dave King, Harvie Andre, and Pierre Bouchard, to propose a steering committee of the five of them to run the campaign from then until the end of the convention. He was leaving early Saturday for three days' rest in Bermuda where he would be out of touch, and when he returned, he would be heading almost straight into the convention program. He would no longer be able to make any campaign decisions. Clark told the five that they should act in concert and in agreement if possible

and proposed Hedlin as chairman. Hedlin had brought
many useful suggestions to national committee meetings
in Montreal and Toronto and it appeared to Clark that
Hedlin was the only one with previous convention
experience. He had run Duff Roblin's campaign at the
1967 leadership convention in Toronto.

All five agreed with Clark.

They thought otherwise the following night after a
fourteen-hour indecisive meeting at campaign headquarters. Until then their style had been informal but
decisive. It was, "Dave, you take care of this, Harvie you
decide on that, and I'll do so and so." And the decisions
were made, jobs done, and all lived with the results. Now
the five found themselves trying to reach a consensus on
everything. Hedlin himself had not been at headquarters;
he lacked the feel for the staff that Hawkes, King and
André had built up. The questions came forward and
begged answers. When would the hospitality suites be
open? Should money be spent on a band? Should more
money be spent on buttons? How should the candidate
spend his time?

Clark acknowledged afterwards that the organization
came close to a rupture that weekend and he took full
responsibility for the situation. "At least we survived it,"
he said. He was worried about the convention. His staff
were enthusiastic amateurs, with considerable skill, but
no convention experience.

"I was the common factor in the campaign," Clark
explained. "For different reasons there was a lot of
loyalty to me. The loyalty involved a confidence in my
judgment. I was playing too active a role. Certainly, if
you take any classical models, I was making judgment
calls more than a candidate should. But I was doing that
because everyone acknowledged that there was no one
better around. While no one challenged my authority,

everyone realized that I was operating under limits of time and strength — so all did their best without jockeying. Often when people are doing their best they're trying to replace whoever is ahead of them on the ladder. I was the only one who was ahead of them on the ladder and they couldn't replace me. That added some peculiar dynamics to the campaign. It might have gone beyond personalities. Our problems arose when we departed from that organization in the last week.

"It might not have been Hedlin versus the others so much as the fact that there was a structure in which people felt uncomfortable. We had been relatively unstructured below the candidate. In retrospect that might have been an advantage."

Hawkes and King had found their original informal style worked well. Only the previous weekend they had been worrying about lobbying delegates at the convention. Hawkes said he would organize the delegate lobby and King agreed to set up a "power lobby" organization. The power lobby would be responsible for approaching the 40 percent of the delegates who were entitled to vote as members of provincial legislatures, members of Parliament, privy councillors and delegates at large. King found there was just too much nitty-gritty to worry about. His hands were full at headquarters and he would not be able to handle the power lobby.

Hawkes decided to call John Sherman in Vancouver. When Hawkes had been president of the student union at the Calgary branch of the University of Alberta in 1963, Sherman had been the arts faculty representative, on the council. Coincidentally, they had met again only recently at a Clark campaign meeting in Edmonton. Sherman lived in Vancouver on weekends but commuted by air to a job as manager of a trust company in Edmonton weekdays.

"John, we're in a bind," Hawkes said. "Can you come down a day or two earlier and head up the power lobbying." Sherman was in Ottawa by Wednesday morning of convention week. He worked with a small group, including Harvie Andre and Allan McKinnon (two of only three MPs committed to Clark), Jim Foster and Fred Bradley (both Alberta MLAs), Jeff Lyons and several other Toronto delegates. They adopted a personal approach. For example, Jeff Lyons found himself in friendly conversation with rival candidate Heward Grafftey. "If it doesn't work out for you, Heward," Lyons had said, "we'd sure like to have you come with us." (After dropping out on the first ballot, Grafftey threw his support to Clark.)

The more formal style Hedlin brought with him to campaign headquarters did not fit well with this easy going yet effective approach.

Hawkes had taken the precaution of asking two old friends, Vic and Beth Bryant, to prepare kits about how to lobby delegates. Vic Bryant, a colleague of Hawkes in the social welfare faculty at the University of Calgary, was also a partner with him in a consulting firm. On his weekly trips home to the university, Hawkes had conferred with them and when convention week came they were ready with material to distribute to the lobbyists. The introduction in their memo to poll workers read: "Clearly the best way to convince people to support Joe is to get them to hear him and meet him. Joe is planning to spend every possible moment meeting delegates. Nevertheless, he won't be able to meet everyone. Therefore, you may have to speak for Joe. This memo is designed to help you do that effectively, by providing a number of points you can raise in convincing delegates to support Joe." The memo said that Joe would play an important role in bringing new people to the party. "Joe is at home everywhere in Canada. He is fluent in French. He is an articulate speaker and à capable House of Commons debater. He will appeal to young voters; over half the electorate in 1978 will be under forty. He is a man from the middle who can unite the party. His momentum is building and with growth potential after the first ballot, he can win."

Every lobbyist was to approach each of twelve assigned delegates every day. Heidi Redekopp of Toronto devised a system for keeping track of voting support. She drew up a master list of all delegates. Lobbyists were to report every night so that volunteers, working during the night, could prepare as accurate a picture as possible of Clark's voting strength.

To her frustration, the master list remained incomplete and inaccurate. Some lobbyists started drinking and socializing around 10 P.M. and forgot to turn in their reports. Others, like John McTeer, thought the system unnecessary. He declined to report the results of his eastern Ontario poll to Marjorie Carroll, the Ontario chairman. "Don't worry, Marjorie, everything will be just fine," he told her. "Yes, but I want to see it," she pleaded. All provincial chairmen and assistants met either late each night or early in the morning in one of the hospitality suites. They were trying, without much success, to follow the strengths and weaknesses among the delegates.

Some delegate lobbyists came to Ottawa armed with files of comments about delegates. These notes from the Toronto section are indicative of the fertile field that awaited their advances.

"York South: Mr. and Mrs. Harner, friendly to Joe, committed Grafftey on first ballot (only?). Staying at Chateau as arranged by Grafftey.

"Finally reached Mr. Ed Wetherall, very friendly, helpful senior member of delegation. He is committed elsewhere but is sympathetic to Joe ('My wife likes Joe very much') and would be happy to talk with Joe and help arrange a meeting with Joe and the delegation."

"York North: Good vote poss. here, especially if Stevens goes out.

"Free and open delegation according to all (except for Miss Clare Williamson, YPC del. — strong Horner worker who was not impressed by Joe's workers). The older members all know Sinc Stevens ('hometown boy') but are intentionally going to Ottawa early (Wed. P.M.) to investigate several of the candidates. Several suggested Joe come for a visit Wed. night or Thurs. and others were very receptive to my sugg. that possibility.

"Very intelligent, thoughtful delegation esp. YPC Malcolm Jardene ('sort of' for Flora), doesn't like Brian, impr. by Joe at forum. Greatest sympathy from delegates Walter Donkin and alternates Barnett and Ron Femson (who saw Joe in Toronto twice and was 'exceptionally impressed')."

"York Centre: Try to see *females* in the group if possible. Men del. (youngish) leaning towards Stevens/ Wagner. Mrs. Godfrey (Paul's mother), Miss Buell (very keen on Joe's NATO and defence stands) are both older, long-time party workers. Miss Seddon likes Wagner but impr. by Joe as well. YPC alt. Jean Copp thinks Joe is picking up support."

Joe and Maureen, meanwhile, returned from Bermuda in time for the staff party at his 200 First Avenue headquarters on Tuesday February 17. They moved into their fourth floor suite at the Skyline Hotel on Wednesday.

Joe's mother Grace Clark arrived from High River and took a suite in the Inn of The Provinces, newest of Ottawa's central hotels. Neither she nor Charles Clark had intended to attend. But as the convention approach-

ed they decided one of them ought to be on hand. They
thought more about commiserating with a loser than
about celebrating a great family victory. But in Ottawa
Grace Clark soon began to see her son as a winner. She
agreed with Joe that his father should be with them. Joe
slipped away from his routine long enough to phone High
River. "Dad, I have a good chance to win this and I'd like
you to be here," he said. Charles Clark caught the next
plane out of Calgary.

As delegates poured into Ottawa, the convention
organization fell together with remarkable speed. For
example, Bill and Carol Herron, who had been instrumental in winning Banff for Clark in the 1972 election,
arrived on Wednesday afternoon and went directly to
headquarters to volunteer. Carol Herron was assigned
with Tia Cooper, wife of Clark's Nova Scotia chairman,
George Cooper, to help and escort Maureen. Bill Herron
joined Jim Foster, the Alberta attorney-general, as
Clark's escort. Foster was particularly effective at
keeping Clark on schedule.

Clark, faced with the need to move on from one group to
the next, would simply say, "The attorney-general of Alberta says I have to go," making the incidental point that he
had the support of a leading Alberta cabinet minister.

Late Wednesday Jim Hawkes found Jenkins, Veale,
Gaston Rivard and Claude Boiselle in a heated discussion
in the coffee shop of the Skyline Hotel. A faction of
Clark's Quebec supporters had rented suite 340 at the
Chateau Laurier for a key club. It would offer jazz and,
contrary to convention regulations, free beer. Jenkins
and Veale were insisting that it was unauthorized and
should be stopped. Rivard and Boiselle sympathized but
said Pierre Bouchard had made it plain that some of
Clark's support depended on the club being left alone.
Since the Chateau had declined to issue scores of extra

keys, the organizers had them made privately. In the end, Jenkins and Veale gave in and the club drew thirsty convention-goers nightly.

Thursday, opening day, was a day for the lobbyists and the candidates to jockey for advantage. Clark's people got into their seats at the Civic Centre just five minutes before the television cameras began to carry the proceedings across the country. At breakfast next morning, Hawkes said they must get into place sooner.

It was really John Diefenbaker's night, but the supporters of every candidate battled it out to impress other camps in the hall as well as the viewers. Clark got a powerful ovation when he was introduced to the convention but so did Paul Hellyer, Sinclair Stevens, Brian Mulroney, Flora MacDonald, Jack Horner, and Claude Wagner.

Brian Mulroney's campaign began going downhill soon after the convention opened.

Christopher Young of Southam News Services reported, "The high rollers in the Mulroney campaign organization continue to overplay their efforts to create a bandwagon. The Mulroney campaign newspaper Thursday carried the incredible statement that 39 percent of Alberta delegates would support their man on the first ballot — and that even more support is expected on the second ballot, including the whole of Premier Lougheed's provincial government.

"Alberta's Attorney-General Jim Foster, a Joe Clark supporter from weeks back, called a press conference last night explicitly to deny this statement. He took care not to blame Mulroney personally for the excessive enthusiasm of his troops but he stated flatly that the claim was untrue."

Hedlin had moved with Pierre Bouchard and others on Wednesday to make sure Clark was properly briefed for the policy sessions on Friday. He pointed out that the Clark people didn't know what tactics supporters of other candidates might devise to present their candidates in a favourable light during the day-long question-and-answer sessions. "We must have people there who can move up on a mike in case somebody tries to do a hammer job on Joe," he said.

With the object of showing up the weaknesses of other candidates, a group of Clark people met on Wednesday and Thursday. Clark himself knew the policy day would be vital to him and he was nervous. The rehearsal for the day became known among his supporters as the "clean tricks" exercise. The object was to plant hard questions on the other candidates, soft ones on Clark. David Jenkins combed Clark's policy papers to devise questions which the papers already answered. The exercise produced mixed results, though on balance Clark won. A "clean tricks" plant brought Brian Mulroney out against the federal caucus position by advocating support for the Trudeau government's sales campaign to sell Candu nuclear reactors abroad. But Mulroney turned another to his advantage. The question was, should the CBC be spending money on a French language television station in Vancouver? He was roundly cheered as he said that if the CBC could finance an English service for sixteen thousand in Quebec City, it could provide a French service for twenty-five thousand in Vancouver.

Supporters of all candidates could play the same game. Clark himself almost fell into an embarrassing pitfall on Canada and the United Nations. He seemed to say that Canada might have to withdraw from the UN. Realizing what he had said, Clark immediately addressed the press corps attending the session and stressed it would only be "as a last resort." Clark expressed concern about Canada's recent tendency to adopt neutral or conciliatory positions in the UN assembly rather than take firm positions on the vital issues.

Clark had worried most about the economic policy forum which was held on Friday. He recognized his own weakness in economics. Yet the economy, the leading national issue at the time, was bound to produce tough questions.

About two weeks before the convention Clark had asked for help from Glenn Carroll, professor of business administration at Wilfrid Laurier University in Waterloo. Carroll, whose wife Marjorie had helped organize southwestern Ontario for Clark, was a twice-defeated Tory candidate in Cambridge-Waterloo. He had met Clark at various conventions over the years. More important, like Clark he believed the future of the country depended to some extent on the strength and growth of small business. He specialized in communications. As the convention approached Clark feared the basic policy material produced by campaign researchers Sandy Borins and Carole Uhlaner lacked polish. On Tuesday afternoon he called Carroll, Borins, Uhlaner and a few other lieutenants to his office and assigned Carroll to write a whole new economic speech for him to deliver on Friday.

Carroll closeted himself with Borins and Uhlaner through Wednesday until two o'clock Thursday morning in his room at the Inn of The Provinces. They threw paper around, paced up and down, snapped at each other, but produced a slick draft. Clark tightened up a few phrases in his own handwriting and delivered the draft in the economic policy forum where it won him a standing ovation. Thanks to Carroll, he had a new theme — that "competence, confidence, and creativity," were needed to stimulate the economy. Borins had expressed reservations about such catch-phrases. At one point during the all-day session he had described them as "pure hokum."

He changed his mind when he saw Clark's success and the subsequent favourable press coverage. The speech had managed to address head-on the main worries of the business community. It identified four main business concerns: stagflation (the phenomenon of inflation and recession running together), the lack of a competitive international trading policy, the need to increase Canadians' control over the national economy and the need for increased efficiency in the public sector. The entire day Friday was an unqualified success for Clark.

Three delegates introduced themselves to John Mc-Teer, Maureen's father, as western Ontario farmers. "We came down here, uncommitted, to listen to the agricultural session. The only one who knows anything about agriculture policy is Joe Clark and you see where we are now."

By nightfall, Clark was exhausted but pleased. He was at home in the question-and-answer style of the various forums. It had been his style in small meetings across the country during the campaign. The day had proven to many delegates that Clark consistently performed well in the give-and-take of question periods.

Friday night a crest of emotion swept over the Civic Centre as the party said farewell to Robert Stanfield. The evening held a special poignancy for Clark. He was listening to the swan song of the man whose speeches he had on occasion written, whose political errands he had run and whose views and policies he closely identified with.

"Our national mission and our political self-interest coincide," Robert Stanfield was saying. "We must see our country and her people as one. This is not a matter of trying to be all things to all people. It is rather a matter of understanding, responding to and reconciling the aspirations, the hopes and the longings of Canadians in all walks of life and in all parts of our land. That is the way to serve our country. That is the way to beat the Liberals. It is not easy. It requires acceptance in our hearts and not merely on our lips of our country in all its diversity. Some of us do not do that, and others notice it and do not trust us."

If one word had to describe Joe Clark's own campaign for the leadership, or even his own political principles, diversity would have served well. For his entire purpose had been to establish a genuine respect in Ottawa for all the nation's diversities.

As they slowly made their way out of the cavernous Civic Centre, Clark shook hands with curious delegates as eagerly as ever. Bill Herron and Jim Foster knew he was exhausted and they persuaded him not to visit his hospitality suites. Instead of resting, Clark went straight to work on his speech for the following afternoon and worked well into the night. Herron and Foster made the round of the hospitality suites and made excuses for his absence.

I was awakened at 7:45 on Saturday morning by the unfamiliar excited voice of Ralph Hedlin. Could I be at his suite in the Inn of The Provinces in about ten minutes? He was sure I would understand, it was one of those things one didn't dare talk about over the telephone. I pulled on my clothes and sped downtown, wondering why my presence should so suddenly be commanded.

Hedlin had heard there was a good chance that John Robarts, the former Ontario premier, would introduce Flora MacDonald's speech at the Civic Centre that afternoon. Like a child who has discovered a new toy, Hedlin produced the name of Allan Laakkonen — not a "name" at all in the party, but one of the dedicated grass-roots workers. He had been writing Laakkonen's speech for him. What did I think of this?

"You don't know me, I have to introduce myself to you," Hedlin intoned solemnly. "We're the ones who ring doorbells. Our wives work in the committee rooms and our children carry signs . . ."

I agreed with Hedlin that he had a great idea. What great contrast and how entirely appropriate. Let Robarts do his damndest. Laakkonen joined us and Hedlin read his speech to him. He said he concurred and would be only too glad to do the introduction. Hedlin said he wanted it published in English and in French in the Clark tabloid which I edited.

I anticipated a problem with the French, I said, because of my experience to date. Nobody was providing copy or translation and I had made do by clipping French press comment and asking my wife Cecilia to write the headings. Hedlin would see to it that the translation was provided. I arranged for a picture of Laakkonen to be taken as he spoke. Our story duly appeared in English only:

"Joe Clark's choice of his nominator at this leadership convention is an example of the individual he is concerned about and the people he appeals to across Canada.

"Rather than choose a well-known caucus colleague and supporter, or one of the leading PC officials present at the convention, Joe chose an ordinary delegate from northern Ontario . . . ." The story went on to quote from Laakkonen's introduction: how he and Joe had met at a party meeting in Barrie, Ontario; how Joe's hand had come out of the crowd with the invitation "come eat with us, Allan," and how Allan had been at Joe's table ever since. As it happened, John Robarts did not introduce Flora. And one of the networks played commercials over Laakkonen's carefully scripted words.

Across the street in the Skyline, Clark was in room 406 rehearsing his speech before a small group that included Maureen, Jim Foster, Dave King, Ian McKinnon and brothers Tim and Peter Woolstencroft. They all knew in their hearts then and there that this was not a great Clark speech, nothing to compare for example with the eloquence of his fund-raising speech in Edmonton two weeks before. At this stage, nobody had the courage or the heart to tell the truth; why bother when it was too late to do much about it anyway?

Before they left, Ian McKinnon and Peter Woolstencroft agreed that it could be better. Foster advised Clark to slow down. He had taken only thirteen minutes in the rehearsal with his rapid-fire delivery. With twenty minutes allotted for each candidate's entire presentation to the convention — speech and demonstrations — and with the demonstration firmly fixed at three minutes, Foster thought Clark could effectively take a little more time.

It was mid-afternoon before Clark mounted the platform in the Civic Centre. After the scare of being almost late on Thursday night, Clark's lieutenants made sure everyone turned out early for the other three days and his cheering section was in place during the noon hour. Clark came fifth in the draw, after John Fraser, Heward Grafftey, Brian Mulroney and Pat Nowlan. Harvie Andre and his convention committee had worried that their presentation to the convention might smack too much of amateurism. It would do them no harm they reasoned, just once, to show the world that if the occasion demanded, they too could be as slick as the Big Blue Machine (or in convention terms as slick as Brian Mulroney or Claude Wagner). In this context, they approved the idea of bringing Joe and Maureen into the arena in an antique landau. It was the brainchild of Frank

Biss and some Toronto colleagues who had volunteered to help about three weeks before the convention. Andre had assigned them the Saturday afternoon program.

As the Ottawa Brass Band swung into the Clark campaign theme song, "I'se the Bye," and two hundred volunteers in yellow T-shirts sang, the doors at the end of the arena swung open and in swept the smiling candidate and his wife in the landau, borrowed for the day from an Ottawa collector. Although the entry has been criticized as superfluous and out of character, it did provide a good visual focus and it was strikingly different.

None of the razzle-dazzle on the floor could be blamed for Clark's tense performance on the platform. He later described the effect of his speech as neutral. It was too long, he thought later, although he had the planned amount of time to deliver it. It was agreed among Clark's group that Mulroney and Hellyer fared badly and Flora MacDonald and Claude Wagner spoke well and helped their causes. Clark probably did no better than hold his own.

The speech disappointed many of Clark's delegates. Its lack of success can be traced to the uncertain organization during convention week. Ralph Hedlin had assumed the responsibility for writing it weeks before. From Toronto he had telephoned several times to Hawkes in his suite at the Bytown Hotel to read lines to him. More than once, Hawkes had warned Hedlin "it's just not Joe Clark."

The problem multiplied during the convention itself because Hedlin guarded the speech as his own preserve. Once Glenn Carroll had cleared the economic speech for Friday, Hawkes pressed him to work on the crucial Saturday speech. On Thursday Hawkes accompanied Carroll to Clark's room at the Skyline looking for Claude Boiselle, who had been assigned the French portion of the speech. Hedlin answered and snapped that he was working on the speech and didn't want to be disturbed. "Now you understand why I didn't want to get involved with the speech," Carroll told Hawkes. "Is there any way I could?

Hedlin indicated the sentences in his draft that he wished translated into French. That was not Boiselle's idea. Nor was it Clark's. Rather, Boiselle was to have provided separate, original French. Later Thursday Boiselle expressed his dissatisfaction to Clark and informed him that he would provide a French text directly to Clark.

Hedlin made a useful contribution with his many hours of work on the speech, but he just didn't have the knack of writing for Clark. Consequently, late in the day an extra burden was placed on the candidate. He felt it necessary to rewrite the speech himself.

Clark had considered making a direct pitch for support from Quebec delegates. He assembled his most politically sensitive lieutenants in his room late Thursday night for a trial reading of the draft. This was meant to detect any remarks that might offend regional sensibilities. And it did. Clark proposed a reference to his strong support for Michael Meighen as the national president of the party: "Thus the party got its first fully bilingual national president, a Quebecer." The phrase was killed after the strenuous objections of Allan McKinnon, MP for Victoria. He pointed out that Meighen's opponent, Donald Matthews of London had had strong support throughout the West. Clark's identification with the struggle for the presidency would do him more harm than good. A potentially damaging reference was dropped.

Thoroughly revised and rewritten, the speech did give Clark's view of the future, with feeling.

"We have a legacy to represent those Canadians whom

others might ignore, or whose rights have been abused, as the rights of women, and of native people, and of small businessmen, have been abused. And we have a tradition of building, of opening new vistas, of closing old wounds. Governments don't build countries. People do. But Canadians can build only if there is confidence in the integrity of government — and only when it is clear that the rules are the same for the powerful as they are for the rest of us.

"I am not going to talk about Mr. Trudeau. You know what I think of him. But Canadians today don't want to know what we are against. They want to know what we are for.

"I am for a government with the courage to challenge — and to change — the way this country has been run for nearly forty years, by one party.

"I am for a greater balance in the distribution of future industry and population — a stronger Parliament, where every member is a somebody — and a government that demonstrates it can control itself before it tries to control others.

"The democratic system works best if parties alternate in power. There have been too many years of Liberal government, too few of Conservative. That has damaged both parties.

"And now that must change."

Delegates struggled through a curtain of snow to their hotels to compare notes, to do their eleventh-hour persuading and to enjoy themselves, if energy permitted.

John Sherman, Jeff Lyons and Hal Veale met in Veale's room at the Skyline for a scheduled meeting of the power lobby. "We're in a lot of trouble," Veale said. The others agreed, such was the impression of Clark's speech. Just as gloom was setting in, George Cooper, the Nova Scotia chairman arrived. "It was great," he said. They went off to discuss with other lieutenants what little more they might do that night.

They could console themselves with one of the best parties in town. Andre had booked the Family Brown band into the Chateau Laurier's Drawing Room, a convenient location just off a well-trodden corridor on the main floor. Crowds milled around every corner of the spacious room and spilled over to the dance floor. After nearly an hour of talking to the happy throng Clark and Maureen had to be dragged away by Herron and Foster.

15
VICTORY

DOWNTOWN Ottawa was asleep as usual on Sunday morning. A heavy blanket of snow greeted Joe Clark as he rose. The stillness of the dawn was disturbed only by the snowplough creeping determinedly along Albert Street. Joe and Maureen slipped off to the Notre Dame Basilica for seven o'clock mass. The question of church was raised the previous day, just before the candidate and his party left the hotel for the convention. Would he be attending church? a CBC reporter asked. No, replied one of his aides, off-handedly. Overhearing the exchange, Clark interrupted to say he really did want to go. Whereupon, the aide corrected himself and undertook to find the most convenient Roman Catholic Church. They agreed on the Basilica; it was closer to Clark's hotel than his parish church.

Jim Hawkes was awakened on an alarming note. "We're in trouble," Dennis Staff, the convention communications man, barked into his phone. All that white stuff had closed in the streets and they were icy too. He didn't see how they could hold a scheduled morning rally for supporters at the hotel and transport them to the Civic Centre in time for the voting. Hawkes took the news into the daily breakfast meeting, put ahead to eight o'clock to take into account the Saturday night partying but not the Ottawa weather. In short order the lieutenants agreed to cancel the rally, spread the word and concentrate on setting up shop in the Civic Centre.

Quickly they reviewed strategy for the afternoon. Non-voting delegates were assigned to cover delegates committed to other candidates on the first ballot. They were instructed to move in when other candidates dropped out to distribute signs and Clark colours.

Dennis Staff, meanwhile, was able to rent one school bus on short notice and it was at the Skyline by ten o'clock. All key staff made the first bus to the Civic Centre. They were concerned about protecting territory in the Centre and organizing their lobbying. Because of this quick change of schedule, Clark had the first significant group of supporters in place. He and his people were there in force when the national television cameras went on the air and focused predominantly on the Mulroney, Wagner, MacDonald and Hellyer camps.

Dennis Staff, an electronics expert, is a friend of the McTeers from Cumberland, who almost single-handedly made the difference between chaos and co-ordination on Sunday. He was the one who arranged to get all the supplies over from Clark headquarters to the Civic Centre. He had designed the convention communication system for the voting day. Based on walkie-talkies with telephone and visual backups, it worked flawlessly and was probably as good as any in the hall.

As far as Clark was concerned personally, by Sunday the fight had been fought. It had been a good and rewarding one.

"It was a surprisingly unemotional day," Clark said afterwards, "partly because I'm a fatalist about these things. It's going to be or it's not, and there isn't anything you can do — at that point. It was like any other election day — the candidate sits and waits." For the lieutenants, hours of worry lay ahead; they could still win over important votes by moving fast and talking astutely. For the candidate, it was a question of waiting, choosing words well when a microphone was thrust in front of him.

As the cameras panned along his benches, viewers saw no powerful figures in the Clark section. No premiers or big names were there. Only three members of Parliament — and they not nationally known names — could be identified: Allan McKinnon of Victoria, the first House of Commons colleague to encourage him to run; Steve Paproski of Edmonton Centre, who later joined McKinnon; and Harvie Andre, of Calgary Centre, who had held out for Peter Lougheed until year's end, then to throw himself enthusiastically into Clark's campaign as convention chairman.

Two rows behind the candidate sat John and Bea McTeer and Grace and Charles Clark, with their son Peter and his wife Marcia. Grace Clark smoked rather self-consciously as the camera passed over them. They ate sandwiches that Mrs. McTeer had prepared.

Even from Alberta, Clark could count on only a handful of provincial members. Three of Clark's strongest supporters, Jenkins, Veale and King tackled national jobs. Although Jack Horner's supporters sometimes overstated the case for support among Alberta MLAs, they and not Clark clearly held the majority.

King commented even before the voting began that the second ballot would be pivotal for Clark. It would indicate which candidates were gathering additional support and what their potential was for fast growth. The Clark group waited tensely for the first vote.

"Clark, 277," called out Michel Coté, chief election officer, announcing the results of the first ballot.

Clark winced. He had been counting on more than three hundred first-ballot votes. His supporters were shocked. A typical comment at this moment: "Two-seventy-seven — we're finished." Disappointment froze the yellow and black cheering section. The chairman continued,

"Fraser, 127
Gillies, 87
Grafftey, 33
Hellyer, 231
Horner, 235
MacDonald, 214
Mulroney, 357
Nowlan, 86
Stevens, 182
Wagner, 531"

Although he had expected more votes, Clark had reckoned on fourth or fifth place on the first ballot. Like many others, he thought Flora MacDonald would be stronger. Here he was, a strong third and the leading candidate outside of Quebec.

Hawkes' voice crackled over the radio system to workers on the floor, "Come on, you guys, let's go, we're right in there." Bill Herron, seated near Clark, jumped to his feet and demanded that everyone within earshot do the same.

Gillies in ninth place with eighty-seven votes dropped out and said he was supporting Clark. Gillies had been impressed by a speech Clark had made in the Commons, critical of the power of the prime minister and had invited Clark to be guest speaker at his annual constituency meeting. Clark had worked hard to win over two Gillies supporters, Regina MP James Balfour and businessman Irving Gerstein. Clark expected their support if Gillies dropped out. Within a few minutes hopeful jubilation replaced despondency around Clark. His workers were just beginning their afternoon of feverish activity.

Already microphones and cameras were being pointed towards him.

Across the area, Sinclair Stevens and his lieutenants were also coming out of a few moments' shock. "I felt there had been a mistake made in the tally," Stevens reported later. He, too, had expected more votes — well over two hundred on the first ballot. When the results board held to the figure of 182, Stevens called on about a dozen close supporters to join him for a private consultation. They found an empty room below the stands for the purpose and closed the door.

Are you in favour of my staying in? was Stevens' first question. To a person, the group was not. Seventh place was simply too far back to offer any hope of victory. Stevens immediately signed a withdrawal slip.

His next question was, which candidate should I support? From his own reading about other conventions Stevens had concluded that a withdrawing candidate ought to name his own preference publicly. It was consistent with any candidate's pretensions to leadership that he try to lead, even as his own cause faltered. And a candidate who stayed in the race after the cause was doomed risked helping a candidate he did not favour for the leadership.

The vote in the small group went about two to one for Joe Clark. Wagner and Mulroney were also considered but Stevens himself leaned towards Clark. Stevens had worked with Clark on various Commons committees and admired him as a scrapper. He considered him a pragmatist in politics. "I knew Clark much better than I knew Wagner," he explained. Wagner had a reputation as a right winger, as, indeed, did Stevens. But in Wagner's case it was based largely on law and order, Stevens thought. He was more concerned with economics and he liked Clark's approach. Also, he was reluctant personally to support a former Liberal for the Tory leadership.

"In the Conservative party," Stevens explained, "there is certainly a great body of true blue. But it is unrealistic to think they represent a majority of voters in Canada. It is wrong to think that we can mould a party that will appeal mainly to true blues and win."

Thus, he reasoned, Wagner might appeal to the true blue but Clark would appeal more effectively than Wagner to the Canadian public.

His decision made, Stevens sought out Earl Rowe, the former lieutenant governor of Ontario who had represented the north end of Stevens' Toronto York Simcoe riding for twenty-five years in Ottawa. "I'm pleased, Clark would be my choice, too," Rowe responded. Stevens learned only later of a friendship between Rowe and the McTeer family. Stevens then sought out William Hodgson, the provincial member for York North. Hodgson said the decision was Stevens' alone to make. If he favoured Clark, that was fine with Hodgson.

Resuming his seat among his supporters Stevens was hounded by reporters, with and without microphones. He first told a CTV reporter he was backing Clark and the word spread like brushfire across the floor and around the stands. Hellyer's supporters radioed to Richard Clewes, Stevens' media manager, that unless Stevens came with Hellyer, Hellyer and many of his supporters were moving over to Wagner. Stevens and Hellyer had been competing for right-wing votes. "Tell them they'd better go to Wagner then," Stevens commented.

Stevens and his wife Noreen then led a group of sad and sobbing supporters to Clark's box, which was five camps away to Stevens' right. Later, Noreen Stevens said it was all she could do not to sob, so infectious was the wave of emotion around her. It was but the beginning of an emotional binge as devoted supporters for one candidate after another released tensions built upon tireless days and sleepless nights.

"I hope you're not too surprised to see me here," Stevens said to Clark. He advised Clark, as the candidate who was gaining strength, to get around the floor and be seen. The two set off to visit several other delegations.

Heward Grafftey, in ninth and last place with thirty-three votes, was automatically eliminated. He now came over to Clark, apologizing for the limited size of his support. Grafftey told the press he had been impressed by Clark's campaigning in Quebec. He thought the Albertan could win there and across Canada.

Word spread that Hellyer had indeed gone over to Wagner. It would have been in Clark's interest for Hellyer to stay in the race longer. There is always the possibility of a bandwagon effect in coventions that can lead some delegates to vote for the candidate who seems to be leaping ahead, and Hellyer's withdrawal and support of Wagner might have given him the momentum to be seen as the likely winner. As it happened there was no bandwagon. Hellyer was unable to deliver all his support to Wagner. For instance, Jake Epp, the MP from Provencher, Manitoba, declined to follow Hellyer's lead and brought several westerners over to Clark's camp.

The news of the Hellyer-Wagner alliance and Stevens withdrawal caused John Fraser to have second thoughts. He had intended to stay in for the second ballet even though his prospects were slim. Although some of his people had already voted their second ballots for him, Fraser said he was pulling out and supporting Clark. "He's an old friend, a great man and a westerner — that should be enough," Fraser told reporters.

The results of the second ballot clearly squared the fight between Clark and Wagner:

Clark, 532

Wagner, 667

Mulroney, 419

Horner, 286

Hellyer, 118

MacDonald, 239

Fraser, 34

Nowlan, 42

Walter Baker, MP for Grenville-Carleton and Hellyer's leading caucus supporter, now came to Clark's box. Flora MacDonald made her way down the floor wearing a yellow scarf. Clark met her. They embraced. Clark put one of her brown scarves around his neck. John McTeer went up to Earl Rowe and said, "Would you mind if I scarved you, Earl?" As Stevens had discovered, Rowe was willing. Meanwhile, Horner was moving into Wagner's box.

David Kirg was trying frantically to persuade Mulroney to release his delegates to ensure Wagner would not win on the third ballot. Mulroney was firm. He was staying in and he was sure Wagner wouldn't win on the next ballot.

"I appreciate his position but I don't think he can control his delegates," King told a reporter at the time. Newfoundland Premier Frank Moores, sweating profusely, tried to change Mulroney's mind unsuccessfully. He said he was committed to supporting him as long as he stayed on the ballot. St. John's East MP James McGrath thought Mulroney was taking too great a risk. He was going to Clark, he said.

When the chairman read out the third ballot results it was clear Clark was gaining on Wagner. He picked up 101 more votes than Wagner between the second and third ballots. The results were: Clark, 969, Mulroney, 369, Wagner, 1,003.

Mulroney knew he could not win, yet still he hesitated. His delegates would decide the victor. He was closer to Clark than to Wagner. He and Clark had fought the Fulton leadership campaign together in 1967.

Jim Hawkes says he took a call from a Mulroney aide saying that if Clark would come across to see Mulroney, he would release his delegates. The word was passed to Clark, who declined. Mulroney disputes the point. He says he wanted nothing to do with the Clark camp. "I wanted to avoid the appearance of screwing anybody." He believed enough supporters would go to Clark to elect him. "If I supported Clark openly it would have looked like a conspiracy against a French-Canadian."

MP Roch LaSalle approached Mulroney on Wagner's behalf. Now was the time to vote for Wagner, he suggested in an unfortunate use of words. "I haven't got a vote," Mulroney replied, "You fellows made sure I haven't got one." (In the bitter battle for Quebec support a Wagner-dominated constituency association had denied Mulroney a vote at the convention.)

Michel Cogger called the Clark camp to say Mulroney would remain neutral outwardly but most of his delegates were going to Clark. "Go with Joe" signs went up in the Mulroney section as Wagner supporters looked on in anger.

Alan Eagleson, Mulroney's campaign manager, climbed into Clark's box, followed by Georges Valade, the former MP, considered one of the most influential Quebec Tories. Valade commented that 80 percent of Mulroney's Quebec vote would go to Clark because of the early alliance between Wagner and Hellyer. "It was too early a kiss," Valade said. "It looked fixed."

Too many Clark delegates thought they had won at this point. Hawkes felt a moment of panic as he tried to keep up the momentum of lobbying. He had met two weeks before the convention with Sandy Borins and Carole Uhlaner of the campaign policy brains trust, who were going to be scrutineers in the counting room during the afternoon. Twenty tables in the room corresponded to the twenty voting lines on the convention floor.

Each candidate's scrutineers were permitted to watch the manual count. Each had the right to object verbally to anything he considered questionable. Hawkes had arranged with Borins and Uhlaner to forward the results to him from each voting line after every ballot. Thus Hawkes knew the strengths of each candidate according to voting lines. Each delegate voted at the same box for every ballot and Hawkes was able to direct his lobbyists to lines where they would be most effective. For example, if Flora MacDonald was strong at box fourteen, Hawkes could direct a lobbyist to that line to shake hands and press Clark's case. Apparently, Clark was the only candidate who arranged for a breakdown according to ballot lines.

The scene in the counting room was not without light moments. Michel Coté, the chief election officer, and his staff were alert for any breach of security or indeed any violation of the rules that might in turn lead to a breach of security. Borins and Uhlaner took to calling him Inspector Clouseau (of *Pink Panther* fame). At one point Coté demanded to see a little black device in Carole Uhlaner's hand. She declined, then decided to have a little fun. She furtively gave it to Hal Veale, Clark's official agent, and dashed dramatically across the room. Veale with all the air of a burglar caught with stolen goods presented the mysterious device to Coté, who was relieved to find not a transmitting device, but an innocent (and acceptable) pocket calculator.

Meanwhile, Clark was writing his victory speech while being fanned by Steve Paproski, the burly MP from

Edmonton Centre. That gave rise to such comments from the stands as, "Hey, Steve, are you a Clark fan?" A CBC reporter craned his neck to see what Clark was writing. Big Bill Herron shifted between them to cut off the view. "Okay," said the reporter, "I get the message." Clark had brought with him the portion of his Saturday speech he had been unable to deliver — the paraphrasing of a song by Gilles Vigneault.

A security officer of the convention quietly approached Bill Herron and whispered in his ear. Clark had won. Nobody was to move, he added, until all the security people were in place. Herron eased over to Clark, squeezed his arm and passed on the news. Herron noticed an instant relaxation of tension. Clark whispered to Maureen. Television cameras relayed their visibly happy faces to two million viewers.

Across the arena, Wagner was being told that he had not won. He sat with his wife in dignified if sad composure.

The final count came over the loudspeaker.

"Clark, 1,187."

Wagner's count, just 65 votes fewer, at 1,122, was inaudible throughout most of the hall in the ensuing storm of jubilation. Delegates were on their feet hugging their fellows, congratulating and kissing each other, clapping and yelling. Others sat quite silently and cried.

Clark hugged Maureen, and received the congratulations of his closest confrères. Now every television camera was upon him. There he stood, the man of the hour for all Canada to see, arms stretched up in triumph.

Then he turned to Allan McKinnon, the MP from Victoria who was his first loyal caucus supporter.

"I bet they don't have any bloody water on that stage," he said, "Allan, will you carry some for me?" McKinnon went out to the corridor for a plastic cup of water. He returned in time to join the party of about a dozen of Clark's lieutenants. Despite a flying wedge of Ottawa policemen they found it hard to make their way through the jubilant crowd of excited well-wishers. McKinnon managed to keep about an inch of water in the cup as he was jostled on every side. It didn't matter because this was one time when Clark's foresight was not needed. There were glasses and a jug of water under the lectern. The Clark group mingled with the other candidates. Only Hellyer was not there; he had slipped away early.

Claude Wagner, speaking in French, told the convention they had shared a great dream. It would now have to be translated into loyalty towards a new leader. "We will demonstrate that we want this party to be the voice and conscience of all Canadians."

In his farewell remarks to the convention, retiring leader R.L. Stanfield paid appropriate tribute to Wagner. "It takes a big man to lose a close one like that." Almost all the rest of his short speech was devoted to the cause of unity within the party. He appealed several times for caucus and delegates to work together. "We will win the next election if we create confidence among Canadians in our leadership and in our party, and if we demonstrate to the people of Canada that we are a cohesive party and that we can work together."

As he finished, the delegates began to chant, "Joe, Joe, Joe." Clark approached the lectern, both arms uplifted and smiling, as the chairman introduced him: "The future prime minister of Canada, Joe Clark."

Clark's hastily prepared speech was remarkable. There was absolutely no question about the party unity Robert Stanfield had belaboured a few moments earlier, Clark said. His would be a team leadership. The old theme of virtue in diversity crept in again — there is more than one way to be a Canadian. It was combative in its partisanship.

And he seized the rare opportunity to appeal to the nation at large on prime-time television. Here was a speech infinitely better than his appeal to delegates the previous afternoon. He had written this one entirely himself in the heat of the convention on a scrap of paper on his knee.

Within fifteen minutes of his election, Clark had laid down the essential course of his first year's leadership. One can see that he has followed closely the tenets laid down in his acceptance speech.

There was no question about the party's unity, Clark said. It would be achieved. "I intend to conduct myself in a way that will make this victory today a victory for all of us." The convention had shown Canadians that the party had a team of talented people capable of proving a strong alternative government. But there was no easy way to win. "We will not take this nation by storm, by stealth or by surprise. We will win it by work." Canada was big enough, Clark said, to have more than one culture in it, "more than one language, more than one way of being a Canadian. In a world that is growing too much the same, we are unique in our diversity."

The delegates jumped to their feet applauding. Clark embraced Maureen. Together, they went to the back of the stage to shake hands with Stanfield and the defeated candidates. After the singing of the national anthem, the decision was made — nobody is sure now who made it — to use the police to move Clark's official party from the stage and escort them from the arena. With Clark on the stage were McKinnon, Jim Foster, Hal Veale, David Jenkins and Peter Woolstencroft. The phalanx of policemen again cut a path through the crowd. "Don't do that — we like him," came the plaintive call of a youthful observer. Clark himself was alarmed at being practically carried away by the police. More than a few delegates commented on the speed with which the system takes over a public figure. Others hoped it would not be a harbinger of things to come. They didn't realize it was not so much "the system" taking over as an attempt to help the new leader leave the hall.

Once outside, the group found a room where they could arrange television appearances and plan the rest of the night. John Diefenbaker found them and came in to congratulate his successor. Ab Douglas of CBC protested to Bill Herron that he had heard the new leader would appear first on "W-5," a rival CTV program. He demanded that the new leader appear first on CBC, citing the network's good coverage of Clark during the convention. Clark appeared first on CBC, then on Radio-Canada, and CTV; afterwards, he gave a full press conference.

Immediately, Clark was asked about unity in the caucus. What about Jack Horner and others in the caucus who had been critical of him? Clark responded that Horner had conducted a moderate and positive campaign. He would play a full role in caucus. As though he had planned his first year carefully, Clark said he would spend less time in the House of Commons than other leaders had done. There would be much organizational work for him to do, in Quebec particularly. There would be no Quebec lieutenant but he would work closely with Wagner. So many federalists in Quebec had lost faith with the Liberal party and could now be welcomed into the Conservative party. Diversity was the nation's strength. Finally, he said he was surprised by the narrowness of his win. He had expected a larger margin on the fourth ballot.

With that, the jubilant but fatigued Clark and his small band of followers made their way across snow-sodden Ottawa to 200 First Avenue and an instantaneous victory celebration at campaign headquarters. The Family Brown, the band that had played the previous night at his Chateau Laurier hoedown, turned up for dancing. An Ottawa submarine sandwich chain produced food. Ottawa lawyer Ron Faulkner had laid in cases of beer and soft drinks.

Clark embraced a few friends and went directly to the television set in the corner of the main room. He sat, as in a trance, eyes glued to the national news. He mouthed the words to himself as he watched and listened to his victory speech of two hours before. Maureen sat on a box and munched a submarine sandwich. She hadn't eaten all day.

16
SETTLING IN

MAUREEN McTeer, in jeans and bulky woollen sweater, was preparing a can of Campbell's Tomato Soup in the kitchen of Stornoway. The time was 6.30 P.M. on Friday March 11, 1976. She had been Canada's most famous law student for two weeks and she was not at all sure she enjoyed it. Apart from the fuss in the papers, there had been all the trouble of moving to this, the official residence of the leader of Her Majesty's Loyal Opposition. Stornoway is quite adequate for a young married couple: nine bedrooms and living and dining rooms to hold a hundred guests for cocktails. The Clarks' furniture was in the den and the master bedroom.

Maureen wished Joe would get home for that soup. They were to attend a black-tie dinner at eight at John Turner's with the American Ambassador. Joe was to get away from the office at 5:30 so he could rest. Next morning he was leaving for a three-day tour of his constituency.

She was thinking about all the fuss in the papers. Reporters wanted interviews the morning after Joe won the leadership. Maureen had talked, in her own forthright way, about herself, her views on teenagers and sex, politics, her career in law — and her name.

Suddenly she was a somebody. At first, rule-conscious editors had made her Mrs. Joe Clark or Mrs. Maureen

Clark, then Maureen McTeer Clark. Some by now had gone all the way. Maureen McTeer, period. Sure she was a feminist, that was true, but not a humourless bitch, as some presentations had suggested. Now the dean of law was pressing her to drop out of her last year at the University of Ottawa. Months of campaigning with Joe had caused her to miss invaluable lectures and study time. The press would be very tough on her if she failed. She resolved to stay in the courses and try to pass, with the odds and the pressure of the media against her.

Joe arrived home at seven bearing a cake from a well-wisher. He announced he had to fly out that night because of icy conditions. That would mean leaving Turner's dinner early. The "scrum" had been longer than usual because of "the judge's affair." (The scrum was the daily corridor confrontation between press and politicians in the Parliament Buildings. The "judge's affair" was the allegation of a Montreal judge that cabinet ministers tried to interfere in the course of justice in a contempt of court charge against Consumer Affairs Minister André Ouellet. It was Clark's first crisis as leader of the Opposition.)

Now he was relaxed, perched on the kitchen stool, changed from his three-piece vested suit into his white woollen cardigan. Maureen was on the other side of the fridge, pouring the soup. Joe flicked on an electric can-opener, flashed an impish grin and asked, "What's that, Mo?" She shook the fridge, thinking there was something wrong with it, before realizing it was merely her husband's sense of humour.

On this, his nineteenth day in the leadership, Clark had won his spurs in the House of Commons. There the mood had been tension and anger and Clark's demeanour had been that of a prosecutor. The question about whether ministers of the Crown had intervened improperly with the judiciary had been simmering during the week. Chief Justice Gilles Deschenes of the Quebec Superior Court had reported to Justice Minister Ron Basford that a telephone call from Public Works Minister C.M. Drury to a Quebec judge was improper. Prime Minister Trudeau had declined either to accept Drury's resignation or to open a public inquiry, as demanded by the Opposition. The tenor of both the Commons and the leader of the Opposition that afternoon was caught in *Hansard*.

MR. CLARK: Mr. Speaker, I have a great respect as a man for the minister of public works. I think it was entirely appropriate for him to present his resignation and I believe that in the circumstances, having regard to a judgment by the Chief Justice of the Supreme Court of Quebec that the minister had acted in a way which the judge characterized as improper, it is inexcusable for the prime minister now not to accept that resignation.

SOME HON. MEMBERS: Hear, hear!

AN HON. MEMBER: The arrogance of power.

MR. LANG: Except you recognize his honour and his distinction.

AN HON. MEMBER: Not yours, Otto.

MR. CLARK: Mr. Speaker, I recognize the honour and distinction of the minister of public works and I regret it is not shared by his leader and perhaps by some of his colleagues. I want to turn for a moment to the question of a public inquiry and the prime minister's refusal to widen the ambit of an investigation which the Chief Justice in his report indicated was limited and restricted to very narrow grounds. The prime minister has said in his statement that the facts are known.

MR. STANFIELD: To whom?

MR. CLARK: To whom? The answer is the facts are not known to the Parliament of Canada.

SOME HON. MEMBERS: Hear, hear!

MR. CLARK: They are not known to the people of Canada, and they are not known to the Chief Justice of the Supreme Court of Quebec. If they are known to anyone they are known only to the prime minister of Canada and he has indicated to us today that despite the evidence of impropriety, despite actions which the Chief Justice of Quebec has described as improper, his standards do not lead him to accept the resignation which the standard of the minister of public works caused him to offer.

SOME HON. MEMBERS: Hear, hear!

MR. CLARK: So the facts are not known, Mr. Speaker. Since those facts relate to the ethics of ministers of the Crown, to the relations between ministers of the Crown and the courts of the land, it is important that the facts be known. It is important that the House of Commons know what the minister of consumer and corporate affairs (Mr. Ouellet) said to the prime minister relative to his own involvement in this affair. It is important that we know what other ministers, if any, what other citizens, if any were involved in any attempt to intervene to use the words of the minister of public works, in decisions by the courts of the country. These are the facts which the Parliament of Canada and the people of Canada have a right to know —

SOME HON. MEMBERS: Hear, hear!

MR. CLARK: . . . if there is to be, in fact, a safeguarding of the independence of the judiciary in Canada. From time to time, Mr. Speaker, Canadians ask about the distinction between major political parties in this country. The distinction is perhaps evident here today. The prime minister has indicated that he is satisfied there has been no impropriety; we, Sir, are not satisfied that there has been no impropriety.

SOME HON. MEMBERS: Hear, hear!

MR. CLARK: We will not be so satisfied until the prime minister has come clean with the House of Commons and the people of Canada and laid before us, this highest court in the land, the facts — all of the facts relating to the activities of the minister of his government and their attempts at intervention in the processes of justice and the activities of the courts of this land.

Members of his caucus congratulated their new leader on his performance. Clark had dispelled the doubt that he could handle himself on the floor of the House.

Being leader of the Opposition did not mean severing the ties with his grassroots supporters.

Next evening, on the floor of the Frank Maddock High School gymnasium, ten local housewives brought tears to Clark's eyes. He was back in Drayton Valley, Alberta where four years before, almost to the day, he had won the nomination as the candidate for Rocky Mountain. Calling themselves the Drayton Valley Entertainers, the women formed a chorus line to sing a revised version of Clark's theme song from the convention, "Look a Little Ahead."

"We're not going to sing it for the leader of the Opposition but for the future prime minister," the chorus leader said as she introduced "the song that won for Joe Clark in Ottawa."

"I don't mean to be so serious," Clark responded, "but as some of you can tell, this is a very emotional evening for me. I'm very much going to need your help in the years ahead." It was supposed to be a dance but nobody danced. Two hundred local folk just wanted to chat with the local boy who'd made it. If they continued to support him, Clark said, he thought he could become the next prime minister.

When he visited the southern end of his unwieldy riding, the weekly newspaper the *Canmore Miner* wrote an open letter to Clark:

"As long as you continue to remain an ordinary Joe in their eyes and don't forget to consider the hopes and dreams of all the other ordinary Joes across this great country, you'll do just fine."

Clark was criticized before he completed his first year as leader because he was, well, ordinary. Where was the charisma? Where was the great wellspring of inspiration? Where was the intellectual? In fact, Clark is an intellectual, if having a master's degree, being a voracious reader and possessing a razor-sharp mind qualifies one as an intellectual. Yet, he was perfectly natural and at home with the folks at Drayton Valley, and all the other small towns of Rocky Mountain.

One of the greatest challenges of his leadership came before the television floodlights on Parliament Hill. Clark had mastered the Commons probably in record time even though he had admitted to being in awe of the Chamber as a "new boy" in the spring of 1973. Three years later he was regularly matched against Prime Minister Trudeau and the cabinet, and holding his own against the taunts and barbs. Unlike Trudeau, he had been accustomed to public political speaking since he was a teenager and had acquired a sense of presence and confidence. On the other hand he had limited experience with television.

Many of his television appearances were filmed at impromptu press sessions outside the Commons. At first Clark appeared on the screens as a sombre preacher, totally out of character with his personality and age. Then he tried to smile slightly to alleviate the sombre mien and he appeared instead to sneer. The solution, which came towards the end of 1977, was simply to be natural. (Clark would be effective, also, in the televised press conference of the kind that Prime Minister Trudeau holds — if he took the time to brief himself properly the way the prime minister does.)

Clark appeared to be the main beneficiary when, in October 1977, television was allowed in the Commons itself. He was often seen on the offensive, scoring points off a smirking prime minister or a complacent Liberal front-bencher.

Politicians sacrifice much of their privacy to their job, they are forced to live so much of their lives in public. What is left of their privacy is all the more cherished and they guard it jealously. They also recognize the natural public curiosity and sometimes try to manipulate it. The Trudeaus apparently saw no contradiction between their wish for family privacy and their voluntarily taking a young child to a formal banquet on Parliament Hill. Or, for that matter, between family political campaigning one month and demands to be left alone the next.

When Ken Pole of the *Ottawa Journal* raised the point of privacy in an interview, Clark responded "I'm inclined to be short with that question. I'm inclined to say 'I don't have to go around proving to people such and such' .... On the other hand I know that I do. We talk about the impossibility of privacy. People do want to know something about one .... If one starts to say deliberately 'Psst, come here and see it, see a new, true side of my character' that by nature is artificial and consequently unreal. I don't know what we do about that." There is probably a feeling on both sides that if only the public could see the politician playing with his children or cross-country skiing, the public would identify with him. And, of course, the politician would benefit at the polls.

The public could draw its own conclusions when Pierre

Trudeau invited the television cameras into 24 Sussex
Drive early in 1977. For years Trudeau had always kept
the public out of his official residences. After a string of
bad polls and after the separatist threat in the Quebec
election, he permitted Télémetropole, the private Quebec
television network, to film the family at home, 24 Sussex
Drive, and at his Harrington Lake retreat.

The media reflected public interest in the new Tory
leader and his young wife from the very first day of his
leadership.

Theirs were new faces. They welcomed the press into
Stornoway the day they moved in. The nation learned
that the young couple had only enough furniture to fill
the den. And Maureen was shown making the bed.

What the viewers, including many of Clark's campaign
supporters, did not realize was how fully his life had
been transformed since that day when he was swept from
his box to the centre stage of Torydom by a flying wedge
of policemen. For the Opposition leader is part of the
political system, which operates mainly in public. As
Clark acknowledged, little of a leader's time is his own
and what is left must be cherished.

The move from the small house on Rockcliffe Way to
Stornoway, a few blocks away, symbolized the trans-
formation. Stornoway is a public house, decorated at
public expense (and modestly redone by the Clarks soon
after they moved in). It is set in half a block of treed
gardens at the exclusive end of Rockcliffe Village, the
gardens manicured by the National Capital Commission.
The Clarks had a minimum of help. After daughter
Catherine was born they hired a nurse for a while then
replaced her with a nanny, finally settling for a
housekeeper who also helped look after the child. The
party provides a car and chauffeur to whisk the leader or
his wife to the airport or Parliament Hill.

After a few months in office, public recognition, so necessary to success, began to encroach on what little privacy remained. As a movie buff, Clark would slip off to an Ottawa cinema, only to be accosted by well-wishers, autograph seekers and curious onlookers while he waited in the queue. To avoid this he sometimes took advantage of managerial courtesy, and was allowed into the cinema as soon as he arrived.

Holidays weren't private any more either. Clark never criticized Prime Minister Trudeau for taking holidays outside the country, as others were wont to do. After the national unity debate in July 1977 Clark slipped away with Maureen, daughter Catherine and sister-in-law Jane McTeer to a quiet cottage in Massachusetts. He insisted there be no receptions by neighbours and that the family be left in total isolation. He arranged to visit friends but only on neutral ground where he was sure he would not become the Canadian leader of the Opposition. Even then, during a day's outing on Cape Cod, he was hailed in a restaurant by some holidaying Montrealers. No longer was a normal holiday possible; a carefully arranged cover for a hermit's holiday became the rule.

But he was able to leave the problems of office far behind. For those few days he could walk for miles along the surf-cleaned private beaches. Public life had its compensations as well as its price.

17
LEADER

WITHIN a few short days in early 1976, Joe Clark went from being a virtual unknown outside of Tory circles to being the leader of the alternative government of Canada. For six months his time and energy had been consumed by his bid to win the leadership. His campaign had been highly personal, supported by only one or two professionals and held together by the enthusiasm of youth. Suddenly Clark found himself in the national spotlight, expected to comment on every national issue, his responses judged as those of a potential national leader. In the United States, a candidate for president acquires a panoply of advisers and support staff even before his party's nominating convention. In Canada there is nothing resembling a transition team.

A new party leader is faced immediately with choosing his advisers. He can, as Robert Stanfield did in 1967, shed his original campaign staff and select a new team. Or, as Jimmy Carter did in 1976, he can move his own creatures, his Hamilton Jordans and his Jody Powells, into new positions of command. Clark chose to blend the two options.

Within forty-eight hours of his election as leader, Clark offered the important post of chief of staff to William Neville. The two had never been close, but they had long admired each other. Neville began his working life as a wire service journalist, then he honed his natural talent for glib verbal barbs as executive assistant to the Liberal cabinet minister Judy LaMarsh. When LaMarsh left government, so did Neville, to take up a career as one of Ottawa's most successful lobbyists. In 1974, he converted to Stanfield Toryism, and forever earned the enmity of John Turner by waging an aggressive campaign against him in the suburban riding of Ottawa-Carleton.

Neville was defeated, along with most of the Tory ticket, in 1974, and Stanfield appointed him director of the PC Research Office in early 1975. During a difficult transition period, Neville skilfully kept the Research Office, with its reservoir of Tory partisan talent, resolutely neutral during the bloody struggle for the Progressive Conservative federal leadership. For his experience, his personal qualities, and his intra-party neutrality, Neville was an obvious — though unexpected — choice for Clark's chief of staff.

As a counterpoint to Neville, Clark chose, for his second senior staff position, Jim Hawkes, a University of Calgary psychologist. In the opinion of many, Hawkes had provided the glue that held Clark's leadership campaign together. He is a shrewd judge of character, a skill acquired through many years as a professional therapist. He agreed to spend his upcoming sabbatical year in Ottawa. From the first, Hawkes was an oddity — or a breath of fresh air, most say — in the bluff-and-bluster world of federal PC politics. As one of Hawkes' assistants later put it, "Jim was unpopular at the Zoo," meaning federal PC headquarters, where fang-and-claw and knife-in-back politics were the order of the day, no matter who the leader, no matter who his staff.

Hawkes was to leave after his sabbatical year had expired to return to Calgary, later to win the federal party nomination in Calgary West. He was succeeded by

Duncan Edmonds, a rather more familiar Ottawa figure
and a former assistant to Lester Pearson and Paul Martin.
But Hawkes left a lasting imprint, one of which was the
Policy Advisory Council. He conceived the idea of a far-
flung network of policy advisers for the Opposition and he
recruited the principal members, including Chairman
Reva Gerstein, an energetic Toronto businesswoman. In
many ways the Council was only an extension of the less
formal and lower-profile group that had advised
Stanfield. Some sneered that the Council was just
another excuse for Clark to avoid taking policy stands.
But the main thrust of the Council was always preparing
to govern, not to campaign.

Deluged with job applications, Clark, Neville and
Hawkes deliberately took their time in putting together a
junior staff. The watchword was team, the leitmotif was
balance. Everyone was supposed to bring a different mix
of talents. Clark himself was insistent that men and
women, francophones and anglophones, those with Tory
connections and those without, Clark supporters and
those who had opposed him, should all be equally
considered on their own merit. Hawkes was harsh on
some, quizzing them on their drinking habits, their
medical record, and anything else that might impinge on
their effectiveness. He was diligent in weeding out people
who thought they were joining an easy coast to power and
privilege. "Don't harbour any illusions," he told one
young recruit. "There are powerful forces ranged against
us. You've just joined the Spartans at the pass — and the
whole Persian army is coming down the pike." Even in the
halcyon days, when the polls were favourable, Clark,
Neville and Hawkes realized that their paltry number
of paid staff were up against what Hawkes called
"Trudeau's captive army" — the immense Public Service
of Canada.

Clark's office was able to recruit most of the people it wanted. A notable exception was Lowell Murray, Clark's long-time confidant, Stanfield's first chief of staff and, at the time of Clark's victory, the alter ego of New Brunswick Premier Richard Hatfield. Murray was about to leave New Brunswick for the calm of Queen's University. For many months he was to stay in the shadows as one of Clark's key out-of-town advisers, until in the autumn of 1977 he became his national campaign director.

During most of Clark's first two years, he suffered image problems of one kind or another. Ironically, although he himself had served Stanfield so well in that very field he was not his own image man and he didn't seem to have anyone who was a match for the professionals in the prime minister's office. The staff of the PMO alone had more than doubled during the Trudeau years, many concerned with the prime ministerial style — pollsters, image men, media directors, the whole panoply of political communications in the seventies. Clark's office never seemed to be quite caught up. An American comment seemed to apply to Clark as he worked away at the nuts and bolts of leadership. During Jimmy Carter's transition period in 1976, his adviser Patrick H. Caddell wrote in a memo: "Too many good people have been beaten because they tried to substitute substance for style." The new president should emphasize style during the early days of his administration.

Critics could say that a leader who substituted style for substance would deserve to fail. But equally, a leader of substance without style is handicapped, particularly when his opponents have both.

Clark's selection of staff left many people unsatisfied. The underpaid and over-worked Research Office staff were annoyed that none of their number, with the exception of Neville himself, had been promoted to the more prestigious and better-paid positions in the leader's office. So every real or imagined weakness in Clark's personal team was quickly magnified and loudly repeated at the National Press Club. Similar growls and gripes, though less well based, emanated from the Zoo, and got passed into the Ottawa gossip mill.

A bitter chorus arose from those members of Clark's volunteer campaign staff who had been passed over. Some of these in fact found themselves in Clark's inner circle; but many did not. In a nasty national magazine article Hazel Strouts, who as paid campaign press secretary had managed to get some good publicity for Joe Clark, leadership candidate, turned on Joe Clark, leader of the Opposition. Specifically, she accused him of allowing his advisers — i.e. Neville and Hawkes — to "package him." The charge was ill-founded. He is — and on this point all his intimates agree — his own man.

The same principles of team and balance that Clark wanted with his personal staff, he applied to his Parliamentary caucus and his front bench. Clark knew that one of Stanfield's albatrosses was the charge that, while he would be an admirable prime minister, he could not form a credible cabinet. So Clark was determined to raise the profile of his front bench. Without bruising too many egos, and without substantially changing the complex Stanfieldian system of caucus committees, he created the impression of a tough and competent alternative government. He did so by introducing an executive caucus group — six policy co-ordinators, the whip, the House leader and his deputy. They meet Clark weekly for lunch. Many MPs credit the innovation with raising the standard of criticism, and keeping the caucus more active and informed.

For his first Parliamentary session as leader, Liberal fumbles — the judges affair, the Sky Shops scandal among others — got Clark off to a good start. Under the Canadian system of government, it is when the ministerial party is caught in error that the Opposition leader shines brightest. And throughout the scandal-ridden spring of 1976, Clark's staff served him well — Bill Neville pounces on Liberal transgression like a lion on a wounded antelope. When the House rose for the summer recess, the PCs stood at 46 percent in the Gallup poll, the Liberals at 31.

Clark's first major fumble came with the big shootout at Bow River, the first public surfacing of an explosive situation that had been simmering for months. Bad luck, bad timing, and bad handling involved the leader himself. Redistribution had given two additional seats to Alberta. But in a province where in recent years the PC nomination has been tantamount to election, there were still not enough seats to accommodate all the ambition. Radical boundary changes had created discord within the all-Tory Alberta caucus, as members jockeyed for favoured constituencies.

As it turned out, Joe Clark and Stan Schumacher, the MP for Palliser, both had their eyes on the new riding of Bow River. It contained large chunks of both members' old ridings — but it also held Clark's hometown of High River. And Clark thought that his High Riverness was an important dimension of his national image.

Schumacher is an amiable man, with a perpetual boyish grin, who often sees things differently from the way that, say, John Kenneth Galbraith sees them. In this case, he saw things differently from the way that Joe Clark saw them. For one thing, he had already put a lot of work into Bow River, well before the leader evinced interest. For another, Schumacher knew well that there was little the leader could do to bring him, Schumacher, to heel. The Canadian system gives few powers to an Opposition leader to control his backbenchers — except the hope of future office. In a Progressive Conservative federal cabinet, Alberta can expect, at the outside, only two or three members in the cabinet. Schumacher, by anybody's reckoning, was very far down the list. He had little to lose by challenging Clark.

All that being said, it is fair to add that Clark himself thoroughly bungled the whole business. Instead of giving in gracefully and quietly right at the start, he chose to make a public fight of it. In an emotional, even intemperate, letter to the *Lethbridge Herald,* Clark wrote: "To be known as 'the man from High River' is a source of personal pride for me and is of very real importance to our party's chances of forming the national government because of the general affinity it gives me for the smaller communities across Canada which remain the bedrock of this country."

The incident was pure Joe Clark. His advisers in Ottawa begged him to back down, as did his close friend David Jenkins and Alberta MLA Fred Bradley. Being "the man from High River," they argued, cut no ice in the suburban swing seats of Toronto and Montreal. These arguments and those of Marilyn Maclean and Morag Oracheski, his local campaign manager and constituency assistant respectively, eventually made him bend. From Newfoundland, he telephoned Mrs. Maclean to tell her he would accept the Progressive Conservative nomination in the new Yellowhead constituency, which also contained part of his previous riding, though not the coveted High River itself.

Bow River was interpreted by some as a sign of weakness in Clark at the very time that many Canadians were asking whether he was tough enough for leadership.

First he staked out untenable ground, then he failed to defend it.

With the Bow River business behind them, Clark's advisers settled down to plan their strategy for the year ahead. They decided that Clark should spend most of his time campaigning in the country at large, leaving the daily rough-and-tumble of trench warfare in Parliament to a reinvigorated front bench. There were those who opposed the decision, but there was much to commend it. For one thing, Clark enjoys personal campaigning, with a fervour unknown since John Diefenbaker. As columnist Geoffrey Stevens, the biographer of Robert L. Stanfield, put it, "Joe Clark shakes more hands in an hour than Bob Stanfield did in a day." In any case, it was those arguments that won the day. Elections, after all, are won in the country, not in the House of Commons — or so it was said in Clark's inner circle.

But there were flaws, too, in the approach. Opposition leaders lack the enormous resources of incumbent prime ministers to mount major media events, the sine qua non of a successful tour strategy. In the spring, Clark had made a brief sally out of the country, to Washington, where he had well-publicized meetings with President Ford and other high officials of the dying Republican administration. That success encouraged Clark and his organization to attempt a much more ambitious tour of Western Europe in the summer.

The European trip in August and September of 1976 was a bad omen of things to come. The Canadian troops at Lahr welcomed Clark warmly, with his hawkish promises of neat, new weapons systems. He was received by the Pope. But the Germans were too busy with their own election campaign to take note of Joe Clark's. In Brussels, nearly everyone seemed to be on holiday, except for the Canadian Ambassador who created a little news by inadvertently calling Clark "prime minister." In Paris, Clark suffered from poor advance work, and bombed badly before an audience of French businessmen. All in all, he gave the impression of a young man out of his depth, badly briefed, and only vaguely aware of the main issues between Canada and the European Economic Community. It was not until the end of his trip that Clark got around to talking turkey — in a thoughtful conservative analysis of the problems of international development in a speech to the U.K.-Canadian Chamber of Commerce. But by that time, most of the accompanying Canadian newsmen had gone home.

The decision to switch Clark's time to the country, rather than to Parliament, does not show up in the statistical records of the House of Commons. If anything, Clark spent more time in the House than the prime minister. He spoke often, including a brilliant reply to the Speech from the Throne, called by columnist Charles Lynch the "best speech by an Opposition leader" in twenty years. Clark spoke on many other issues: the James Bay Settlement, federal-provincial fiscal arrangements, unemployment, the budget. He often led off in the daily Question Period. He was diligent about showing up for recorded votes. But for the long months of the third session of the Thirtieth Parliament, from October 1976 to July 1977 Clark often left the Commons to his front bench.

From the beginning, the public opinion polls were the touchstone — for good and ill — of the Clark leadership. Since the 1950s the Canadian Institute of Public Opinion has asked a representative sample of Canadians about their party preferences. The survey (popularly known as the Gallup poll) had been irregular, sometimes only once or twice a year. But, for reasons best known to itself, Gallup started monthly surveys in the summer of 1975, just as the PC leadership race to succeed Robert Stanfield was heating up.

The Gallup poll had never been kind to Stanfield. He'd had one moment of soaring glory, just after he'd been selected as party leader in 1967, but it had soon dissipated. In almost nine years as leader of the Opposition he never pulled ahead of the Liberals. At times, such as the October Crisis in 1970, he dipped near the teens. At other times he even fell behind the New Democrats. Later, when Clark was to lose some ground in the polls, one of Stanfield's old assistants cracked: "I don't know what Joe's people are so gloomy about. When we got *up to* where Joe has gone *down to,* we broke out the champagne."

Immediately after Clark's leadership victory, in February 1976, the Gallup recorded a stunning jump in PC fortunes — from 36 to 47 percent. It was to stay there for exactly a year. Month after month Gallup reported uniformly favourable results (in the 40s) for the Conservatives, uniformly bad results (in the 30s) for the Liberal government. Month after month pundits would go on television to solemnly discuss changes of two or three percentage points — changes which were well within the range of sampling error. The media became, it is fair to say, obsessed with the monthly Gallup poll.

But throughout the long months of frontrunning, a sense of unease took root in Tory ranks everywhere. After fifteen years in the wilderness, it all seemed too good to be true. And there seemed no sound reason, beyond the momentum of the leadership convention itself, to justify the lead. One observer put it this way: "Clark's ahead because he's not Trudeau and he's not Stanfield." Members of Parliament brought back to Ottawa the restiveness of their constituents. Clark's vagueness, his failure to take crisp positive policy stands, and his foolish frequent admissions that the party had no detailed "policies," all contributed to the incipent problem.

Clark himself repeatedly reminded audiences that the Gallup lead could not be sustained forever. His private comment with each new piece of good news from the pollsters was "We have another month of grace."

All the same, the polls bred a kind of cockiness in the Clark camp. And it led to an unhealthy conservatism in the making of political strategy. The inevitable answer to any suggestion of change was a glib "We must be doing something right" — followed by a recitation of the latest poll results. In short, the polls became a kind of camouflage to hide weaknesses of policy and organization.

The election of the Parti Québecois on November 15, 1976 crystallized the widespread sentiment that the PC lead was somehow artificial. Nearly everyone realized that the crisis precipitated by the Quebec election played directly into Trudeau's long and strong suit. The idea that the Trudeau Liberals would immediately jump ahead of the Clark Conservatives, because of the Liberals' presumed status as the guardians of national unity, became the coventional wisdom. The first post-election poll was to be released in early January. Clark's staff awaited the news with taut nerves, but their anguish proved unnecessary. When the poll results were released they showed that the Tories had not lost ground, in fact they had gained. On the orders of the leader's office, the Zoo issued a strident, triumphant pamphlet headed: "PC Support Hits Seventeen-Year High." The pamphlet claimed, on the basis of utterly unreliable provincial totals, that the PC and the Liberals were "running even" in the province of Quebec.

The January Gallup poll reinforced a view in Clark's

circles that, in the words of one staff member, "the historic vote-jam in Quebec has broken up." The belief was that many Quebecers had voted on November 15, not for separation, but for simple change. Clark said as much in his speeches. The personal assessments of Tory organizers in Quebec echoed the views of the national leader, as for some strange reason they almost always do. Private party polls, although thought amateurish by many, solidified that idea. There were five parliamentary vacancies in Quebec, and they, plus the wide PC lead in the polls, formed a neat nexus in the minds of Tory strategists. Clark drifted towards a major political gamble. He would spend most of his time campaigning in Quebec in the hope of electing at least one member. But Fate and the Liberal party were preparing some rough blows. The first fell in early March; for the first time in a year, the Tories fell behind the Liberals in the polls, 37 percent to 41 percent. After that, much else was to come unstuck.

Clark himself heard the bad news privately in his office. His wife was less fortunate. She was in a more public situation in the Research Office, gathering materials for one of her speeches. She was in the middle of an impromptu lecture on her enthusiasm for an election when a messenger arrived with the news. She finished her discourse anyway. Across the street from Parliament, at the National Press Club, where there had been a growing dislike of Clark, and his equally confident wife, there arose a chorus of hoots and huzzahs.

The March poll confirmed the punditry of the late fall. Richard Gwyn, the syndicated columnist probably went too far when he likened the unity crisis to the Battle of Britain, and congratulated Canadians for having had the good sense to "rally around their national leader." "Canadians," Gwyn wrote, "have rejoined the main-

stream of political history." Over-reaction, yes, but he
reflected a mood among the media that Clark's long lead
had been unjustified.

Within a few weeks the government called five
byelections in Quebec for May 24, Victoria Day, plus a
sixth that had been pending for many months in a vacant
Tory riding in P.E.I. This was the opening shot in a
massive Liberal offensive against the PCs, such as they
had never bothered to mobilize against Stanfield. Clark,
now behind in the polls, was left in the lurch with no
choice but to bull ahead with his byelection gamble. Bad
luck, complacency and confusion in the Clark camp was
to turn a normal swing in the political pendulum into a
PC rout.

Clark appeared in person at all the five nominating
conventions in Quebec, where he spoke about his vague
ideas for restructuring the constitution. He never made it
to the sixth nominating convention, in Prince Edward
Island. Everywhere, Quebec's sycophantic Tory organizers turned out good crowds. And the same crowds
responded encouragingly well. At least Clark didn't put
the French language throught the same torture as
Stanfield had in three previous general elections. In most
ridings, the PCs presented good, solid candidates.

But in the Montreal suburb of Terrebonne, the local
blues nominated Roger Delorme, a radio hot-liner who
pronounced his pro-Palestinian sentiments against the
State of Israel in the presence of Clark himself and dozens
of other embarrassed Tory dignitaries bused in from
Ottawa. The Delorme nomination was to trouble Clark
for months to come, even after the byelections.

Clark is passionately devoted to the idea of the State of
Israel. In 1976, in one of his first speeches as PC leader,
he had aroused the fury of Arab-Canadians by the
intensity of his commitment. But Clark is also committed

to making the Progressive Conservative party a people's party, open to all. The two commitments clashed. He extracted from Delorme the promise to toe the pro-Israel party line on the Middle East.

As the byelection campaign came to a close, Clark and his advisers could read the writing on the wall as well as anyone. Tory party polls showed that the Liberals would probably sweep the five Quebec elections but that the PCs might still pick up two or three if the vote split just right. Clark again gambled on the latter possibility and Quebec consumed ever more of his personal schedule. Just before May 24, he and Maureen spent two exhausting days working in the riding of Verdun on be-half of Pierrette Lucas—a beautiful young woman whose sea of perfect teeth, manicured hands, and elegant clothes seemed, in the eyes of many, inappropriate to the working class constituency formerly represented by Bryce Mackasey.

May 24, 1977 was a low point in Clark's leadership. He lost the Prince Edward Island seat the PCs had held for two decades, and which he had virtually ignored throughout the campaign. And in the five Quebec constituencies, the PC candidates went down in flames. Pierrette Lucas ran third and lost her deposit. Ironically, the best showing of any PC candidate was made by Roger Delorme. Clark's office pointed out that the PC vote had gone up substantially over the 1974 general election but the press gallery wasn't listening. The news was that Clark's gamble had failed.

With the Victoria Day disaster only a few days behind them, Joe and Maureen, tired and depressed, set out on a gruelling campaign-style trip through British Columbia. It seems to have been originally planned as a sort of triumphal tour to bask in the glory of PC victories in the byelections; it turned out, understandably, quite differently. In Vancouver, Clark faced a press which was, if possible, even more sceptical about him than that in Ottawa — both the city's dailies had run editorials bitterly critical of Clark's economic policies. And the popular columnist Allan Fotheringham had for months regularly heaped scorn on Clark.

But elsewhere in the Pacific province Clark's people usually had only themselves to blame. In a frantic tour of small coastal communities, dismal on-the-ground organization and poor advance work turned out only tiny crowds. Everywhere, as on his European trip many months before, Clark seemed unaware of the basic facts of local issues. In Kitimat, he seemed ignorant of major legislation at that time before Parliament. In Prince Rupert, he was scooped by an important announcement by a Liberal cabinet minister. CTV's Craig Oliver filed a devastating critique of the tour, referring to Clark's "faltering" political career. The next day, Maureen, tired and nervous, publicly scolded the same reporter. That, too, became news; in fact, it was just about the biggest news to emanate from the whole trip. A downcast Joe Clark returned to Ottawa to confront a Gallup poll that showed him running almost as low as Robert Stanfield had exactly six years before.

Back in March, one of the first to react to loss of the Tory lead in the Gallup poll had been the PC Member for Crowfoot, Jack Horner. He told reporters he thought that Clark and his advisers put "too much faith in polls." The unleashing of the byelection campaign had been the first prong of the Liberal attack; in the months to come, Horner was to become the target of the second prong — probing for weak spots in the Tory caucus itself.

Horner and Clark had never been close. But they had never been enemies either except insofar as Horner regards most of the world as his enemy. But they are different types of men. Once, before either was an announced candidate for the Tory leadership, they had appeared together on "Canada A.M.," CTV's morning talk show. Horner was on about his favourite topic — the Toronto-centred conspirators who control the media, the PC party, and most of the rest of Canada. Clark interrupted him, to say, "Jack, I don't know who you're talking about." Horner shot back: "You ought to know, Joe, you're one of them."

Popular wisdom has it that Jack Horner has been handled unfairly by the press and there may be some foundation to the charge. For example, Horner raises cattle on several square miles of land in Southern Alberta, a spread which lends itself to the term "ranch." So Horner finds the press calling him a "rancher-politican." On the other hand, Horner himself is not entirely blameless in the matter. At times during the long leadership campaign he behaved badly. For example, at an Ottawa press conference he broke the candidates' unwritten code and lashed out with vicious remarks about his fellow Tory competitors. At the convention itself, during the voting, Horner got himself into what amounted to a fistfight with a reporter. The following morning Horner appeared on "Canada A.M." Obviously still strung out from the tension of the day before, he again attacked the Canadian media, and told a puzzled interviewer, "I wouldn't send my sons to fight for the 'free' press, because it isn't free."

In the months that followed, Clark and Horner worked at getting along. Clark left Horner in the important Transport portfolio in the new shadow cabinet, where the latter served creditably. Clark was careful not to say anything to set off the volatile Horner, in private or in public. For his part, Horner praised the new leader in public and worked at patching up his own press relations.

In private, however, Horner continued to treat Clark with disdain, just as he had undermined Robert Stanfield for his nine years as leader.

While Horner was mending his media fences in Ottawa, things were going downhill for him back at the ranch in rural Alberta. Under redistribution, most of his riding of Crowfoot had been swallowed up by another constituency, represented by a fellow PC, the likeable young Arnold Malone. In a move reminiscent of the Clark-Schumacher squabble, Malone had moved in and poached on Horner's turf. It is often difficult to figure impending nomination battles, but it appeared as if Malone would easily win the PC nomination over Horner. Horner demanded that Clark intervene by exercising his powers under the Canada Elections Act and refusing to sign Malone's papers as a PC candidate, should the latter defeat Horner's bid for the nomination. Clark, who seems to regard that section of the Act as a dangerous step towards centralization of the parties, refused to do so — just as he had declined to use the same powers on his own behalf, against Schumacher. Other available ridings were already occupied by other powerful Tories. So by early 1977 it looked as if Jack Horner would not be able to get a PC nomination anywhere in Alberta.

By the end of March, it was an open secret in Ottawa that Horner was meeting with high officials of the prime minister's office. The same officials let it be known that they, and presumably their boss, thought highly of Horner. In the next weeks "will-he-or-won't-he?" became the most popular topic of conversation on Parliament Hill. Horner's new approach to the press seemed to pay off, as reporters discovered new and surprising qualities in him. Habits previously thought of as eccentricities — such as keeping a bottle of whisky under the seat of his tractor while on the ranch — were now seen as evidence of his manliness. The columnist W.A. Wilson called Horner "a man of integrity . . . and intelligence" and urged him to change parties "in the national interest." A week later Horner announced he was a Liberal; a day after that he was sworn into the Trudeau cabinet.

Horner was later to say that Joe Clark had made it "easy" for him to cross the floor. There was some truth in that. Clark had not intervened in the Malone-Horner struggle. Later, fed up with Horner's quasi-public dialogue with the Liberals, Clark had tossed him out of the shadow cabinet. Horner had sympathizers among other Tory members, but when the caucus met to discuss the issue, it was Robert Stanfield who best reflected the mood. "Joe," Stanfield said, "You've handled this matter with just the right mixture of firmness and understanding. You deserve our support." The former leader, who had suffered Horner in silence for nine years, sat down to thunderous applause from other members. Later, Stanfield, was to repeat the gesture in public. At the exact moment that Horner took his place in Parliament on the government side, Stanfield walked up to Clark and shook the leader's hand. Again, the Tory caucus erupted in thunderous applause. They were expressing their support for the leader, but more than a few Tories were glad to see Horner go. Said one, embittered, "The Grits could have had Jack ten years ago. They just didn't need him then."

In June, Hochelaga MP Jacques Lavoie went over to the Liberals. In his short parliamentary career, Lavoie had never really fitted into the party. His victory in the October 1975 byelections, against Liberal superstar Pierre Juneau, had been a useful symbol of a possible Conservative breakthrough in Quebec. And Clark, then

an unknown Alberta MP, had campaigned vigorously
for Lavoie, and took some pride in the triumph of the
self-described "little guy from the neighbourhood." But
Lavoie brought little else to the Tory caucus. The media,
jaded after the labour of reporting on the drawnout
Horner defection, paid relatively little attention.

Later, when some other Tory MPs drifted away, there
was even less attention. The young John Reynolds went
back to Vancouver to seek his natural metier as a hotline
radio host. The even younger Sean O'Sullivan left to
follow his own natural vocation as a priest. Gordon
Fairweather, a man of integrity and intelligence, left to
become chairman of the new Canadian Human Rights
Commission, an agency for which he had long fought in
Parliament. In their announcements of their departures,
Fairweather and O'Sullivan were at pains to express
admiration for Joe Clark. Reynolds was equally at pains
to express his admiration for himself.

In early July, Jōe Clark faced two more problems. The
first was the announcement of what was to be the worst
poll yet. The PCs were to sink to 27 percent in public
favour; it was a respectable enough figure by pre-1976
standards; but the foot-soldier PCs had come to expect
better. The other problem was the national unity debate.
For months the Opposition had hounded the government
to bring that important question to Parliament. The
government had at last agreed. With four months of good
polls and the byelection victories in May behind them,
and with Jack Horner on their side, they could afford an
act of charity. Besides, the Liberals reasoned, the
Conservatives had nothing to say on the subject.

The Liberals had good reason to operate on that
assumption. For months, Clark had dallied on the issue.
Throughout the byelections he had hesitated to attack
separatist ideas. Instead, he chose to court the Quebec

nationalist vote, through vague talk about new constitutional arrangements (pointing out to Quebecers that they were not the only ones dissatisfied with Trudeau federalism) and an emphasis on economic issues. He was right of course — polls invariably showed that most Quebecers want change in the system short of separation, and prefer good jobs and low prices to Quebec independence. But Clark failed to grasp that the issue was, and is, emotional and symbolic, not legal and constitutional. While Clark tried to appeal to the currents of change in Quebec, his Tory clientele in English Canada, which wanted thundering rhetoric against separation, may have drifted away.

When Clark rose in the House of Commons to speak in the national unity debate on July 5, 1977, the ministerial party expected little of the Opposition leader. Fortunately for Clark, the prime minister chose to lead off with a rather tedious recitation of his own achievements in bringing Canada together, and the announcement of yet another task force on national unity. The response to the prime minister's speech, even from the government side, was desultory. The PCs had wisely spent the previous evening in caucus, psyching up themselves and their leader for the debate. There was really little new in Clark's speech, nothing he had not said before. But his style, backed up by the exuberance of his caucus, was terrific. At last, Clark had responded to his anglophone clientele by bluntly saying that language policy alone was not enough to keep Canada together. "We must face the fact that difference of language and culture tend to divide, not to unite," Clark said, as he called for a new emphasis on economic development. The PC caucus responded with wild enthusiasm, and most of the media were only a little less impressed with Clark's performance. By common consent, Clark and the Tories had bested the government in the national unity debate, the Liberals' own ground.

A month later, Clark repeated his performance under rather similar circumstances. For months the Opposition had been demanding that the government bring before Parliament the issue of a northern gas pipeline. In August, the government, seeing yet another opening to embarrass the Tories, summoned Parliament back to a steaming, humid Ottawa so they could "seek the advice of the House." The ministerial party reasoned that the Tories would have nothing of interest to say since they, the Liberals, possessed more information. Moreover, Clark had badly bungled the early stages of the pipeline issue, when the Berger Report had been issued in the spring. Then Clark's office had issued a written statement which Clark, through an unfortunate choice of words, seemed to contradict before the television cameras. Sneered one ministerial assistant: "It's going to be the 1956 pipeline debate all over again. Only this time it's the Opposition that gets screwed in the ear."

But, again, the Liberals led with their chin. Government House Leader Allan MacEachen began the debate with a speech so embarrassingly pedantic and dry that even government members failed to pound their desks, even once. That made the contrast that Clark was to strike all the more vivid. Clark spoke about the pipeline and laid down some tough conditions for the acceptance of the Foothills Route — which by then appeared to be the only logical choice. But he used the occasion to savage the government's energy and northern development policies, saying "This is more than a debate about a pipeline. It is, instead, a debate about the future shape of our country." Then he went on to lay out his own programme for Canadian self-sufficiency in energy. It was one of the few times that Joe Clark had spoken so convincingly, obviously using his own words, about his feelings on Canada's future.

As the summer of 1977 drew to a close, and the autumn campaign of the political wars drew nearer, Clark was to pull off another coup. Since the Gallup turnaround in March, the earlier murmurs of party discontent had taken on a new dimension. There were rumours of cabals against the leader, as strong as those of plots against Trudeau a year before, when the prime minister was the one trailing in the polls. The annual meeting of the PC Association of Canada in November was the natural focus. It would automatically take a vote on leadership review.

It is one of the features of the Canadian system of government that any first minister anywhere is more influential than any leader of the Opposition in his own domain or anywhere else. It is one of the humiliating crosses that federal Opposition leaders have to bear that any provincial premier of his own party is more powerful and commands more attention than he does. Drew, Diefenbaker, Pearson and Stanfield have all in their time and turn suffered from this fact. But it is a special problem for Joe Clark, since he is not only less powerful than Bill Davis, Peter Lougheed, Richard Hatfield, Sterling Lyon or Frank Moores — he is also younger.

So it was something of a surprise when the four PC premiers accepted Clark's invitation to meet with him in Kingston, ostensibly to discuss the constitution, the economy and other dull matters. But to reflective observers, the meeting was reminiscent of one of those medieval gatherings when the King of France, with little more than moral authority to back him up, would summon his nominal vassals, the powerful regional dukes, who had great feudal armies behind them, to pay homage. The joint statement of Clark and the premiers, or the Kingston Communique, as Clark's office grandly called it, was little more than a rehash of Clark's recent speeches about language policy, economic progress, and regional development, with each of the four premiers' favourite hobby horses tacked on.

The government party in Ottawa tried to upstage the event by announcing yet another one of Trudeau's musical cabinet shuffles on the same day. But the importance of the Kingston meeting was that it took place at all. The subliminal message of the great dukes of Torydom was this: *Clark is the leader.* The message was not lost on the lesser vassals and foot soldiers. There would be no rebellion against the young king. At least not yet.

Nothing could have been more effective in reinforcing that message than the introduction of television in the House of Commons in October. Not only was Clark the leader, he was seen to be a match for Pierre Trudeau on the floor of the House. Tory MPs had been saying as much since the scandals of early 1976. Columnists had applauded Clark occasionally. Now television viewers could see for themselves. It wasn't the emperor and the upstart, as the Liberals had complacently assumed, but equals. Frequently Clark was seen, right hand pounding home a point, while Trudeau sat smirking opposite. Some viewers told Clark they hadn't even realized he had the same sized desk as the prime minister and sat directly in front of him. Thanks to Clark's introduction of a caucus policy executive, its critics were better informed, more capable performers on television.

The fourteen hundred delegates from Tory associations across the country were in fighting spirits when they arrived in Quebec City for their annual meeting during the first week in November. "Our determination to win is greater than our desire to fight among ourselves," one said. Effective performances by Clark during the national unity and pipeline debates, the Kingston meeting and television had replaced early summer gloom with late autumn optimism. Although the Liberals still led in the Gallup poll the Conservatives had climbed from 27 percent in July to 32 percent in October. While party unity was uppermost in the minds of the dukes and almost all the foot soldiers, the national obsession with national unity was close behind. A strategy memo circulated among top Tories before the meeting asserted grandly, "This is where Clark reasserts his leadership, where the party reasserts its primacy in the national debate and where our 1978 election campaign begins."

Clark had no choice in placing his leadership on the line. The party's constitution required a vote on calling a leadership convention. First, however, the convention organizers arranged for a pep rally to preview "the selling of Joe Clark, 1978." Toronto ad-man Ron Lillie showed some commercials featuring the leader wearing a shorter hair style, relaxed and authoritative, speaking from his prime ministerial office on Parliament Hill.

The vote later in the day was anti-climactic. Only 72 of the 1,031 delegates who voted favoured holding a leadership convention; 93.1 percent endorsed Clark by voting against one. The organizers had achieved their goal, to demonstrate that Clark's grip on the party was even firmer than Pierre Trudeau's over the Liberals. When the Liberals voted on the same issue in 1975, 19 percent of the delegates supported a leadership convention.

The Tories have been known to split into left and right over the election of party presidents. In 1974 Michael Meighen, whose campaign Clark had managed, narrowly defeated Donald Matthews for the presidency. Meighen's support came heavily from the party's progressive wing,

Matthews' from the conservative side. Robert Coates, the member of Parliament for Cumberland, Nova Scotia, is a staunch defender of former Prime Minister John Diefenbaker and a man whose stands on a variety of issues suggest he would draw his support from Tories of right-wing inclination. He had been campaigning for the presidency for months, and went to Quebec without any declared candidate in opposition.

Clark as an ordinary MP would probably not have supported Robert Coates; they belonged to different schools of politics. However, at Quebec the delegates who voted so overwhelmingly for Clark's leadership also gave generous support to Coates as president, though many decided not to vote at all. He received 678 votes to 108 for late challenger John Gamble, a Toronto lawyer.

After the byelection disaster in May, Clark had been forced to pay less attention to Quebec. His critics thought he had been wrong to campaign so vigorously for what they thought was a hopeless cause. Clark hoped this convention would restore the party's interest in Quebec.

Attendance by Quebecers showed the distance the party had yet to travel within that province. Only 166 of an expected 350 Quebec delegates turned up, and a majority of those came from predominantly English-speaking ridings.

Those who came were told bluntly by Sterling Lyon, the newly elected premier of Manitoba, that western Canadians do not share the federal government's "overweening preoccupation with linguistic and cultural"matters. He said French Canada must understand that English Canadians are more concerned with job security and economic security than with preserving the French language and culture in Canada.

For their part, Quebec delegates reflected their province's priority — its concern about its place in

Confederation. Rodrigue Biron, leader of the Tories' Quebec ally, the Union Nationale, challenged them "to recognize the equality of two distinct communities, two linguistic and cultural communities, one the manifestation of anglophones which is found throughout Canada and the other the manifestation of francophones, found essentially in Quebec." Mindful of the party's troubles a decade before when it adopted and later abandoned a two-nations concept of the country as official policy, delegates avoided any conclusion.

Media coverage in Quebec was one of the party's considerations in holding the meeting there. But the meeting was overshadowed in the news by the triumphant visit of Quebec Premier René Levesque to France and its drumbeat of sniping between Ottawa and Paris. In addition three Quebec newspapers, *Le Soleil* of Quebec and *La Presse* and *Montreal Matin* of Montreal were on strike and not publishing.

Nevertheless the meeting made a splash on television networks in the province. Clark, speaking French fluently, told Quebecers there is a federalist alternative to the Liberals and the Parti Québecois. A national Conservative Clark government would be prepared to modify federalism, to give the provinces greater control over cultural and educational institutions.

After Quebec Clark was able to reflect on nearly two years of work towards unity within the party and the country. He could say with justification that the party was ready to fight the Liberals rather than themselves. He had demonstrated within the party an ability to heal old wounds, to bring people together. A few weeks later he bragged to a reporter: "Anyone who can bring the Conservative party together can bring the country together."

EPILOGUE

THERE is an element of truth in most of the labels applied to Clark. But they oversimplify and some are misleading.

A loner? He keeps his own counsel, as a leader must. He isn't one of the back-slapping, booze and backroom boys. He is good at meeting people and thrives on friends and associates. He has never really wanted to be alone for any length of time. The label is inappropriate.

A Red Tory? As an ordinary member of Parliament and before election Clark was at home in the progressive wing of the party. In principle, he favoured the Official Languages Act, as well as the abolition of capital punishment. He could more correctly be called a moderate, for he has steadfastly rejected socialist solutions. During his campaign he advocated denying the right to strike to public servants in essential services. Government spending must be reduced, he said, and some social security payments should be made on the basis of need.

Boy politician? Clark's youth has been a favourite subject for caricaturists. Inexperience goes hand in hand with youth. On the other hand, youth isn't necessarily a problem when nearly a third of the electorate is under thirty. Clark was thirty-six when he became leader of the Opposition. Although there have been no prime ministers of that age in modern times, William Pitt became prime minister of Great Britain — a highly successful one — at the age of twenty-four. Today, British Foreign Secretary David Owen is a year older than Clark. In Canada, Ed Schreyer became premier of Manitoba at thirty-four and Robert Bourrassa was thirty-seven when he was elected premier of Quebec. In terms of Parliamentary experience Clark had four years before he became Tory leader, the same period as Pierre Trudeau before he became prime minister. The label has been applied to Clark probably because, until recently, he looked younger than he was.

An idealist? History may consider him one for his respect for diversity. He believes that the way to keep the country together is to allow communities and regions to preserve their identities. Central government should not impose its will on them. He likes to quote Northrop Frye, the University of Toronto literary critic, on the danger of confusing unity and identity. If Canadians insist on unity in such a diverse country, they destroy local identity. And national identity is the sum of regional and local identities, not an additional super identity, Clark argues. "One of the great disuniting factors in Canada is to have the Toronto idea of Canada, or the Montreal idea, or indeed the High River idea imposed on places where it doesn't fit." Most leaders have certain ideals before them as they struggle with mundane political problems; Clark has his share, though not necessarily more than others. Idealist isn't a fitting description of him.

A pragmatist? It's a label Clark himself wouldn't reject. He has always placed much more emphasis on policy than on philosophy. His first instinct as leader was to heal the wounds of the leadership campaign. He united his caucus. He recognized the party's control over its finances. He set up a new electoral strategy committee.

These were all practical achievements and they make the term pragmatist appropriate for Clark's first two years in the leadership.

Ordinary? Clark has frequently been called ordinary, scornfully by detractors, approvingly by supporters. Clark does indeed have qualities usually considered ordinary and they are, on balance, an asset because they are shared by most voters. He has simple tastes, in food, in reading and in entertainment. He'd rather go to a movie, any movie, than the ballet. He'd rather watch a ball game than go deep-sea diving. Although he has earned his living in politics and journalism he can talk with the farmer and the miner on their terms; he projects an interest in their problems despite his lack of direct experience.

Ordinary, like other labels, contains its own paradox. For ordinary means "commonplace" or "not exceptional." Clark can't be considered commonplace in, for example, his understanding of Canada, or in his willingness to tackle daunting tasks. His elections — to Parliament and to the party leadership — were won the hard way, step by step from the bottom up.

Of all the labels, populist is most apt. It was the populist who dropped his books at home and rushed off to see John Diefenbaker in 1957. It was the populist who in 1971 went to bat for the Polish immigrants in Pincher Creek who had been denied Canadian citizenship for years. It was the populist who, during the best speech of his leadership campaign, called on his party to be the home for all disenfranchised Canadians. And it was the populist who won the leadership without the support of any important political figures or alliances. Modern populism is usually defined as the political advocacy of the interests of the ordinary citizen, especially as contrasted with special interest or privileged groups. It fits Clark. Even better is the definition offered by Peter Jenkins of the *Manchester Guardian*. "It is only useful to use the word at all," he writes, "if it conveys a distinctive political manner or style, rooted in the politics of country against city, or small against big, expressive of a frustration which transcends mere divisions of wealth and status, a combination of attitudes which might seem incongruous to urban political sophisticates but which makes more sense to ordinary people the more it seems to cut across party lines."

INDEX